The
QUEST

A Novel

The QUEST

A Novel

O. F. Ursenbach

Bookcraft

Salt Lake City, Utah

Litho in U.S.A.
by
Publishers Press
Salt Lake City, Utah

FROM the summit of many a roof garden in Jerusalem, the inhabitants were enjoying the evening coolness, following an intensely hot day characteristic of the Holy Land at this season of the year; and, as long had been the custom in Palestine, prelates, astrologers, and men of science could be seen studying the star-studded heavens.

In a beautiful roof-garden, reposing in a hammock beneath spreading palm branches, waited an anxious mother whose silvered brow told the story of a long toilsome life, and whose face at this time presented a troubled mein. Since the demise of her husband some years past, she had been left with a son in whom she had reposed explicit confidence. She had been unsparing in giving of her substance for his education to the extent that he had been successfully graduated from the best colleges of the land and was now a doctor of Jewish law, for he had already been ordained a rabbi. It was his seeming indifference to the Jewish faith that caused his mother's sadness. She would rather have had her son as of former years than be forced to the realization that, with all his learning, he had largely forsaken Judaism. Suddenly she heard approaching steps that assured her that her son, Homer Ben Arden, had arrived.

Coming softly to her side and giving her the usual loving embrace, he greeted her with: "So, Mother, you have been patiently awaiting my arrival. I hope my lateness has not caused you undue concrn, but I have had a prolonged conference with Rabbi Kelvi relative to some existing conditions in which I did not concur. Will you pardon my delay?"

"Yes, Homer, dear," answered Mrs. Ben Arden, "yet I have been lonely without you, especially tonight."

"And why tonight, my dear? What is tonight more than other nights? Perhaps you have allowed yourself to drift into a state of melancholia. So, come, cheer up! you must know I feel more dutiful to you than ever before in my life."

"Homer, my boy, you have always been kind and considerate of me, and until recently have caused few tears to flow, but now—"

Amazed, Homer returned wonderingly: "Why, Mother, what have I done to cause you sadness? Have I in some manner injured you?"

"No, you have not injured me, but I am apprehensive that your intensive learning is driving you mad. I have heard some rumors as to your attitude and indifference toward the faith of our fathers. I know, Homer, there is something to it, for I have detected this very thing in your life of late."

"Mother, I am not indifferent to the faith of our fathers Abraham, Isaac, and Jacob. But to modern Judaism with its cold, spiritless shell buried in pomp and ceremony, I confess that I am apathetic. My ambition, you know, has been so to educate myself as worthy of becoming a member of the chief rabbinate, of which Father was an honored member."

"Yes, Homer, that was Father's dying request, and you well know how I have sacrificed to that end that you might have the essentials. I have assisted you to gain the best there is in Jewish education that would place you among the greatest minds in Judaism."

"And, Mother, I hope I have attained somewhere

near your ambition in my behalf, excepting a position in the chief rabbinate, which to me is nothing less than a futile piece of pomp and ceremony."

Mrs. Ben Arden gasped: "Why, Homer, those are hard words, and especially from a man of your balance and temperament. I am baffled."

"That may be true, Mother, but understand me. They are not meant for the thousands of honest hearts in the land who worship fervently and with purpose, but I am opposed to the selfish sham and unrealism that I am forced to meet on every hand among the prelates of Jewry."

"Ah, Homer, I plead with you, do not allow the actions of individuals to undermine your faith in the true and living God."

"Mother, I would to heaven that our people did worship such a God, but in lieu thereof, the present conception of Deity seems to be founded upon a doctrine comparable to that of Baalim that has been the stumbling-block of Israel through the centuries to the extent that we now, as in former years, are abandoned to our fate. Mother, we are a lost Israel. Our house is left unto us desolate, with faith gone, and all we seem to have salvaged is a cold, ineffectual form of godliness."

Intently his mother replied: "Homer, dear, things might not be as spirited as your young spirit may demand, but you must remember that the race is not to the swift, but to him that endures. Therefore, go slowly and be very cautious of your criticism."

"Mother, until recent years, as you are well aware, I have been largely deprived of access to the Holy Scriptures, but since that has been my privilege, I have lost little opportunity to delve deeply into those sacred writings. I have read of God's handiwork with ancient prophets, and I have longed to experience that power enjoyed by the patriarchs of old—Abraham, Isaac, Jacob, Elijah, Elisha, and others, together with their marvelous conquests over the enemies of Israel. It has caused me to yearn for that power of God unto salvation—that power that I have been pleased to name 'The Priceless Pearl,' that once was, but now is not found among us. My life ambition, Mother, is to begin a quest for that power."

"But, my son," returned his mother, pleadingly, "do not forget that with Israel reposes the gift of godliness. The covenant with Abraham must be continued in his posterity."

Homer became very emphatic: "Mother, you must remember this, that the tribe of Judah is but a fraction of Israel, and more, that all prophecy and promise is contingent on obedience to God's work. A tree must be known by its fruit, and all I can see in the present Judaism is a barren, fruitless system. The love we once had has waxed cold. Our faith is dead, leaving us as a legacy, the curse of heaven under which we are a deluded people. Our land is a desolation; even the once beautiful Mount of Olives is a waste. We are a hiss and a by-word in the world of men."

"Really, it cannot be that bad, Homer. I cannot think that a just God has abandoned us to such a lamentable fate. I know we are struggling under some yoke of oppression that has been upon us for long centuries. There is, no doubt, some fundamental cause. Yet, the day must come when the 'Shiloh shall come to break our chains of seeming bondage.'"

"That bondage, Mother, we brought upon ourselves, for when we crucified the Nazarene—I mean Jesus of Nazareth—we there and then assassinated the very Shiloh, the Messiah. In our rage, we invited heaven's curse that his blood should be upon our heads. It came, and two thousand years of curse should be manifestation to us of the fact."

"Why, Homer, you do not mean to tell me—"

"That very thing, Mother. I mean to tell you that I am a devotee of Jesus Christ, the Lord. With your indulgence, I wish to tell you my story, and I feel sure you will agree that I have come to my decision advisedly."

Mrs. Ben Arden faltered perceptibly. "My son, after the shock I feared was coming, I feel somewhat prepared for anything. I know not how to express my feelings, Homer, other than to say that now all seems blank, and the faith of a lifetime blasted."

"You will, I am sure, see just the reverse, Mother, when the true story of life and salvation is disclosed to you. Then you will see that our yoke of bondage is about to be lifted from us, for in the life and death of Jesus Christ the very ransom was wrought of which our prophets through the centuries have foretold. Mother, I have feared to open my soul to you lest I wound you. Yet, I knew well that the break must come sooner or later."

Mrs. Ben Arden's face seemed to blanch as she sat motionless. At length, she replied: "The sincerity of your devotion, my boy, has aroused in me an urge to listen attentively to your experience and findings. I want to know what it is that has brought about such a change in your life."

"You do me honor, Mother, and it makes my heart light to avail myself of this privilege, for I have dreaded to disclose to you my convictions, despite the fact that I well knew your keen sense of right and wrong."

"At least, Homer, I have an open mind, and you will find me an ardent listener."

Homer leaned back in the large armchair, then began: "Well, in the first place, I have learned that

Judaism has lost its power, and is today in a state of gross apostasy, the same as she was prior to the birth of the Nazarene. Even then, she had but a dead form left with multiplied pretentions of her divinity. When Jesus came, we were divided into several contending sects such as the Pharisees, Sadducees, Essenes, Herodians, and others.

"Furthermore, Mother, in my studies of prophecy and sacred writings, I learned concerning the coming of the Messiah, and found to my amazement, that Jesus of Nazareth fitted into their fulfilment so precisely that there remained no grounds for doubt. Moreover, I discovered that the long-lost Priceless Pearl of which I have spoken was marvelously restored under his adminis-tratiton, in that the very winds and waves obeyed his mandate; sick were healed; the lame leaped for joy; lepers were cleansed; and the dead were raised to life again; and then came the wondrous resurrection of Jesus from the dead, following which many of the saints came from their graves, appearing as living sentient beings to friends in this city. This divine authority—aye, this Priceless Pearl, remained with the Christian apostles long after his ascension into heaven.

"As had been promised, the Messiah came to his own people, but in our apostasy, we rejected him. We had built false hopes that the Messiah would come with letters so that he could be crowned our king and re-deemer, and we were so disappointed in Jesus that, in our disdain and hate, we crowned him with a crown of thorns, asking that his blood be upon our heads and those of our children. Well, have we not reaped, in pain and sorrow, the seed we had sown?"

For several minutes, Mrs. Ben Arden maintained silence, for she was deeply perplexed. "Your narration, Homer, is indeed interesting, and I hardly know how to

reply or what to say, other than that at this late day to
have my faith blasted, is not easy to endure. However,
I am free to confess that the remarkable manifestations
that you are pleased to name your Priceless Pearl, do
not seem to continue among us today. If the cause is
as you indicate, then, of course, I can not blame you for
changing your faith."

Homer gave his mother a fond embrace. "Mother,
I have resolved that I shall not falter until I find that
lost power which, perhaps, still exists among some people, somewhere. The church that can satisfy me that it
has this power unto salvation is the object of my quest.
There is nothing under heaven that can cause me to
retract. Oh, Mother, I hope you will not censure me
unduly in being true to my convictions and determination, for in the love and necessity for the salvation of
our souls, I have felt impelled to abandon Judaism and
apply myself to the object of my quest."

At length came the soft answer, "I repress, with
difficulty, the emotions of my soul. I have listened to
you with profound interest, and I confess that it might
not take much to make me think as you do."

"Mother, would to heaven you could; then we could
be one in faith and devotion. Little would I care for
the rebuffs and jeers of men. One more word, Mother:
Do you blame me for my stand, even though it mean
my apostasy from the Jewish faith?"

"Homer, I have every confidence in you. What my
heart desires at this moment is to know, sense and feel
in my heart as you do. By the way, Homer, before I
forget, Rabbi Ben Hooda has asked the privilege of a
special conference with you tomorrow evening. Will
you consent to meet him?"

"Why, most decidedly, Mother. He shall have a
welcome, even though he may find me somewhat of an
aggressive listener."

CHAPTER II

SUNRISE found Homer Ben Arden ascending the Mount of Olives. From this elevation he took a long and careful view of the city of Jerusalem, for, according to his anticipations, he would soon sever his connections with this great city. His heart was softened almost to tears, for the joys and reminiscences of his boyhood came in legions. Returning, he came to his mother's bedside and with satisfaction found her softly sleeping. Almost audibly, he whispered as he gazed into her careworn face: "Never before have you seemed sweeter to me, my dear. How cruel that I should disturb your faith after seventy years of Judaism."

While Homer gazed in love and admiration, his mother opened her eyes and smiled.

"Homer, my boy, I slept very little, for the experiences of last evening drove all sleep from me until near the dawn. Is the hour late?"

Homer smiled: "No, Mother, the sun is not more than an hour high, so I must insist that you remain at your rest for a few hours longer, as the evening might be long and tiresome for you. Mother, dear, I express with deepest tenderness my profound appreciation for your long years of goodness to me. Truly, I feel more dutiful this morning than at any previous time of my life. Today life seems to me more majestic and exhilarating than ever before. There is more to live for. At dawn, Mother, I was on the summit of Mount Olives, from which I saw Jerusalem as I have never done before. Now, I leave you, and shall be away until evening."

Evening came, bringing a serene atmosphere, following another day of intense heat. Homer and his mother had taken seats on their roof garden preparatory to receiving the distinguished rabbi.

A servant announced the arrival of Rabbi Ben Hooda with some other gentlemen of the prelate class, and several minutes elapsed in the formalities of receiving the visitors and making them comfortable.

"You are most welcome, sires; I pray you to be composed and comfortable," said Homer, sincerely.

"Truly, we thank you, Rabbi Ben Arden, but we hope our coming has not deranged your plans."

"Oh, to the contrary," returned Homer, "I cancelled some business, but it can wait until tomorrow."

"That is kind of you, Homer, for it is inspiring to meet here under the star-studded heavens where we may enjoy the majesty of God's handiwork, which at best, makes one feel his infinite smallness as one considers the starry realm in all its divine glory."

"Very true, my sires, and especially to one who has learned by experience to know that his Creator is a living, tangible personality."

At this remark a tinge of uneasiness was detectable upon the faces of the visitors, and to change the trend of thought, Rabbi Hooda began: "Mrs. Ben Arden and friend Homer, we may as well come directly to the object of our mission here this evening. We are appointed by the rabbinate to call to discuss vital matters pertaining to the welfare of Israel. You are well aware, Rabbi Homer, that your father, the well-beloved Rabbi Ben Arden, a profound doctor of Jewish law, was foremost in the rabbinate. Since his passing, Jerusalem has suffered an irreparable loss. We have, however, watched, with anxious anticipation, your educational development, as you were successfully passed from school to school in

this great city, and we have fondly presaged the exalted
position once held by your father to be honorably filled
by his son. The only apparent obstacle that is a barrier
to your now being made one of the rabbinate is your
seeming indifference to all that savors of Jewish procedure. As to your degrees and knowledge of Jewish law,
we know there are few, if any, who are your peers. For
this reason, Homer, our mission here tonight is a pleading one, to induce you to retrace your steps and become
devoted to the Lord. To apply your life as we, your
seniors, have applied ours to service.

"We are living in a fast age, Homer, when events
chronicled by our prophets of old soon will reach their
culmination. The time is near when the Messiah—the
Shiloh—will appear from yonder East. This great event
is to be at a time when we are sorely oppressed, then will
he come to fight our battles, to be our solace, our refuge,
and our strength. Israel will then be redeemed, and
Palestine once more adorned with her pristine splendor.
The law of carnal commandments will then be fulfilled,
and the dispensation of Shiloh will hold undisputed
sway. The great millennial reign shall come in which
the lamb and the lion shall lie down together, for there
will be no more destruction in the Lord's holy mountain.
It is written, as you know; 'Be ye glad and rejoice forever
in that which I create, for behold, I create Jerusalem a re-
joicing and her people a joy; and I will rejoice in Jerusalem, and the voice of weeping shall be no more heard in
her, nor the voice of crying. There shall be no more an
infant of days; for they shall not build and another in-
habit, for as the days of a tree are the days of my people.'

"We are old men, Homer, and may not live to behold the Messiah, but you are young and will, no doubt,
live to witness these grand events. By the time the Messiah comes, you will undoubtedly be the most exalted in

Israel, and the one whom he will call the most blessed of men. Will you therefore, Homer, turn from the delusions that threaten to drag you down to the very jaws of death and hell, whereby you would lose your soul and eventually be damned? Then I am sure your aged mother, now blanched to snowy whiteness, can pass to the great beyond with the assurance that her son is in very deed, a man of God. What do you say, Homer?"

Homer had listened to the long pleading discourse of Rabbi Ben Hooda, while his mother seemed to acquiesce to the masterly plea from the distinguished rabbi, and she feared lest Homer might come back with a retort that would mar the serenity of the occasion.

Homer broke the silence "My dear Rabbi Hooda, I have listened with interest to your narration of future events, some of which naturally strike a responsive chord in my soul. We are living, or rather, worm-like, existing, in perilous times. Yet, your picture of eternal bliss on the one hand, and the anathemas of damnation on the other, are insufficient to induce me to depart from what to me is grand and noble. As you know, I was educated with a view to becoming some day a qualified and worthy member of the chief rabbinate; but as my learning advanced, more lofty ambitions came into my life."

The rabbi interrupted, "Do you imply that there could be a more lofty calling than to become one of the rabbinate?"

"With all due respect to you gentlemen whom I deem my friends, I must answer, yes. I have no ambition to be even a cog in the wheel of an engine that has lost its steam; or to be part in a dynamo from which the current has been disconnected. I hope you understand my meaning."

"You talk in parables, Homer," returned the rabbi, somewhat perplexed. "Please be more explicit."

"If I have not made myself sufficiently clear, Rabbi Ben Hooda, I shall do so. I mean I shall not affiliate myself with a church or creed that has lost its power of salvation, and that has lapsed into cold, rank apostasy to the extent that Judaism has."

"I do not care to tolerate this insolence, Homer. Perhaps you forget to whom you speak."

"I have not forgotten, for I am talking to my sires to whom I bow in homage, but not to my superiors in priesthood, for I consider my ordination as a rabbi futile, and yours spurious. Neither of us has a vestige of divine authority."

Rabbi Ben Hooda was terribly shocked. "Homer, I am astonished—dumbfounded."

Homer was insistent: "Rabbi Ben Hooda and friends, please listen to me while I review your plea for what is left of poor, deluded Israel. In all kindness, I wish to assume the aggressive, and I trust you doctors of the law will be frank in answering me. You frequently referred to the power of God. Will you kindly tell me something of his nature? This question is to the point. May I have an explicit answer?"

With great confidence in his ability to reply, Rabbi Ben Hooda began: "Yes, Homer, God is a spirit omnipotent and omnipresent in space. Were it not so, he could not manifest himself in every moss and cobweb. It is thus that he can create, maintain, and control the universe with its myriads of solar systems and all that dwell thereon."

"His power, Rabbi, I fully admit, but as to his all-pervading self in the universe in his personality, I take radical exception. To me, it is the very dogma of Baalim, that old delusion that has confused Israel through the ages. In fact, we can point to very brief periods when we were free from the infusions of these falsehoods.

Your theory being as stated, Rabbi Ben Hooda, will you tell me how man can be made in God's image, when the god you describe is an imageless nonentity? How could such a myth appear to Adam; to Abraham on the plains of Mamre; wrestle with Jacob, who bore solemn testimony, saying: 'I have seen God face to face'? How, also, could he be seen by, and converse with Moses? How is it that he has been seen by many prophets of Israel who have left faithful testimonies of his personality? Will you please answer these questions?"

Seeming to be staggered somewhat under the tirade, Rabbi Ben Hooda replied: "It is written, Homer, that God is spirit; and while it is true that, as has been written, he appears to men in the flesh, we must meet the situation in a rational sense. Man, as you know, is crude and mortal, and God at times has made his appearance in bodily form for momentary duration, simply to establish faith in the hearts of men; but immediately he has again become invisible as he did with Jacob, Moses and others. But to infer that he is a corporal being is contrary to good reason and judgment."

"Which, of course, is the only answer remaining for a religion steeped in Baalism to offer in order to reconcile the concept of Deity with monistic-pantheism, and to do this, God naturally must be figured out of his very existence as a tangible being. You brethren, of course, believe the sacred records."

"Why, indeed," returned one of the visitors. "They have been our guide through the ages. I am sure you will agree to this."

"Then, gentlemen, why do you refuse to believe the written word relative to God's personality? On what grounds can you, as doctors of Israelitish law, consistently spiritualize your Creator out of his tangibility? If you are content thus to do—to accept—that God is an imageless nonentity; that he is so deceptive to man that he will appear in personal form momentarily, then dissolve himself into nothingness. I say if such is the God of your conception, you are at liberty to adore that essence. For me, I shall worship the God of Abraham, Isaac, and Jacob, entirely devoid of the thought of an absolute God being a cosmic substance of the universe. Moreover, gentlemen, you are believers in prophecy and other divine gifts."

"Indeed, Homer, for holy men in all ages have spoken under that divine power, and we today are witnesses to some of the marvelous fulfilments of prophetic utterance in earlier ages."

"Of course you are, Rabbi Ben Hooda. But tell me what that power is—what does it signify? I mean that power by which one can forecast future events, that power that delivered the children of Israel from Egyptian bondage; that brought fire from heaven to confound the priests of Baal; that caused the River Jordan to divide; healed the sick; raised the dead, together with many kindred operations of natural law for the benefit of man."

Rabbi Ben Hooda was quiet, hesitantly replying: "The events you indicate, Homer, are scripture, and I have no doubt but that they occurred as written. Those holy men of old were in touch with the heavens to the extent that they could do many things that this age knows nothing of."

Homer smiled. "I am glad, my friends, to hear you make so humble a confession. Now, will you next tell me what is wrong with modern Israel that she has lost this precious power?"

The visitors looked from one to the other in seeming discomfort. Eventually, Rabbi Ben Hooda returned: "I hardly know, Homer, save it be that since we are

under the law of carnal commandments we seem to
have all that is necessary to lead mankind to the higher
light. In generations to come, however, our people will
probably realize anew these blessings, but I doubt that
they will be restored before the Shiloh comes."

"Yes, Rabbi Ben Hooda, the law of Moses was given
to fallen Israel to lead her from her former apostasy
following Egyptian bondage, given as a schoolmaster
to lead her to faith in God. You referred to the coming of the Shiloh or Messiah. Will you indicate your
conception of that majestic anticipated event?"

Emphatically, Rabbi Ben Hooda spoke with assurance: "The scriptures are very explicit in this regard.
He will appear in glory, coming to yonder east on a day
when we are sorely oppressed. The Mount of Olives
will part in twain. Israel then will reach the end of
her oppression."

"Then, Rabbi Ben Hooda, you do not think he will
first be born into mortality as men are born?"

"To think, Homer, of the Shiloh coming to earth
through mortal birth would belittle him in the minds
of thinking men. Were it so, wherein were the redemption of Israel? The very thought is nothing less than
Christian delusion, and as such is unworthy of the conception of Judaism. Moreover, it is in sharp contradiction to the prophecy that he will come in splendor in
the east."

Homer was calm, composed, yet insistent as he replied: "Now, my dear sire, permit me to present some
of the scriptures you say are conflicting with the thought
of the Messiah's entering mortality as a child. Please
follow me as I read from Isaiah, 'Behold, a virgin shall
conceive and bear a son, and he shall be called Emmanuel,' (which means, of course, God with us) . . .
'For unto us a child is born, unto us a son is given, and

the government shall be upon his shoulders, and his
name shall be called, Wonderful, Counselor, the Mighty
God of the Everlasting Father.' Mark you, gentlemen,
a child to be born of a virgin to be Emmanuel, the
Mighty God. Could you ask scripture to be more explicit? Before now, I suppose you have discovered that
I am of Christian persuasion."

"My boy, I would to heaven that I did not know it.
The thought that you have shipwrecked your faith for
Christian heresy is lamentable to contemplate."

"Be that as it may," smiled Homer assuredly, "let
us consider this thought of Jesus of Nazareth a little
further. Will you agree with me that inasmuch as
Messiah may come to mortality as a child, so strongly
supported in Jewish scripture, that the prophecies receive a striking fulfilment in the life of the Nazarene?"

"Homer, Christian intrigue has concocted a pretty
story with which to delude weak-minded people. As
for me, I take it all with a grain of salt. The very thought
of the low, unlettered Nazarite's being the Messiah is a
burlesque indeed."

Homer smiled. "Yes, perhaps I am one of those
weak-minded people, all of which I take good-naturedly.
But, to continue: 'He is despised and rejected of men,
a man of sorrow and acquainted with grief, as we hid
as it were, our face from him.' Just as you do, Rabbi,
and more: you call him a low, uncouth Nazarene, hence,
once more I read, this time from the Judges: 'For lo,
thou shalt consecrate and bear a son, and no razor shall
come upon him: for the child shall be a Nazarite from
the womb of God.'"

"It would require more than that, Homer, to interest me in the thought that Jesus of Nazareth could
possibly be the Messiah. That is silly rubbish, Homer,
silly rubbish."

"As you choose, Doctor Ben Hooda, but you must confess that it is striking evidence of Christ's divinity. And here is another: 'But thou, Bethlehem Ephrata, though thou be little among the thousands of Judea, yet out of thee shall come forth he that is to be ruler in Israel; whose goings forth have been told of old from everlasting.' We all admit, of course, that this refers to the Messiah. Now the very fact that Jesus was born in Bethlehem is another strong evidence of his being in every deed the long expected Shiloh. In face of all this scriptural evidence, how, I ask, can you rabbis do other than confess that there is a possibility that he might be the very Messiah?"

"Mr. Ben Arden," interrupted Rabbi Ben Hooda, "do not think for one moment that we would accept the low-born Nazarene as the Shiloh. Do you really think that God would go to such low life, as the channel through which Jesus of Nazareth came? The very thought of his questionable birth and parenthood would suffice to condemn him."

"So we agree, Rabbi," interrupted Homer, "that the Son of God, the Messiah, the Mighty God of the Everlasting Father, Immanuel, the Prince of Peace, as it is written, may after all be born of a virgin in mortality?"

"It seems hard to say, Homer, much as I dislike believing it, but I confess that it might be so."

Homer smiled in his amusement: "Good enough, you might yet become a Christian yourself if you continue. Now, as to his birth. Christianity has eliminated the Jewish accusation of his questionable birth. Listen to this scripture, for it is sublime. It is where the angel made his annunciation to the young woman, Mary: 'And, behold, thou shalt conceive and bring forth a son and shall call him Jesus. He shall be called the Son of

the Highest, and the Lord God shall give unto him
the throne of his father David, and he shall reign over
the house of Jacob forever, and of his kingdom, there
shall be no end.'"

"But, Homer," interposed the rabbi intently, "you
do not expect us to consider Christian scripture as anything but fabulous, do you?"

"Perhaps not," returned Homer, somewhat hesitantly. "But your condemning it as fabulous does not
in any manner destroy its authenticity and truth, for
even you, and in fact the entire Jewish people, might
be deluded."

"Homer, even though the scripture does indicate
that the Messiah is to be born into mortality to become
the Shiloh, Mighty God of the Everlasting Father, I
positively refuse to recognize Jesus of Nazareth as the
fulfiller of that scripture. There can be no immaculate
conception as claimed by Christians. He will never
come through any such questionable progeny, never!"

"Rabbi Ben Hooda, what could be purer than the
little Mary, and what more majestic for the Father
than God himself? Listen again to more Christian
scripture, as the angel announced to Mary: "The
Holy Ghost shall come upon thee, and the Power of
the Highest shall overshadow thee, therefore that holy
thing which shall be born of thee shall be the Son of
God.' I am sure you will agree, gentlemen, that the
analogy herein presented, as compared to our own scripture, is decidedly striking."

"While it seems strong, Homer, it is, without doubt,
a malicious concoction of Christian intrigue. To me,
it is trash. The thought that he would come through
such low-down, uncouth lineage, hated and despised of
all men, the hiss and by-word of the entire Hebrew
populace, is rot. No, Homer, it is not so."

Rabbi Homer Ben Arden quickly turned over pages of scripture. "Rabbi, each time you speak, you suggest new scripture in refutation of your statements. Listen to this, from Isaiah: 'For he shall grow up before him as a tender plant, and as the root of the dry ground he hath no form of comeliness, and when we shall see him, there is no beauty that we should admire him. He is despised and rejected of men.' Rabbi, that is just as you have implied. 'A man of sorrows and acquainted with grief; and we hid our face from him, and he was despised and we esteemed him not.' How completely, gentlemen, this was fulfilled in the life of Jesus and his treatment by the Jews. Again: 'Surely he hath borne our griefs, and carried our sorrows, yet we did not esteem him stricken.' Here is another: 'He was wounded for our transgressions; he was bruised for our iniquities, the chastisement of our peace was upon him and with his stripes we are healed!' . . . All have gone astray, 'we have turned every one his own way, and the Lord hath laid upon him the iniquity of us all. He was oppressed and afflicted, yet he opened not his mouth. He was brought as a lamb to the slaughter.'" Homer looked straight into Rabbi Ben Hooda's eyes. "To Calvary, Rabbi Ben Hooda. But, to read on: 'And as a sheep before the shearer is dumb, so he opened not his mouth.' Brethren, in face of this from our own scripture, how can you do other than confess that Jesus of Nazareth may not have been the very Shiloh?"

Rabbi Ben Hooda seemed very much perplexed as he struggled for an adequate reply which, with a degree of positiveness, came: "Homer, when your Nazarene idol was on earth, his life works were met and dealt with by the Hebrew people. He was examined as a man, his doctrine thoroughly weighed and found wanting, contradictory, and false. He was proved to have been an impostor, finally tried and convicted of blas-

phemy against God, hence he justly paid the penalty at
Calvary."

"Yes," quickly interjected Homer, "just as Isaiah
said the Jews would do to him. But, Rabbi Ben Hooda,
I grieve to hear you say that his crucifixion was a just
penalty. I really wish you had left that unsaid."

Rabbi Ben Hooda seemed somewhat irritated at the
statement, yet he returned with positiveness: "Why
should I, a Jew, be ashamed of the act—ashamed of
justice and judgment?"

"Simply this," answered Homer with emphasis, "I
repeat that it grieves me immeasurably, for therein you
become an accessory after the fact and thereby ally yourself with his murderers. I hope you understand me,
Rabbi."

Ben Hooda was reflective, and for several moments
looked off in space. "That, Homer, depends entirely
upon the point of view. However, I retract my impetu-
ous words. I apologize."

Homer accepted the apology graciously, although
he felt that the apology did not come from the deep
recesses of the soul. "But to continue, friends, let us
recall the wondrous events of divine power under Moses,
Joshua, Elijah, Elisha, and numerous other prophets,
wherein the very mandate of power was obeyed. The
Red Sea was divided; the walls of Jericho fell; armies
were smitten; water supplied to famishing armies of
Moab; the dead were raised; then the wondrous event
at Mount Carmel under Elijah; men immunized from
the heat of the fiery furnace; Daniel freed from the den
of ferocious lions, with all of which you gentlemen are
familiar. Now, comparing this to Israel today, how do
you measure up, and have we measured up during the
past two thousand years and more? I am very sure you
will agree that the handwriting on the wall indicates

that we have been weighed in the balance and found wanting, that we have apostasized from the Lord. We have lost that divine power, and have as a legacy but a cold form of ineffective godliness."

The prelates sat motionless, without speaking a word, for they seemed to realize the defeat of Judaism. Homer continued: "Next, come with me to the dispensation under Jesus Christ, wherein the winds and waves obeyed, the sick were healed, water was turned into wine, the lame walked, dead were raised, and last, but not least, the glorious resurrection and ascension of the Shiloh into heaven, and the workings of mighty powers with the apostles after his passing. It is useless for you gentlemen to deny this, for history affirms that majestic life and works. True, gentlemen, we have tried to deny it, only to meet lamentable failure. Rabbi Ben Hooda, there is but one conclusion before us, and that is, that the divine operations of divine power with ancient Israel, and with Jesus Christ, were one and the same in power and authority. We are forced to admit that nowhere in present Judaism can we point to the effectiveness of this mighty power that I am pleased to name The Priceless Pearl, which is the power of God unto salvation. You are forced to admit that we have lost that power, which implies our being rejected, and not recognized of heaven. Gentlemen, for centuries we have been a lost Israel."

"Homer," interjected Rabbi Ben Hooda as an avenue of escape from the intellectual tirade that baffled them: "it is said that your much learning has driven you mad. You know there is such a thing, yet—"

Homer listened, but no further word escaped the rabbi's lips, for the members of the rabbinate present seemed to have no reply. Looking the visitors squarely in the eyes, Homer continued: "Brethren, the hour is already late, yet I feel that I must present one more topic and that is: When our people crucified Jesus at Golgotha, we cried that his blood be upon our heads and on the heads of our children. You will also remember how we were nettled when he told us our house would be left unto us desolate, and that we would become a lost people. The point I wish to make here is this: That from that day to this we have been a hiss and a by-word, dispersed throughout the earth, and devoid of our national home. Our once lovely Palestine is a desolation. We have struggled under the stress of our self-invited curse these many centuries, and will still continue to do so, perhaps, until the Messiah—Jesus Christ—shall return in his glory. Yes, brethren, he, as you have already indicated, is to come in the dire distress of our people about to fall by the sword. It is then he shall appear fully undisguised to fight our battles and to bring us victory. In the words of Zacharias, we shall stand aghast. We shall look upon him whom we have pierced, and one will say unto him, 'What are those wounds in thy hands?' He will answer that they are those he received in the house of his friends. It is then, my rabbi friends, that Judaism shall know that this Jesus of Nazareth is indeed the very Shiloh of our aspirations, the very God come of the Everlasting Father."

The visitors arose to leave, and Homer Ben Arden extended his hands warmly, giving them a hearty shake, concluding with: "Brethren, for you are my brothers and friends, I hope you understand the cause of my apostasy from Judaism. You may impart all to the rabbinate. Tell them also that Homer Ben Arden has determined to make a world-wide quest for the Priceless Pearl that must be somewhere, with some people on earth. With this I bid you good-night, and may your declining years be abundant and pregnant with joy."

CHAPTER III

THE early marketing in Jerusalem had come with its usual bustle with donkeys by the hundreds laden with fruits, vegetables, and other edibles in the several marketplaces, while buyers by thousands were in evidence. Homer Ben Arden had arisen early to witness once again the interesting movements of the people. He sauntered leisurely from place to place of interest, none knowing better than he the motive of his very close observations. When he returned home, it was nearly the noon hour, with the sun in all its splendor semaphoring her effulgent rays and intense heat over the massed buildings.

Mrs. Ben Arden had risen late, for the experiences of the evening before had greatly wearied her.

At breakfast, Homer ate heartily, while his mother merely made a gesture of eating.

Noting her lack of appetite, Homer spoke solicitously, "Mother, you seem to have little appetite this morning. I fear the emotional strain of last evening has been too much for you. Tell me, are you ill?"

"Homer, my boy, I cannot express my feelings other than to say that I feel like a stranger in a strange land. Having had my devotion and faith of a lifetime crushed at this late hour, is something so devastating that I am sure you cannot realize what it has done to me. The fond aspirations of life seem to have forsaken me, and I am obsessed with deep concern lest I pass on to the great beyond, an unworthy stewardess. A life of toil, with hope of a glorious end in sight, now to be forsaken for another faith, beautiful as it is, nearly overcomes me. Homer, I am in a spiritual and mental state of wonderment."

Homer reacted quickly: "You don't mean to imply, Mother, dear, that you, like your wayward son, have turned Christian?" Homer waited as he forced back the lump in his throat.

"What else could I do, Homer? Your masterly exposition of the prophecies of old which we have, it seems, not understood despite our faith in them, was bafflling and your able argument relative to the Messiah, which point by point you clinched, culminating all in the life and works of Jesus of Nazareth, really convinced me. Besides, your narration of the wondrous powers of God that once maintained, but now lost to modern Judaism, which you have been pleased to name your Priceless Pearl seems to have driven all doubt from me. Even so, it comes with a pang. I hope you understand me. I am now sure, Homer, my boy, that Jesus was indeed the Christ."

Homer had listened with deep attention as his mother disclosed her feelings, frequently forcing back her tears. He was amazed to hear his mother confess her belief that Jesus was indeed the Christ. He arose, taking his mother in his arms, and for several moments neither spoke a word. The silence was finally broken with: "Mother, this is really more than I could have dreamed for. I felt alone in Jerusalem regarding my convictions, but since Jehovah has seen fit to plant in your heart true faith, as he has in me, I feel joy abundant. What care I now that men revile? What care I now though all ministerial Judea turn the cold shoulder against me, as they will now do. What though my friends ostracize me from their circles? Far greater than all, Mother, is the assurance of your devotion and conviction that means more to me than all else in this great metropolis."

"Really, Homer," returned Mrs. Ben Arden, reassuringly, "it is a source of consolation to know that I mean so much to you, for, you know, I am aged and have but a short time left me before I go to where father is, where I hope some sort of tangibility and intelligence continue. Homer, I wish I could set my mind at ease on a subject that of late has given me great concern, in fact, ever since father died."

"Mother, what is it? Father was a noble man, clean in thought and action, living the best he knew, so you may rest assured that there is a just reward in store for him in the eternal world."

"Of that I feel assured, Homer. The thing that concerns me is the tangibility of life after we pass on. It has always been very vague to me, and the rabbis have never been able to give me anything like a reasonable solution. Homer, there must be some sort of tangibility of life and its continuity beyond the grave. Should there not be, then life with all its effort were futile and worthless."

"Mother, this has been uppermost in my mind for years. The teachings of Judaism are so vague regarding this most important of all issues, that I was at a loss to know what man's future would be, if there were one at all. But now that light has come, I see more clearly into the majestic workings of the great plan of salvation. Do you feel sufficiently strong, Mother, to listen while I disclose my findings in this regard?'

"Yes, Homer, and if I did not, I feel that I could not postpone the opportunity to have my soul enlightened, for I have had some very queer sensations that have caused me much uneasiness, so I cannot procrastinate."

Homer was not unmindful of a strange look in his mother's face, and would have gladly postponed further conversation, but his mother insisted.

Placing her comfortably on a divan, Homer took a seat near her, and at once began explaining his convictions and findings. "Mother," said he softly, "The tangibility of resurrection and eternal life beyond the grave has always been obscure to me. But now I have no doubt as to its actuality. I feel assured that, as we lay our bodies down, so shall we arise in the full stature and completeness of structure, with nothing lacking. Heaven is providential, and man, God's masterpiece, was not born to be annihilated, but to be perpetuated throughout eternity, and that in strict obedience with law and order. I am satisfied that the entire human family is preordained to a resurrection of some kind, good or evil. I read from the Prophet Job: 'I know that my Redeemer lives, and that he shall stand at a latter day upon the earth; and though, after my skin worms destroy this body, yet in my flesh shall I see God, whom I shall see for myself, and mine eyes shall behold though my veins be consumed within me.' Could there be a more tangible hope than this, Mother?"

"That is beautiful, Homer; it gives me solace, a picture of what continuity might be. Besides—" She was about to arise.

"Mother, please lie at your ease and listen. Now, let me refer to the vision the prophet Ezekiel had of the valley of dry bones. After having the vision described fully, the Lord gave him the full significance of its meaning in the following: 'Then said the Lord unto me, Son of man, these bones are the whole House of Israel; behold, they say, our bodies are dried and our hope is lost; and we are cut off from our parts. Therefore, prophesy and say unto them: Thus saith the Lord God;

behold O, my people, I will open your graves, and will bring you into the land of Israel. And ye shall know that I am the Lord, when I have opened your graves, O, my people . . . then shall ye know I have spoken it and performed it, saith the Lord.' Mother, the very fact that Jesus the Christ was resurrected, together with the fact that many of those that slept have arisen and appeared to friends in this city, is reassuring indeed."

"Homer, it is majestic to contemplate, yet how can it be—how can it be? I cannot fathom it."

"No, Mother, nor can we fathom the myriads of events of natural science and philosophy in the phenomena that are everywhere presented for our astonishment. The very mystery of birth, life, thought, memory, the metamorphosis of insect life, with thousands of unanswerables come for our astonishment and bewilderment, yet they are forced upon our very experience that we have no room for doubt in their actuality. Many of them must be as incomprehensible as death and resurrection."

Mrs. Ben Arden sat motionless and deeply pensive, at last saying: "Homer, I seem to envision a great expanse of eternity; it is lovely to the eyes of my spirit. My time, my boy, is short. Perhaps shorter than you think. However, you had better allow me to repose quietly for a spell."

Having made his mother comfortable, Homer retired to the large garden in the rear of the mansion where, in the profundity of his thoughts he reviewed his situation from many angles. On the one hand, his acceptance of Christianity; it meant the loss of friends, social standing, and power in the community; it meant he would be ostracized, shunned, abused, and hated. Could he stand the test? He meditated long when the mental vision of his Priceless Pearl seemed to flash across his mind, and he became resolute in his determination.

Homer was still in the spacious garden, when a servant rushed to him, announcing that his mother had suddenly been stricken ill, and he at once rushed to her side. He was startled to find the family physician near her. "It is a sudden heart attack," explained the doctor, "from which she may not rally." The words staggered Homer.

Grief-stricken and motionless, he watched the sands of life slowly ebbing away.

News of Mrs. Ben Arden's demise spread rapidly throughout Jerusalem. Friends were solicitous of rendering service in Homer's hour of trial, and in effecting funeral arrangements.

The funeral was a sumptuous one, the great synagogue being packed to its capacity, for the Ben Arden family was of the foremost in Jerusalem.

Homer consented to have the funeral conducted according to Jewish rites, saying, "It will not add or detract from mother's conviction of the hereafter."

Returning to the home, Homer experienced loneliness for the first time in his life. The home of his youth, where love and motherhood had reigned, now seemed to mock him in cold, uninviting defiance.

During the next weeks, Homer Ben Arden attended to the settlement of his affairs, selling the palatial Ben Arden mansion for a fabulous sum.

For many days Homer visited and bade farewell to his many friends, teachers, doctors of the law, and ecclesiastical associates. He knew in his heart that this parting was more final than they dreamed. He had no intention of returning to Jerusalem.

CHAPTER IV

IT was with moistened eyes that Homer Ben Arden bade farewell to the city and experiences of his youth. He had just returned from his last visit to the Mount of Olives, from which he had taken a final view of Jerusalem in all its splendor. He was exceedingly meditative as he thought that in this great city the Christ should some day make his appearance when he returned in his glory. "May I," he prayed, "be worthy to greet him when he comes. Until that time, Jerusalem, I bid thee farewell."

Homer on this occasion was not without tense anxiety, for he had not the slightest idea what lands and climes would be his to encounter. All he seemed conscious of in this moment was his indomitable urge to discover the Priceless Pearl. History of modern Christendom, quite familiar to him with its decline and loss of the Power of God, had dissuaded him from seeking, for the present at least, in those fields. On the other hand, statements made by champions of oriental religions, that Christianity had its birth in their beliefs, and that India had long since been considered as the "headwaters of thought," seemed to impel him to begin his quest therein. Being conscious moreover, of the fact that nearly two thirds of the earth's population came under oriental philosophies, he made his decision to go first into those fields in search of his Priceless Pearl.

The journey to Joppa, on the east coast of the Mediterranean Sea, was anything but pleasant, owing to the heavy winds and dust storms so incident to the Holy Land.

Arriving at the quaint old seaport, he at once began working out his itinerary. At Port Said he was to embark on an English vessel en route to Bombay and thence go to Calcutta.

The journey through the Suez Canal was interesting, and while many people seemed kind and gentle, nevertheless the uppermost thought on his mind was his self-appointed mission, and he was anxious to get to his destination.

As the vessel, in due time, approached the Gulf of Aden, a heavy gale was suddenly encountered, causing the ship to roll from side to side. The evening of the third day found the storm still unabated, continuing through the entire night, the shrill whistle of deckhands being audible to those below. The dawn, however, brought a change, and by noon the great liner was sailing through calm water.

The first view of India that the rabbi had was in the late afternoon, and in the early evening the ship was safely anchored at Bombay, whose picturesque surroundings, quaint architecture and diversified characteristics of the people were curiosities of the voyagers.

On land, Homer Ben Arden soon realized what it meant to be a stranger in a strange land, alone and friendless. Just how to proceed with his task was a problem, indeed. However, he resolved to meet any obstacles squarely and intelligently. He was gratified to observe that many people could speak the English language, even among the natives.

No time was lost securing a guide, and soon Homer was lodged in a hotel, not far from the wharf.

Before releasing his guide, who spoke good English, the rabbi made known his mission, urging that he be brought in touch with some of the great religions of India.

The guide assured him that he would return on the morrow with a priest of Parseeism. "You will appreciate this venerable gentleman," said the guide," as a man with a big heart, pleasant, affable, and kind, also eloquent in his explanation of Parseeism, to which he is dearly devoted."

Ben Arden arose early, and wandered leisurely through the winding streets of the quaint old city. Arriving at his hotel at noontide, he felt reassured that after all, there were many warm hearts and real human beings in India. Fatigued and weary, Ben Arden ate a hearty meal, then sat for hours on the hotel veranda that overlooked the city. Here he witnessed the moving mass of humanity in the busy din of commercial enterprise. As evening approached, the setting sun was partially hidden by crimson clouds, and presented a spectacle of exhilarating splendor, that impelled the rabbi to exclaim in ecstasy: "How gracious that the great Creator is pleased to bless the nations with such vistas of beauty. Would that I had learned in bygone years, how to appreciate the Master's handiwork as I now do, for I look upon the grandeur of natural things understandingly. To me they speak profoundly of creation's power that transcends all things mortal. Who, in the face of such wonders, could deny the existence of an All-seeing Master, for in each vista there is to me a wondrous something that always sings."

While Homer was enjoying the majesty of the sunset, a servant announced the arrival of his expected visitors, and as he gazed at the approaching people, he was amazed at the peculiar headdress, tunic, and robe of one, who he was sure must be the Parsee priest.

"Good evening, my rabbi friend," began the guide, "I hope you have rested well after your long, tiresome journey. Now, permit me to present Mr. Zulus, a priest of the Parsee religion of whom I spoke yesterday."

"The pleasure is mine," spoke Homer. "Indeed, I am gratified to know you. I pray you to be seated."

"My dear rabbi," returned the priest, "I am really delighted to meet you on this occasion, for your guide has spoken to me, praising you to the extent that I was eager to have a conference with you. Moreover, it is singular, is it not, to hear of a Christian Jew. Rather a paradox, is it not?"

Homer smiled with an air of amusement. "Well, yes, I confess it is rather unusual. Yet, I am happy to present myself as a firm and devoted follower of Jesus Christ."

Rabbi Ben Arden handed the guide a substantial tip, who, with a polite bow, left the room.

"It is my very good fortune," began the priest, "to meet you in this famous old city. You little know how much I appreciate this privilege."

"And I," returned Homer, "am equally gratified, for I had no comprehension that I should find such warm hearts in India. To my satisfaction, however, I feel that I am among friends, and your teachings, I am sure, will add much to my store of information."

"On the other hand, my Christian friend, it is I who shall be the recipient of the greater benefit."

During the ensuing hour descriptions of Jerusalem and Bombay, with their peoples, manners and customs, educational advantages, civics, and other topics were freely exchanged. Finally, the occasion presented itself wherein the rabbi deemed it opportune to speak of the power of God, as manifested throughout the dispensations of his great handiwork with the children of men, especially stressing the object of his quest in India. "To this end," he continued, "I am eager to investigate the internal workings of Parseeism. I desire to learn of the workings of your religion as regards the power of God, and also of the principles of your faith as regards the immortality of the soul."

"That shall be my delight," answered Mr. Zulus eagerly, "to unfold to you the majestic workings of the great God of Fire as understood by the devotees of Parseeism. We sincerely believe that, unique as we are, we have completely solved the question of creation and physical existence. I desire to refer you to our very long chain of historical descent through the past, whereby you will clearly observe that it dates back to the earliest ages of human experience.

"In the earliest days of Chaldea and Assyria, our religion was already realizing salutary effects. We point with pride to the very remote period when the great Ormadz flourished. According to our reckoning of time, and of course yours, he dates back to twenty-four hundred years before Christ. Of the illustrious achievements of Ormadz, I shall say little at this time, other than that no man before or since has been so great as he."

"Permit me to ask," interrupted the rabbi, "as to your source of information. Is it traditional or have you a written history?"

"Tradition, Rabbi, is a powerful medium by which great truths are conserved to future ages, and while much of our information comes of that source, yet we have it written in the very oldest books of existence. You Christians speak of Moses as being God's first pen. But we can produce records that antedate him by many hundreds of years. To us the very ancient records known as the *Gathas* are our principal guide. One division of these records is known as the *Zend Avesta*. To the

Parsee this is all, or perhaps more than your Bible is
or can be to you Christians. In it the wondrous workings of God are disclosed clearly, building for us the
various sources of our devotion."

The rabbi was quiet for a few moments, then said,
"Mr. Zulus, am I to understand that you are polytheistic
—having numerous gods and sources of devotion?"

"Yes, Rabbi, we are largely polytheistic," returned
the priest with something of an ostentacious air, "as you
will observe. In the first place, we point to the great
sole principle that is self-existent in the universe, and the
fundamental cause of all that tangibly exists. In a word,
it is the Absolute—the superlative of superlatives. From
this all things radiate, including even the great planetary
systems. All are of him a part."

"Then," interrupted the rabbi, "I am to understand
that your fundamental postulate is a principle—a substance, or essence, and not an object?"

"Exactly so. Now, to define him further. He is
eternal fire, radical as this might appear to you, a Christian. At times we see him flash in mighty power in
the heavens, which the misunderstanding mind calls
lightning. But for this power there could be no action
in the physical universe by way of creation."

"I hardly conceive," answered Homer, somewhat bewildered, "how you construe fire as a basic principle
that could be operative in creating worlds or solar systems. I therefore ask that you be more explicit."

"That I shall, Rabbi, by asking you a simple question. Did you ever see a meteorite, commonly called
a thunderbolt?"

"Well, no. But I am informed that there is one
weighing many tons that has been exhumed from the
desert sands near Alexandria, Egypt."

"Exactly so, my friend. And it is just that principle

in operation through phenomenal combinations that creates worlds. You will agree with me that a meteorite is never formed except as a result of fiery forces operative in the heavens. Occasionally, some immature bodies fall to earth; but the gigantic ones are set into revolution in space, maintaining themselves in their revolving and rotating orbits, and it is thus worlds come into being. All this, mind you, is by strict design of the great fundamental principle."

"May I ask, Mr. Zulus, by what name you designate this principle? Do you call it God, or have you some other name for it?"

"We call it Ilu, which means, that it might be clear to your understanding, God par excellence, since he is the superlative of the gods. He is, in a word, the All Soul of the Universe, every particle of which is infinite and all-pervading and manifested in all tangible things of existence."

Homer was still insistent: "This being the case then, how do you account for mortal life on earth?"

"That is just as logical and philosophical as the creation of worlds. We teach that it came about in this wise: In a mysterious manner a triad of actual beings came from Ilu, known as Bel, Bin, and Anu. In their order comes first, Bel, the organizer and creator of worlds; then Bin, known as the divine son. Lastly, Anu, the god of darkness. From this triad ultimately came the human family, hence the inhabitants that swarm the earth."

Urgently Homer continued: "This being fundamental with you, why, I ask, do you worship the planets to the extent that you do when you indicate that the superlative of all is Ilu?"

"My answer is this, Rabbi. When the sun rises in his morning majesty, we know that Ilu is reflecting his fiery power through that medium to bless and warm the earth. Understand me, that we are not idolaters in that we worship planets as such. But we do adore the planets as mediums through which this all-pervading power of Ilu is reflected. In fact, fire of any nature whatsoever, to us is a thing of devotion. It might be interesting to you to learn that a Parsee does not smoke tobacco as you Christians do, for we believe that by so sacrilegious a use of fire, we would displease Ilu.

"Your philosophy, Mr. Zulus, is interesting and somewhat understandable as you explain it. However, I cannot say that it appeals to me as much as you might anticipate. Your philosophy evidently had its birth ages ago."

"Yes, Rabbi," quickly interrupted the priest, "as it will also endure to ages *ad infinitum*. It has been the feeder and superstructure of the world's religious beliefs, even including Christendom."

"You really do not imply—"

"Indeed, my Christian friend, I certainly imply that even Christianity is an offshoot of Parseeism. I have here an English copy of the *Zend Avesta,* also a copy of your Bible. Moreover, I am somewhat of a student of the many contending sects of Christianity, in all of which I discover Parseeism outstandingly manifested, even though at times it is disguised almost beyond recognition. It is nonetheless there."

Rabbi Ben Arden, suppressing a revulsion that suddenly arose in his mind, returned calmly: "A very radical statement, friend Zulus, is it not? I fail to see the slightest comparison."

"Then listen to me," quickly interjected the Parsee. "You agree, of course, that the conception of God is fundamental in all religions. You Christians delight in Dershaven's famous hymn that speaks of the presence bright that all space does occupy; filling existence with himself alone; being whom you call God and know no more. Then in your articles of religion you teach that God is an incorporal substance. Am I not right?"

"As regards some creeds, nominally Christian, yes. Yet many are grossly in error in this conception."

"Well, Rabbi, we taught that same doctrine many centuries before Jesus Christ was born in Bethlehem. You also teach the workings of creation with so little variance from what we have taught for ages, and it is easy enough to find its source in Parseeism. You teach of the Divine Son. We taught of him long, long before you Christians ever conceived the idea. You boast of the sublimity of the New Testament, but we present its antecedent in the *Zend Avesta* that is much superior, and was written long before the days of Abraham."

"I confess, Mr. Zulus, that I am somewhat at a disadventage, hence to an extent unarmed because I am unfamiliar with your *Zend Avesta*. Yet, I feel free to affirm that my faith is unshaken in my conception of the true and living God. I have often read of his wondrous workings among men, in which I have failed to see even a trace in your philosophy. Whatever you have must be some extract of an earlier dispensation of God's marvelous gospel to the remote peoples of the earth. The power I have sought, and now seek, does not seem to be known to you Parsees, and beautiful as the ethics of your religion is, I fail to see the least shadow of my quest."

The priest registered disappointment in the rabbi's reaction, yet he was interested in what the rabbi called his quest. "May I ask, Rabbi, what you mean by your quest?"

"Indeed, my reverend friend: it is this. There is a power of God that has during all time been manifested among men, in that the very elements of nature have obeyed. Fire has been brought from heaven. Armies have been stricken. The sick have been immediately healed; lepers have been cleansed; and in a word, multiplied workings of a divine authority given to men, even to the raising of the dead to life. This authority and power has come during periods of righteousness, and departed when righteousness waned. It was with ancient Israel, then was lost. Then it was strikingly manifested under the reign and dispensation of Jesus Christ, only to be lost when Christianity became paganized. Now, Mr. Zulus, to find this authority that I have been pleased to name my Priceless Pearl, is my quest, for I feel in my soul that it must be somewhere, among some people sufficiently righteous to be beneficiaries of this rare power."

Reluctantly, the Parsee priest honestly replied: "Rabbi Ben Arden, I am free to confess that what you seek does not seem to have place in Parsee experience. The sublimity of it all is baffling to me. I confess that I have read of these things in your Bible, but I did not take them as other than unreal and emotional."

"To me, Mr. Zulus, they are most tangible to the extent that where that power does not exist, the true church of God is not."

The priest was exceedingly thoughtful. Finally he continued: "Rabbi, I am sorry you are disappointed. However, I shall be pleased to present you with this English copy of the *Zend Avesta* with my good wishes and brotherly love. Will you accept it?"

The rabbi's eyes were suddenly moist, as he answered sincerely, "It is my great joy, my friend, and I promise you that I shall give it a very careful perusal, aye, a very careful reading."

"You have aroused in my soul, Rabbi, something

newly born, and I am going to ask of you one earnest favor—"

"And that is?" returned Ben Arden as he looked kindly into the priest's eyes. "This, Rabbi: That when you shall have found the power you are seeking—your Priceless Pearl, as you name it, will you promise me that you will advise me of your findings, irrespective of where in this great world you may be?"

Homer Ben Arden replied earnestly: "My dear friend, I give you my solemn promise, for I feel assured that I shall not fail in my quest, thought it take years to realize."

"This, Rabbi, is more that I am worthy of or could have hoped for. I know you, being a man of God, will not fail me."

They arose from the extended interview, each enjoying the other's handshake of friendship, the priest retiring full of admiration for Homer Ben Arden. On the other hand, the rabbi was exceedingly satisfied with the interview, also with the thought that there were warm hearts in India, far beyond his anticipation, although he felt sorrow that he had not found his Priceless Pearl.

CHAPTER V

FOR several days Homer Ben Arden busied himself in the deep perusal of his treasured copy of the *Zend Avesta*. Despite the fact that he was somewhat out of harmony with its teachings of a cold spiritless philosophy, he was amazed at the great amount of ethical teaching, and elements of character building. Yet, in all he failed to see anything that gave him a clue as to object of his quest.

Fatigued and weary from his intense study, he laid the book aside and strolled down to the docks to witness the arrival of another English liner en route to Calcutta.

While on the wharf, he was greeted by his genial guide, who informed him that a noted Brahmin was seeking a conference with him in view to presenting a resume' of that great religion. "He wishes to see you," continued the guide, "without delay, as he is scheduled to leave on this ship. Will you condescend to meet him?"

"To meet the gentleman," returned the rabbi, "will be my pleasure, and that at the earliest moment."

"He told me," continued the guide, "to meet him here, and I am to escort him to your hotel. I assured him that he would be at your apartment within an hour from now."

Thanking the guide Ben Arden was soon at his hotel awaiting the arrival of the new visitor. A privilege of meeting a real Brahmin was an occasion for him. Often he had read, and heard much of the Vedic philosophies, but the prospect of meeting a champion of that great religion, was exhilarating to him, more so because he knew the taboos with which a Braham must protect himself.

Within the appointed hour, the guide escorted Mr. Brigha, a priest of Braminism, and soon the two men were comfortably seated, and the formalities of getting acquainted ensued. Thereafter, each one became much interested in the other's story.

"My dear rabbi," began the priest, "the guide informed me that you have had a long conference with Mr. Zulus of Parsee persuasion. Yet I feel confident that you learned but little that was of interest to you."

Quickly and with great kindness, Homer replied: "Much to the contrary, Mr. Brigha, I have gleaned much that has been satisfying and intellectual. Besides, I have found in Priest Zulus a personality that is intensely interesting. To say, however, that I have found a trace of my quest in India, would not be true for I see nothing in Parseeism that I could adopt."

"I shall not attempt at this time to inquire as to the object of your mission in India, Rabbi, but I urgently desire discussing Brahminism with you at the earliest moment, for I feel that the mighty Vedic religion will be intensely appealing to you. It is something that will bring peace to your soul as no other religion can. However, I have called to ask you to arrange to accompany me at midnight tonight on my trip to Puri, and during the ocean voyage there will be ample time to make a thorough investigation of the great mysteries of Brahminism. What do you say?"

Homer pondered for a time, then he returned: "Nothing would give me more pleasure, Mr. Brigha. But the notice is altogether too short. Can you not wait until the next steamer? It will arrive within a few days."

"Impossible," returned the priest with emphasis, "for

it is now the seventh of June, and on the eighteenth of the month the great Festival of the Juggernaut will take place. Under no circumstances can you afford to miss this gigantic affair, for it will be the pinnacle of your life experience. Will you accompany me?"

Ben Arden had often heard and read of this great festival, and a sudden urge gripped him to go along. He pondered a few minutes, while Brigha awaited with patience. At length Homer had made his decision: "Yes, Mr. Brigha, I shall accompany you. Really, I congratulate myself upon this rare occasion. And more, I express my gratitude to you for the invitation."

Following full understanding and a hasty parting, the rabbi began to pack his baggage preparatory to the voyage. The thought of having, in so surprising a manner, the way opened for the anticipated experience was incomprehensible to him. The Brahmin's visit, although short and business-like, had impressed him favorably, and he marveled at the ease with which the priest spoke the English language. That he was an educated man, Homer knew, for his words were choice and came with seeming ease and correctness.

The midnight rush at the docks was intense, for Hindus by the hundreds were embarking for the voyage.

From the larboard side of the ship, he was gratified to see Brigha approaching, escorted by many prelates and dignitaries, the pomp and ceremony of which seemed to imply that his host was a personality of no little moment.

On deck, the rabbi and priest were enjoying a pleasant conversation, as the deep guttural whistle announced the time of departure, and within the next few minutes the liner slowly put to sea.

Although when they started, the ocean was rough and choppy, by morning the ocean was more calm. Ben

Arden, an early riser, was enjoying a thoughtful period. As he gazed at the glowing sun he agreed that the Parsees had some reason after all for their devotion, for the sun sent its beneficent rays in all her splendor. "Why," said he in a low voice, "has man so departed from the conception of the true and living God? On the other hand, when one is devoid of faith, what remains for him but to worship some object peculiar to his environment? How logical," said he in his soliloquy, "that most pagan philosophies are nature worshipers, especially when nature smiles as it does this morning. To them when nature smiles, and all is calm and serene, the gods are bestowing benedictions. Conversely, when the skies are covered, winds blow and thunder rolls, the gods are at strife with human beings. Man has gradually fallen from the worship of God, to the worship of what he has created."

While the rabbi was in his reverie, Brigha came forward saying: "So Rabbi Ben Arden, you are already on deck. I feared lest you would be one of the hundreds that are down below this morning, for the water was pretty rough during the night."

"Quite to the contrary," smiled Homer. "I think I have passed my *mal de mer* period. I hope so at least, having had a siege on my way from Port Said."

"How serene the breeze is this morning," returned the priest as he reveled in the beauty and calmness that maintained. "It seems that kind Providence has been pleased to bestow her benedictions lavishly. Do you observe the rare cloud formation in yonder heavens? See the majestic blendings from a deep purple, through red to yellow, culminating higher in the sky, an azure blue. Is it not a manifestation of divine art?"

"Indeed, Mr. Brigha, I have been enjoying that for

some time, to the full capacity of my appreciation. You know, through just such vistas as these, I have learned to understand God's great handiwork."

"Changing the subject, Rabbi, it is a real treat to me to have you here, and the privilege of conversing with you about Jerusalem, so widely known to ancient history as the land of Israelitish lore. I have read extensively of your people, but this is my first opportunity of meeting with one directly from that famed metropolis. However, the thing that makes me curious, if not perplexed, is that you, a Jew, are a Christian. I did not think such a thing were possible."

"Mr. Brigha," answered the rabbi with a smile, "one might find very few Jews in Jerusalem of Christian persuasion. In truth, I know of none. I was reared and educated until I was eventually graduated as doctor of Jewish law, and eventually ordained a rabbi. But as my information increased, I began to see in Judaism but a dead form, or branch of an erstwhile tree. So I severed my allegiance with that faith. I learned to my satisfaction, that the power I sought was strikingly potent in bygone ages, and wondrously manifest during the life of Jesus of Nazareth, perhaps more so than during four thousand years before his birth. However, in modern Christendom I fail to see that mighty power perpetuated. I resolved to begin a quest for that power. I mean that power wherein men, holding divine authority, have caused the very forces of nature to obey, such as recorded of Moses, Joshua, Elias, Elijah. Then men were saved from the fiery furnace, from the den of ravenous lions. Sick were healed, lame walked, the blind saw, and the dead were raised to life again. This power then, Mr. Brigha, is the object of my quest. Having vague conceptions of the great philosophies and religions of the Orient, I have come here to begin my search, for that power must be extant somewhere, among some people on earth."

Mr. Brigha, intensely interested in the brief narration, yet seemed so sure of his ground that he said immediately, "You have selected wisely, for you certainly make no mistake in coming into this fertile field, and among a people that even you Christians point to as being the headquarters of thought in religion, philosophy, and science."

Homer was restrained as he replied. "I must confess, Mr. Brigha, that I am somewhat uninformed. Will you tell me of your conception of India being the world seat of learning, or the source from which intelligence, according to your conception, originally sprang?"

"Mr. Ben Arden, I have but to refer to the writings of some of your illustrious Christians, among whom are Victor Cousins and Max Muller. One of them wrote: 'We (Christians) must bow the knee before the philosophies of the Orient.' And another wrote: 'Every philosophical, religious, or scientific thought known to this age, has been spoken by someone, at some time in India.' In the face of these statements, coming from such eminent gentlemen, outstanding translators of Indian writings into English, I feel sure you will agree with me that India has certainly been the cradle of thought, and consequently the source of knowledge."

"To an extent that might be true, Mr. Brigha. Yet, we Christians point to historical events of achievements in intellectuality and human progress that antedate anything you can point to."

Mr. Brigha looked Homer in the eye as he spoke with determined zest and fervor: "Be not too sure of your ground, Rabbi, for the great Vedic religion flourished long before your prophet Abraham was born. How much it antedated that time, I am not prepared

factually to state, other than that it flourished antedating
all history. Even your Christian writers point to our
records known as the *Vedas,* as being the oldest books
in all the world."

"Yes," answered the rabbi, advisedly. "I am free
to concede that you date far back in history. But the
thought that concerns me, is the extent to which the
Lord's dealings with your people have been, and still
might be manifest in power and glory. I desire to know
your conception of Deity and your relationship to him."

The question was thought-provoking to the priest.
Yet, with an air of confidence, evading a direct answer,
he stated: "Nothing will afford me greater pleasure,
Rabbi, than to take you deeply into the very fundamentals of Brahminism, for I feel assured that in the
disclosure you will see for yourself that there is no power
on earth or in the heavens to equal ours. Surely you,
like other learned men who have come here for intellectual food, will be forced to admit that here lies the parent
thought and postulate of all religious conception,
from which the diversified religions of the earth have,
directly or indirectly, come to being. You will concede,
I feel sure, that even your modern languages came from
the Sanscrit tongue."

Homer thought this a daring statement, answering,
as one in search of truth: "You may be right, Mr.
Brigha, and yet, so far as I know, some things you
present might be more inference than truth. Be that
as it may, I wish to direct your attention more to the
fundamentals of your religious thought."

"We are coming to that, Rabbi," returned the priest,
with an air of seeming impatience. "Now, to begin, I
wish to call your attention to what is known to us as
Dyaus—Mother of the Gods—the Self—the Absolute of
the universe—the Superlative of superlatives. It is known

to us as substance, or essence pervading all space in its infinity. Now, following Dyaus, exist subordinate powers, known as Varuna—God of the Sky in all its brightness and grandeur. Next comes Indra—God of Atmosphere."

"But, tell me, Mr. Brigha. Are you polytheistic in belief? If so, which of these gods do you worship as the central object of your devotion?"

"Rabbi, I prefer answering that later on. Dyaus consists of that which is invisible, and even that which is visible. One third of him has been created into solar systems and worlds, comprehending all mineral kingdoms, flora, and fauna thereon. But the remaining two-thirds is unorganized, omnipresent, and omnipotent in the vastness of space."

"Which implies, Mr. Brigha, that Dyaus is in no wise a personality, but an all-pervading essence."

"Fundamentally so. However, get this thought: that from Dyaus radiate the subordinate Gods with whom we, in obedience, have to deal—Varuna and Indra, gods of sky and atmosphere already referred to. From this wonderful combination radiate in turn, Agni, God of Fire, who later became Brahma; then, Indra, God of the Sun, who became Vishnu, and lastly, Siva, all of whom are indirectly subservient to the mighty Dyaus, and it is through these mediums that we worship the great superlative head."

"All these gods, as you state, are subservient to Dyaus. Am I right?"

"Exactly so, Rabbi, yet bear in mind that, while they are subservient to Dyaus, they are each of him a part. For the human mind to essay defining Dyaus would be an absurdity as he is beyond analysis."

Ben Arden still seemed unable to grasp the thought to his complete satisfaction, hence, he asked: "You mention the power of these gods, Mr. Brigha. Will you kindly explain which is the greatest of these?"

"That is not known fully, Rabbi. We teach, however, that all are equally invested in authority. This thought has been pretty well explained by one of your Christian writers, who penned the following stanza:

'In these three persons the one god is shown,
Each first in place, each last not one alone;
Of Siva, Vishnu, Brahma, each may be,
First, second, third among the blessed three.'"

This was decidedly confusing to Homer, as he questioned for more information: "Do I understand that this triad, trinity, or trimurti, represents the Dyaus principle?"

Mr. Brigha answered emphatically: "Yes, both as to trinity and individuality. However, the power of each is indefinable."

"That is too deep for me, Mr. Brigha. I must think more to comprehend even the elementary principles of it all. However, passing that up for the present, will you explain to me your conception of man, his origin, mission, and place in the universe? His final destiny?"

"Well, Rabbi, one third of Dyaus became material as represented in solar systems, worlds with all flora and fauna thereon. Hence, man, being material in his physical make-up, is of Dyaus a part."

"That being the case, Mr. Brigha, how do you account for his final destiny? In other words, will he always exist as a material entity as he is today, or will he, at some future time, become a resurrected, tangible being?"

The priest smiled. "Both wrong, Rabbi; decidedly so. That is merely Christian fallacy. I assure you that it has no place in Brahminism. That man is mortal we do not deny. But that his mortal shell is to continue eternally were the greatest curse that man could experience. Even the gods, Brahma, Vishnu, and Siva, were once mortal, and would have, perhaps, remained so had they not extorted from Dyaus the immortality they now possess. Self-denial through torture and suffering are the true mediums through which this mortal shell is ultimately thrown off. That alone makes man immortal."

Homer thought profoundly. "The term immortality to you seems altogether different from what it means to me. Please explain more fully."

"To me, Rabbi, it signifies entering into what is known to us as the state of Moksha. It represents the soul's entry into perfect rest: subduing of all ambition or desire; indifference to joy, pain, good, or evil; freedom from the curse of birth or death; absorption of self into the universal soul of Dyaus; into the Elysian fields."

Homer Ben Arden pondered the seeming absurdity, as he returned: "If I understand you correctly, it means that man's future is comparable to life's candle having blown out. Am I right?"

"Your figurative expression, Rabbi, quite logically covers the truth. The thought that we shall be relieved some time of this mortal frame, with all the weaknesses and vicissitudes attendant thereto, is reassuring, indeed, to us."

Ben Arden thought a few moments. "Then, Mr. Brigha, I am to understand that this union of body and the spark of life is, after all, a negation rather than a blessing. Do I conceive the thought rightly?"

"That very thing, Rabbi. Mortality is a curse rather than a blessing to life and existence, placed upon us by divine ordinance whereby we are purged through the school of experience. Here we learn to appreciate by the things we suffer. I am sure that when we arrive at Puri, you will observe this more intensively than words of mine could explain."

Homer seemed to philosophize a few moments, then: "Now, Mr. Brigha, if man is a part of the one-third of Dyaus created into worlds, with its flora and fauna, then he must be, in a way, related to all forms of life, mammal, fish, and fowl. Is my inference rightly drawn?"

"That very thing, my Jewish friend, and we have a philosophy that accounts for all diversified conditions of life, irrespective of its classification or differentiation."

"That being the case, Mr. Brigha, what is there to prevent your coming back at some time from the element of Dyaus, to be reborn to some lower form of life?"

"I am pleased you are leading me into this thread of thought, Rabbi, for that is embraced in our great philosophy of existence. The only preventive against such a possibility, for there is a possibility of such transition, is through the principle of self-denial, whereby man may extort from Dyaus an assurance that he is immune to such a deplorable destiny."

"Are you really sincere in that, Mr. Brigha?"

"Were we unsure of our ground, Rabbi, we would be foolish, indeed, to endure what we do in order to merit it. Now, in support of the philosophy, I want to refer you to the sacred ordinance of what is known as *suttee,* which, though suppressed by the British government, still remains true to principle."

"Yes, I have read frequently something of your *suttee,* and I assure you that a description first-hand will be illuminating and interesting."

"Very well, Mr. Ben Arden, but in so doing I ask that you keep your mind upon the sacredness of its observance. Briefly, it means that a widow of a deceased husband, voluntarily enters a funeral fire to be burned alive with the body of her deceased husband, or even subsequent to his death and burial. But allow me to read its motive and sacred rite from one of our sacred books, known as the shasters and puranas. Listen to it:

" 'If a woman despise her Lord, or has done what is contrary to his mind from mercenary motives and fears, or from suspicion or reasoning power, die with her husband, she shall be purged from all crimes. As the snake-catcher draws a serpent from its hole, so she by burning rescues her husband from hell, and rejoices with him. The woman who expires on the funeral pyre with her husband, purifies the family of her father, her mother, and husband. If her husband is a banminicide—the greatest of criminals—his wife, by burning, purges away his sins. There is no greater virtue than for a woman to burn herself with her husband. So long as a woman in her successive migrations should decline burning herself like a faithful wife, so long shall she not be exempted from springing into life again in the body of some female animal. Dying with her husband purifies three generations on her father's and her mother's side, who will enter into felicity with her. With them she shall enjoy heavenly choirs while fourteen Hindras reign.' "

Rabbi Ben Arden had difficulty in suppressing his disgust at so queer a doctrine of paganism. "This transcendental doctrine, Mr. Brigha, must apply to all humanity, does it not?"

Impressively, the priest replied: "Decidedly so. Even the great Vishnu, one of the triad of gods, passed through ten incarnations in the following manner and order. A fish, tortoise, bear, lion, dwarf, Rama, Ravana, Kirishna, Buddah, and lastly Kalkhi, the mighty one who is yet to appear."

"If I understand you correctly," urged Homer, "man became human by reason of some erstwhile merit. But for this he would, perchance, have become a monkey or some other form of lower life."

"Your inference is right, Rabbi. I see you are well on the road to become a typical Brahmin," replied the priest jocularly. "But let's carry the thought further that you may more fully comprehend our philosophy. His future emancipation from mortal slavery, together with the horror of sometime becoming some lower animal, is secured only by long and painful suffering and self-denial."

Homer's mind was working with rapidity: "Then, Mr. Brigha, how do you regard the animal kingdom? I mean from a standpoint of life preservation?"

"A Brahmin, Rabbi, kills no animal lest in the act he disturb some unfortunate soul struggling for higher planes in the scale of transmigration, wherein eventually he might become even as we are now."

Rabbi Ben Arden, feeling considerable disgust from the exposition of what he considered the acme of ridiculous philosophy, sought to bring the present conference to a close. "This conversation," said he, "has been intensely illuminating, and in that we have several days before we arrive at Puri, I propose a brisk walk up and down the deck, for we have conversed long."

Together the two men walked, edging their way through the very large cargo of massed humanity, nearly all of whom appeared to be fanatically imbued with the coming Festival of the Juggernaut.

Suddenly Ben Arden stopped, looking aloof: "Look, Mr. Brigha, I see land. Do you know where we are?"

"Yes, Rabbi, those are the Lacadive Islands, which means that we are now very far from Bombay, and at least half way to Ceylon. If all goes well, we should soon arrive at the south end of the Arabian peninsula, there to begin our northward journey."

CHAPTER VI

WHEN next Rabbi Ben Arden and the Brahmin priest met, they exchanged geographical explanations of India on the one hand, and of Palestine on the other, in which peoples, manners, and customs, were quite fully discussed and explained.

The ease with which each spoke the English language, became an interesting topic. "How wonderful," said the priest, "that wherever one goes, the English language is spoken, for one has little trouble in finding people who speak the tongue."

"It is quite different in Jerusalem, Mr. Brigha, for in my experience I have not encountered much English. What knowledge I have of the language comes as a result of diligent study. I had a college professor, a tutor of mine, who spoke English fluently. The euphony of the tongue was so musical to me, that I appealed to him for tuition. He tried to discourage me, but I was insistent. So he taught me, carefully coaching me for three years. Now, it is said that I speak the language with almost as much freedom as I do to my mother tongue. I take it, of course, that in Bombay, being a seaport city, you had greater opportunity and facilities to acquire the language."

"Yes, Rabbi. I have had the privilege of meeting and speaking with many English people. However, I have spoken the language from the time I was a lad. Many years ago, my father desired that I learn the language, and to this end he employed an officer in the

British army, then stationed in Bombay, to become my
tutor. The officer seemed to take a liking to me, and,
as a result of his patience, I learned to speak with quite
a marked facility. Since then I have spoken very much
English. You understand, there is but little comparison
in the grammar of the Hindu language and that of English. Yet, somehow, it came freely."

The rabbi and priest were seated on comfortable
deck chairs, with warm robes, when Rabbi Ben Arden,
eager to air some thoughts that had come to him during
the night, began: "Mr. Brigha, suppose we continue
our conversation of yesterday. I am anxious to differentiate between Brahminism and Buddhism, for in the
expounding of your philosophy yesterday, I seemed to
detect much that I thought belongs to the latter. I confess that I am somewhat confused."

"Briefly, Rabbi, I make but a brief answer at this
time, as I wish to go on to that later on. I state merely
that Buddha merely tried to reform Brahminism, but
in so doing, he excluded much of the fundamental
philosophy. You understand, Rabbi, that taking the two
great religions together, fully two thirds of the earth's
population is embraced. But to continue our conversation of Brahmin philosophy, I hope you have found
much beautiful ethical and sound philosophy in yesterday's presentation."

"I confess, Mr. Brigha, that some of your teachings
and explanations are ponderable, and I am not at all
surprised at your mighty following. Now, Mr. Brigha,
will you kindly explain further the following: Part of
Dyaus, as you stated, became man, and in that transla-
tion, I ask, was there a breaking of some law of natural
philosophy. If so, is there to be some form of atonement for the violation of law and order that man may
revert back to what you consider his destiny?"

The priest seemed to register some displeasure at the question: "Why, Rabbi, emphatically no. To me, the thought is a burlesque on logic and reason. It is no more or less than Christian deduction from fundamental philosophy, with apologies to you, of course, a Christian. Were I to admit such a conception, I would be placing Dyaus in the negative. No, Rabbi, the *modus operandi* of all creation is a progressive one, and to this end Dyaus is transmitted into solar systems, comprehending the vast millions of creations that study the great immensity of infinitude. By this, man becomes individualized with a distinct identity, purified through suffering until ultimately he can extort for himself a welcome dissolution into the reality of repose and rest. The very thought of such a thing as an atonement, has no place in Brahminism. What better were that than mortality which in itself is a negation, and the thought of resurrection even less? My aspirations, Rabbi, are to become emancipated from this crude shell—from the body I am compelled to drag along through my mortal career. I hail the time when I can shake it off forever."

Ben Arden, after giving the argument due consideration, turned to the priest, answering firmly: "Mr. Brigha, it will be a long time before you can convert me to that phase of your philosophy. For my hope is to realize a continuity of my self and individuality, to some day come from my tomb a tangible, resurrected being, with faculties such that I may progress throughout eternity. So, you see, there is an unbridgeable chasm between us as regards our hope of the future."

Priest Brigha smiled, taking all in good nature: "That does not discourage me, Rabbi, in the least, for I would be foolish were I to expect you to fathom the depth of our philosophy at a single bound. Please remember that it has taken many centuries for us to develop this great philosophy."

Ben Arden had another thought that he wished discussed by the Brahmin priest. "Permit me, Mr. Brigha, to ask you pointedly regarding the equality or inequality of human beings on earth. Do you regard all men born of one flesh and blood with an equality as coming of one common source? I have a specific reason for asking this question."

"Very unequal, my friend. Men are born within specified castes, from which they can never transcend during life."

"I have often read of this, Mr. Brigha, hence my pointed question. It seems to me very unreasonable to accept the caste system. That I might be unfortunate enough to be born in one of your lower castes in which a goodly life on my part can never raise me above it, to me is unthinkable."

"Speaking directly, Rabbi, as well might an ape aspire to become a man, a peach an apple, or a thorn a rose. A crocodile, for instance, is such by reason of some demerit. The same may be said of all lower forms of life, up through all animal life to man in his varied degrees. What is man that he should dare to change the caste the creator gave him as his destiny? Above his destined caste, he can never evolve. If he be a pariah, which is below the castes, a pariah he must remain. Above this comes the Surdas, or servile caste; then the merchant caste, the warrior caste, and, highest, is the priest or Brahmin caste."

"Meaning, Mr. Brigha, that you are one of the Brahmin caste, and so I take it that you have little directly to do with them of lower castes? Am I right in my deductions?"

"Only as a beacon light to show them the better way, to elevate them, if you will, to the loftiest degree within their destined caste."

"But, Mr. Brigha," persisted Homer, "is it not a mockery and discouraging torture to the soul below you, for you to teach man that there is no progression beyond the circumference of his limited circle?"

"That may be so, Rabbi, but what more can he expect but to be the result of his destiny?"

"Then, I am to understand that a pariah, for instance, may never become one of the servile caste. Why, I ask?"

"Simply this, Rabbi, to bring about this change would be an act of transmigration, which may not occur while man lives in mortality."

While the argument seemed absurd, Homer was determined to go to the bottom of the weird philosophy in this regard. "Suppose, Mr. Brigha, you have in your Brahmin caste, a savage, a renegade. Can such sink below that caste?"

"I thought, Rabbi, I had made that sufficiently clear. I say no, for it would be as impossible as for a man to become a monkey. The thought, to us, is not worth considering. With apologies to you, of course, my friend."

Home smiled good-naturedly, as he glanced at the great horde of Hindus on deck. "However do you distinguish between them, for they all look alike to me. Do you have distinguishing marks?"

Mr. Brigha arose, saying: "Come with me, and let us walk the deck out through this vast crowd, and I shall point to you some distinctions. I feel sure that you, with a little experience, will be able to distinguish somewhat for yourself. Now, see that miserable piece of humanity standing by the railing, and study his unintelligent face, for he is a pariah, as proud of his caste as I could ever be of mine, with no disposition whatever of evolving above it. I take it that you have observed that the most ignorant of men are the most egotistically inclined."

"Yes, Mr. Brigha, I have. But am I to understand that whenever I see such an unfortunate, he is a pariah?"

"Generally so, Rabbi, but not always. However, I doubt very much that you, in all India, could find one of this class dissatisfied with his caste. To such, it is the best commensurate with his adaptation. He would be uncomfortable and unhappy were he out of his soul-measure. Now, let us walk up the deck and I will point out to you one of the Surdas caste. But you must be sure to keep his shadow from falling on you. Ah, here comes one, and I ask you to mark well the difference in facial expression and general make-up. You easily observe, I am sure, a more brilliant personality."

"The difference is quite apparent, Mr. Brigha," returned the perplexed rabbi, "but I fear it would require much experience for me to be sure of my decisions."

"Quite so, quite so," answered the priest. "It comes only by one being possessed with power of delineation and character reading. Yet, on the other hand, the lowest as well as the highest can detect the difference by long experience. Furthermore, there are distinguishing marks that indicate the castes."

Homer was becoming deeply engrossed in his study of the Hindus as pointed out by the priest. "This is indeed interesting, I assure you, Mr. Brigha, and it must be fascinating to be able to differentiate between the castes."

"Just so, Rabbi. Now for the merchant caste. I saw one pass a few minutes ago. You might be able to detect him yourself."

This gave Homer a new ambition. "I have a jolly thought. Why not permit me to select him?" His eyes flashed as he looked at the hundreds of Hindus on deck.

"Very well," smiled the priest, "and I shall watch you closely to observe your ingenuity in delineation."

Together the two made their way through the crowd, Mr. Brigha carefully avoiding any physical contact and always keeping in the sun where his shadow would fall away from him so that no one's shadow might fall on him. Some were in conversation, some playing games, and others gathered in bands of a hundred or more. Together the men walked, while the rabbi was trying his skill. Finally the rabbi stopped. "There, I take it that this man is of the merchant caste. He must be commercially minded. Am I right in my selection?"

"Bravo," returned the priest, as he clapped his hands. "Now, tell me, how did you come to select him?"

"Well, Mr. Brigha, it was mostly guesswork. However, I seemed to observe from his narrowed eyes and firm countenance, that he might be some calculator."

"I doubt, Rabbi, that there is one of the warrior caste on board. At least, I have seen none. So now for the priest or Brahmin caste. This might test your ability."

In view of discovering one comparable to the priest, Homer went to work. Soon he stopped, and pointing to an individual, he returned: "There, I would say he is a Brahmin."

"And how did you know, Rabbi?"

"For the simple reason that, to me he is a mystic, such as I have not seen elsewhere in the crowd." Homer looked at the priest as the thought came to him. "Of course, Mr. Brigha, this with apologies to you."

"Well, Rabbi, you win. I take the inference in good nature, with the admission that all Brahmin priests are more or less of a mystic, or divining nature."

"One more question, Mr. Brigha. Do those of lower castes look up in reverence to the caste above them? For instance, do those of lower castes look up to you?"

"Well, yes and no. You have observed how hundreds have given me homage as they passed us. Other than the priest or Brahmin caste, however, there is little recognition, as each thinks himself the equal, and often the superior of his fellows or members of other castes. By the way, Rabbi," said the priest, as he pointed off to the leeward of the ship. "Do you see those white massive cliffs far ahead of us?"

Homer looked off, later replying: "If you see land, you have better eyes than I have."

"Not so, Rabbi. Just fix your gaze northward and look carefully to the white cliff above the clouds."

"Yes, yes, I see it dimly. It becomes clearer as one fixes his gaze firmly upon it. You know, Mr. Brigha, I have often observed the weakness of the eye, especially when on the ocean, and how slowly the first vision of land is shown in very dim appearance. I wonder what land it is."

"That particular land tells us that we are now in the Indian ocean, and have come at last to the extreme southern end of the Indian peninsula. You observe that we are bearing to the eastward now."

"I have not noticed it," returned the rabbi. "I have been too much engrossed with the days of conversation to think of directions. Is that the mainland in the distance?"

"Not so, Rabbi, for we are many miles from land. What we see is the island of Ceylon, and soon we shall be docked at the quaint old city of Galle."

"It is regrettable that we shall arrive in the darkness. I would that we could see the old landmark in daylight. Will the ship remain until dawn?"

"No, for we shall be en route an hour or so after our arrival. Then for a midnight cruise, and when we arise in the morning, we shall have partly traversed the Indian ocean toward the Bay of Bengal."

"Which implies, of course, Mr. Brigha, that the sun

tomorrow will rise on the opposite side of the ship than it has been doing since we left Bombay."

"Exactly so, Rabbi, and do not be surprised if you lose your bearings altogether."

"Which," returned the rabbi, intently, "is quite possible. However, to test my sense of direction, I will point to where I think north should be."

"Bravo," laughed the priest. "You are pointing southwest. Have you so soon forgotten that the ship has changed its direction?"

"No, Mr. Brigha, I have not forgotten mentally, but I confess that my sense of direction has not changed."

"Well, Rabbi Ben Arden, when the sun fails to rise in the morning where your tardy intuition suggests it should, do not think the gods have turned the world topsy-turvy, but that it is one of those mental illusions that humanity is subject to experiencing."

"I have, in my travels, Mr. Brigha, often lost my cardinal points, and I confess that there is no feeling that can be more distressing and uncomfortable, to endure."

CHAPTER VII

THE moon was shining in all her beauty when the vessel docked at Galle. The rush of changing mail, freight, with the bustle of the longshoremen was intensely interesting to Ben Arden, and especially to witness the large group of passengers board the already crowded ship. Turning to the priest, Homer suggested: "It seems to me that fully three hundred passengers are boarding the boat. I cannot understand why they are joining us."

Placing his hand carefully on the rabbi's shoulder, the priest replied: "Why, my dear rabbi? Have you so soon forgotten that we are en route to Puri to witness the great Festival of the Juggernaut? These people have the same objective as we have, of course."

Homer seemed to marvel deeply: "Upon my word, will all India be there?"

"Well, you will witness the massed human horde of all your life experiences. Do not be surprised to find yourself one of many millions of people in one vast throng, many of whom have, no doubt, camped at Puri for days in anticipation of the great event."

The deep fog-horn-like whistle announced the time of departure, and soon the grinding of the machinery was clearly audible.

During the next few days the ship rolled, and it was with difficulty that the berths held some of the passengers. Ben Arden, for one, felt quite alarmed as the ship encountered a severe windstorm. However, he was informed by the steward that it was one of those gales incident to that section of the sea. "It might continue," said he, "until about nine in the morning, at which time, all being well, we shall be nearing the Bay of Bengal."

More days passed, with the ship still rolling and fighting a forty-five degree gale; even some hoisted sails did not seem to reduce the rolling. Waves swept the deck and all were ordered below, leaving the sailors alone to man the ship through the seeming mad and troubled water.

As soon as permitted, Homer Ben Arden found his way upon the deck, when, seeing a burly tar approaching, asked: "Mister Sailor, do you think this great human cargo will endanger the ship?"

The crude derelict gave the Jew a staring glance as he gruffly replied: "Danger, mon—lawd, no. Dos't think a bloomin' bunch of humans 'ud mattah to a ship like this? By the bloomin' 'ell, thee must be crazy."

"Well," returned the humiliated Jew from so sound a snubbing. "I certainly apologize. I meant no offense, I assure you."

"Ah, bosh, Sheeney, keep the change, cos I was poor onct mesself." With that the tar went up the deck.

Rabbi Ben Arden was dumbfounded and bewildered, for such a reproach was new to his experience.

An English-speaking gentleman who had witnessed the scene with amusement, approached Ben Arden with: "Come, friend, do not take it so seriously. You know, you can expect nothing but a kick from a mule. Remember, he is only an English tar, and a crude one at that."

"Crude," replied Ben Arden, as he looked into the gentleman's kind eyes. "I think it a very mild way of expressing such discourtesy. To me it was a kick that struck home. I am not accustomed to such deportment."

"Which implies, my friend, that you are not used to the fraternity of the sea. You should take the hardness of his lot into account and consider the source. Don't allow such as that to mar your peace for one moment."

"Thank you," returned the rabbi. "I shall profit by your advice. I had no idea, by the way, that I should find another English-speaking gentleman on board. That man spoke a dialect that, if English, it was scarcely understandable."

"Very true," replied the gentleman. "My experience in traveling over England is that in each town you visit, you are likely to encounter a new dialect peculiar to the locality, until it is with difficulty, at times, that one understands the people. There are idioms by the thousands, and each group seems to have them different from the others. This may be stated of the entire nation, especially in country districts."

Rabbi Ben Arden seemed amazed as he listened to the clear ring of the gentleman's voice and his musical enunciation: "I note, sir, that your voice has a pleasant ring to it, and a euphony different from the English I have been used to. Will you kindly tell me your nationality?"

The stranger smiled whimsically: "Why certainly, I am an American, and I come from the United States. You know, throughout our vast enlightened nation, we have but one dialect of the English language. While many below the mediocre class often abuse the use of verbs, we have but one dialect."

"This is my good fortune," returned the rabbi, appreciatively. "This is the first time in my experience to meet a real American. May I ask your name?"

"Surely. My name is Mordon—John Mordon, and I hail from Indianapolis, in the State of Indiana. And your name—?"

"Is Homer Ben Arden, commonly known as Rabbi Ben Arden, and I am directly from Jerusalem."

Mr. Mordon seemed to enjoy making the acquaintance of the rabbi, for he smiled, at the same time extending his hand, a hearty handshake following. "Well," smiled Mordon, "this is certainly my pleasure, to be sure, for the first time in my life to shake the hand of a Jew directly from the Holy City. But what perplexes me is the fluency with which you speak English. Certainly they speak little of that tongue in Jerusalem?"

"Very little, very little. I learned, by persistent effort, from one of my college tutors, and I have been so fascinated by it, that I am making it my language instead of my mother tongue."

"The only fault I find with your English," returned Mr. Mordon, with a smiling vein of accusation, "is that you should spend a year or two in America to wear off that accent of yours."

This seemed momentarily to stagger the rabbi, who had thought his accent good, but now that it was challenged, he was sufficiently broad to take the criticism. Earnestly, he replied: "My friend, it is just like the experiences of life, is it not? One so often thinks he has the best there is, until something superior is presented. You have given me a new ambition. All being well, I hope some day to visit your wonderful country, perhaps in search of my quest, and I assure you I shall profit by your suggestion."

"You speak of your quest, Rabbi. Will it be asking too much of you to indicate what you mean by it?"

"It will give me the greatest of pleasure, Mr. Mordon. As you observe, I am a typical Jew." Smilingly, he pointed to his nose.

John Mordon smiled, for the racial physical evidence was unmistakable. "In my youth," continued the rabbi," I knew nothing of religion other than that of Judaism. As I grew older, however, and obtained access to the Holy Scriptures, I observed how in bygone ages there had been dispensations of the gospel bestowed upon Israel, under which the higher laws of heaven were strikingly realized, whereby the very elements were brought under divine power and authority, such as during the times of Moses, Joshua, Elijah, Elisha, and others. Came the time when this power and authority was lost. As I turned my attention to Christian scripture in the meridian of time, those powers were again marvelously restored to the extent that the very winds and waves obeyed, sick were healed, the blind saw, while the lame leaped for joy. Even the dead were raised to life again. To me, Mr. Mordon, this is the sign of the true gospel that I have been pleased to name my Priceless Pearl. To find this is the object of my quest."

John Mordon seemed amazed at so lofty an ambition. "Your quest, Rabbi, is a marvelous one, indeed. But a Christian Jew, is a combination that one seldom sees, is it not?"

Ben Arden smiled. "Perhaps so. But in Jerusalem and Judaism, I saw a dead form of worship buried in an admixture of cold pomp and ceremony. A dilapidated wreck, if you will, and so I turned my attention to Christianity. In Jesus Christ, I saw the very manifestation that has been the insignia of God's work throughout the ages of his dealings with righteous people. In fact, I saw in Jesus of Nazareth the true Messiah, and in his dispensation the veritable Priceless Pearl. But, alas, I also saw a subsequent falling away into complete apostasy, until I am quite sure the Christians have little of the power I seek." The rabbi became deeply earnest: "Can you tell me, Mr. Mordon, "is there any place on earth that I may find it?"

Mr. Mordon replied: "Indeed, Rabbi, I cannot. Your quest is one to be much admired, and I truly hope that some day you will be rewarded to your soul's full satisfaction. You know, I have often thought of the words of Isaiah, who wrote: 'The hand of the Lord is not shortened that he can not save; neither his ear heavy that he can not hear; But your iniquities have separated between you and your God, and your sins have hidden his face from you that he will not hear.' More modern writers, in fact, some of the humble confessions of prelates today, fully confess that this lost power is nowhere to be found among Christian creeds."

"That is just as I have learned, Mr. Mordon."

John Mordon drew a loose-leaf notebook from his pocket: "While on the subject, Rabbi, you might be interested in a clipping I have here from a discourse from an honest minister, a Rev. T. H. Martin of Meaderville, Montana. Surely you will be interested in what he said. I shall read it:

" 'Is the Church anything but a social organization? Is the Christianity of our day the true doctrine of the Christ of the Bible? Has the so-called Christianity of today anything in it that ought to attract more than any other creed that is supposed to help humanity? Is not the Church today boycotted, and that justly? Are we not today concocting questionable schemes to operate our churches? I know that such interrogations will not be very savory to many people, but knowing something concerning the Church from top to bottom, and as I fear God and would rather be true than esteemed, I fearlessly propound them. The Christian community of the present is loud in its acclaims of conquests and remarkable victories. We are invited to see its acquired wealth, its tremendous expansion, and to hear the clang of its enormous machinery. But with all this, I maintain that the Christianity of the present is face to face with a lamentable loss. The Christianity of today has acquired much but in its getting, it has lost its own soul—it has lost the Holy Ghost. No true Christian dare refute this argument, for, go where you may in Christendom today, you will find that our religion is void of the supernatural element which the Bible claims it must have in order to exist. The Christian religion today is merely a social code and has nothing in it whereby it could claim a divine origin. It is truly pitiable to behold the Church trying to save this sinful world. We have lost our magnet. The Christ, who said he would draw all men to him, if lifted up, is disobeyed and ignored in the multiplicity of our present church life. Since we have presented many substitutions to the world for genuine spiritual power, they are of no more value in saving the sinner than an artificial heart would be pumping blood through the arteries. We are like an engine trying to run without steam. The Church of today is the church of man and not the church of God.' "

Homer had listened with intense interest, for the writing struck a responsive chord in his soul. "Would you mind my copying that article, Mr. Mordon?"

John Mordon smiled as he removed the leaf from his notebook. "Here, you may have it, for I have pretty well memorized its contents. You know, Rabbi, I agree fully with that honest minister. I presume that I might be termed an infidel to the creeds, yet I am a Christian at heart, even though I do but little at appearing one."

The rabbi sat motionless in deep thought. At last, he exclaimed: "This is interesting, indeed, Mr. Mordon. Really, it is a source of satisfaction to find for the first time, a mind that seems to run in the same channel as mine. I feel sure you can appreciate, to an extent at least, the object of my quest."

"I certainly do, Rabbi, but why are you here in India? You certainly do not anticipate finding your Priceless Pearl among these pagans, do you?"

"That I know not, Mr. Mordon. One thing I do know, and that is that modern Christendom owes much to Oriental thought and philosophy for some of its choice tenets and religious conceptions. Moreover, one might stand about as good a chance here as among Christian creeds, in that India is known in philosophy as being the headwaters of thought. Thus, I deemed it advisable to begin my quest here."

"Well," returned John Mordon, "perhaps you are right. However, I cannot help feeling that your search in India will be a fruitless one."

"Yes, Mr. Mordon, I might have to spend years in my search, but I have both youth and wealth in my favor, all of which I shall apply unreservedly to the end of my elected quest."

"Are you traveling alone, Rabbi?"

"I was alone, but I was fortunate in forming the acquaintance of a Hindu priest, a Mr. Brigha, now on this vessel. In return, Mr. Mordon, may I ask your business in these parts?

"Indeed, Rabbi. I am an American merchant, and am taking my doctor's advice to leave business and its cares for a season that my system may be somewhat rebuilt. Moreover, I have an American friend, a Mr. Johnson, in Calcutta, connected with the American Embassy, who has frequently insisted that I pay him a visit. So, you see, I am killing, as it were, two birds with one stone. Of course, you are going to Calcutta?"

"Yes, but not direct, for I shall disembark at Puri, where the great Festival of the Juggernaut is to take place on the eighteenth of this month. I could not think of missing that event, for I am told it is the experience of a lifetime."

"And this, Rabbi, accounts for the tremendous throng of Hindus on this vessel? I have wondered what it is all about."

"Exactly so, Mr. Mordon. Can you arrange to stop over and accompany me? Then we can go on to Calcutta together."

The American pondered for a few moments and then said, "I should be gratified to accompany you,

Rabbi, for I have read much of the Juggernaut, and know that it would be an unusual experience. I shall see the purser and see if a stopover can be arranged. When do we arrive at Puri?"

"All being well, we should arrive within the next two days."

"Good, Rabbi. I shall write my friend Johnson at once, sending my letter along on this boat, informing him of my delay. Now, what say you if we pace the deck awhile, now that the sea has become calmer?"

"Agreed," answered the rabbi, "and while so doing, let us study carefully the faces and characteristics of these sailors, for they seem a curious lot to me."

For a time they were silent, and then the rabbi said, "You know, I long for the time when I can go to the United States, for I realize that a little more wit and humor than I possess will give me a new slant on life. For my part, I sense that I must have some of the old landmarks of antiquity effaced from my make-up to prepare me for better progress in a strange world like this."

"Yes, Rabbi, you are right, and while you seem to marvel at me, I am a very common type of American. I assure you that some hair-raising experiences await you when you shall arrive in my country, which you need to put the necessary pep into you."

"Be assured that I shall shape my affairs to that end. It might be within the next year or two."

"And when you do, Rabbi, remember that your headquarters must be with me in Indianapolis, for I shall be glad to consider you my guest."

"Very kind of you, Mr. Mordon, and I shall look forward with pleasure to being in America. Already, you have given me much that has been new to me."

John Mordon looked up the deck, seeing a tar approaching, when, nudging the rabbi, he smiled. "By the way, Rabbi, here comes your friend, the tar. See the look he wears on his face. Does he not remind you very much of a bulldog?"

"Hello, Sheney," scowled the gruff tar, boisterously. "How's old father Abraham? I see youse got his nose. Jist you listen to this: 'France boasts of her lily, England of her rose,'" he pointed to the rabbi, flipping his finger under his nose. "'Jerusalem has the sheney, and the sheney's got the nose.' By the bloomin' 'ell, yer it."

"Well, puppy," retorted Mordon, showing his disgust at the intrusion. "What has the old cat dragged in this time, a thing like you."

The tar was immediately nonplussed yet enraged as, shaking his fist in Mordon's face, he growled vindictively: "Look 'ere, ye blasted American bull-dozin' Yankee, yez 'ave butted into a hornet's nest this time, to be sure. Now, it's up to yez to swallow them words, an' do it quick." The tar at once began rolling up his sleeves, when suddenly a dozen sailors appeared on the scene, witnessing Mordon preparing to remove his coat. Seeing the American meant business, the tar withdrew somewhat, only to meet the jeers of his comrades. A sailor's voice rang out. "Hey, Sandy, ye have met yer Wellington this time, I bet ye. I thought ye had too much sense to stir American ire."

"Aw, 'ell," returned Sandy, "'e's easy. Say, Yankee, does ye mean business? We'll jist try the gloves Bedad I'm jist akin' to get a smack at yer monkey-face."

"Well," replied Mordon, dryly, "I don't mind a few solid rounds, but take my advice and start nothing you are not prepared to carry through. Even a tar like you might run into a snag."

Sandy at once began to show the white feather, seeing which, the sailors shouted: "Bluffed, Sandy, bluffed."

Ben Arden's face blanched: "Do you really mean, Mr. Mordon, do you mean—"

Mordon smiled: "That very thing, Rabbi. I mean that an American cannot be bluffed; besides, I am pretty well experienced, for this is one of my pastimes in the gymnasiums at home."

The gloves were soon produced, and a ring of sailors was formed, each eager to witness what the outcome would be. Sandy, who had been the terror of the ship, was now reluctant to enter the ring until his fellows forced him.

Before round one was over, the sailors saw the American was scienced, and cheer after cheer went up as the American landed blow after blow, the tar leaving ample openings in his lack of defense.

At the end of round one, Mordon stepped up to the rabbi. "The tar has no skill at all. I am sure I can finish him at will. I'll spar with him for the next round, then you watch the third round."

During the second round Mordon playfully dodged Sandy's clumsy drives, toward the end receiving a staggering upper from Mordon that sent him reeling. Then came round three, that opened furiously. Sandy was floored as fast as he could arise before the count of ten. Again and again he fell under Mordon's intense battery, until finally he was completely knocked out.

The sailors danced with glee, as one said: "Bully for the Yankee, the first man to knock old Sandy out."

Mordon advanced, assisting Sandy to his feet, Sandy eventually saying, incoherently: "Well, Yankee, yez put me in bad, didn't yez? I'm licked to a frazzle."

"So it appears," returned Mordon, calmly, "and now, unless you want another dose, there is one thing you must do without delay. You apologize to my friend, the rabbi, for your insolence."

Like a whipped puppy, Sandy apologized, while the sailors enjoyed the old bully's humiliation.

Slapping Sandy on the shoulders, Mordon said, intently: "Bravo! Now you just get out of here, and when you pass this way again, see how nearly you can act like a white man." And Sandy withdrew.

The mate advanced, and grasping Mordon by the hand, said: "American, the congratulations are coming your way, for that bluffer has held sway on this ship these three years. The lesson will be his making."

"Mate," returned Mordon, calmly, "I do not profess to be a pugilist, nor do I approve of such work. However, it is a good thing to have a little science in times of emergency, you know."

Turning to the rabbi, Mordon said, thoughtfully: "Now, Rabbi, do not think me altogether savage by such conduct. I feel now that your urge to come to America, among such a ferocious people, will be changed."

"To the contrary, Mordon, you little know how much you interest me, and have intensified my urge immeasurably to become something more than I now am. I wish I could be in your company continuously, then, perhaps, I might amount to something as a well-rounded human being."

"Rabbi," answered Mordon, calmly, "you have a great time in store for you, to be sure, when you come to my country. I think I know how you feel. However, there's the dinner bell, and I for one am hungry as a wolf."

Taking the rabbi by the arm, they descended the stairway to the dining room.

When the two men returned on deck, whom should they meet but Priest Brigha, who had been pacing the deck vigorously.

"Well, began the rabbi, cheerfully, "if here is not my friend, Brigha."

Following the formalities of getting acquainted, the trio took seats under the canvas veranda in comfortable deck chairs.

On learning that the American had decided to accompany the rabbi on his trip and visit at Puri, the priest expressed deep satisfaction and gratitude. "I confess that I have been perplexed somewhat as to just what to do with my Jewish friend, since I am scheduled to take a very active part in the festival. Everything will be arranged, gentlemen, as I have a suite of rooms reserved at a hotel, and you will have ample quarters assigned for your comfort. So, now I wish to have a little time with you by way of instruction when you arrive and for your conduct during the festival."

For fully an hour the trio were deep in conversation, the priest freely advising them as to safe procedure, even suggesting a locality as a point of vantage from which they could best observe the momentous festival.

CHAPTER VIII

LATE that evening they debarked at Puri, and soon the two men were settled in a hotel that was quite clean and comfortable.

The following morning, after a hearty breakfast, the priest led the two men to the hotel veranda, from which he pointed out various sights, and especially the magnificent temple of the Juggernaut in the distance, and advising them as to their deportment during the day, concluded: "Now, friends, I must leave you, but expect to return sometime tonight." So saying, the priest withdrew.

"How peculiar," began Ben Arden. "Mr. Brigha has been so cool and composed during our voyage from Bombay, but today he seems wrought up to a high pitch."

"Judging from the faces of this Hindu horde, Rabbi, they all seem fanatically emotional. I have often read stories to that effect. How a rational being can be thus wrought up is beyond me. On the other hand it is, after all, quite understandable. You know, even in America, I have seen things just about as revolting. Why, I have really seen women robed in silks, rolling idiotically in the dust in revival meetings, shouting that they had found Jesus, and such tommy-rot."

Pointing off in the distance, the rabbi said in his amazement: "Just look at yonder hillside. It seems alive with human beings. They must be there by the millions."

"Let me suggest, Rabbi, that under any and all con-

ditions, we hang closely together, lest we become separated in the crowd. A lone stranger, you know, might
not fare any too well. On the other hand, when two
are together, there is always less to be concerned about.
Now, let's stroll along that boulevard yonder. The
tropical verdue seems inviting after our long sea voyage."

The walk was exhilarating, for everywhere were
spreading trees, ornamental shrubs and flowers to gladden
the eye. Frequently, they stopped to admire the beauty
of their surroundings, and more especially were they
attracted to the masses of human beings on every hand.
Frequently they were accosted by mendicants, and Ben
Arden was free with giving coins, until Mordon took
him to task. "You know, Rabbi, unless you desist, you
will be stormed by thousands begging for pennies."

"Very well," answered the rabbi, "I shall do as you
suggest." Stopping suddenly, the rabbi continued.
"Upon my word, what is this? A man wearing a heavy
iron collar about his neck, and see how filthy he is. It
seems to me he has not washed for months."

"Or perhaps years," interjected Mr. Mordon. "This
must be a Hindu fakir, extorting through self-inflicted
punishment and torture, divine assurance that he will
not pass through unpleasant transmigrations. But look,
here is another, holding his hand in the air. See how
skinny are his arms; also, look at his fingernails. They
have grown inches long. He probably has held his arm
in that position for years."

Ben Arden watched him closely. "I think I am
safe in saying that he has not smiled in years. What a
life, what a life, to be sure!"

"Indeed," chuckled the American, "he reminds me
of a funeral or something worse. Look, here is another
freak. This fool is torturing himself by having his legs
wrapped around his neck. Surely he is one that has
to be fed what he eats."

As they passed leisurely along, Ben Arden stopped suddenly. "Just look at this. This fellow is actually lying on nails, point up. How could he endure such torture?"

"Well, I'll be ———," returned Mordon. "That is the limit, if there is a limit to this fakirism, which is the height of imbicility. You know, Rabbi, I have read of fakirs hanging to a pole extended in air with hooks in their flesh, and kindred self-inflicted tortures. You know, Rabbi, things I have seen in human beings when emotionally wrought up, has made me feel estranged from what often goes in the name of Christianity."

Arm in arm, the friends worked their way through the crowd, ever growing more dense as they advanced. They eventually arrived near the court of the temple. Here they stood amazed at the gorgeousness of the architecture, beautiful stone-cutting, symmetry and finish, decorated with marble, mosiacs, frescoes, and friezes. With all this the frenzied emotion on the faces of the thousands of Hindus did not go unnoticed.

"Seems to me, Mordon, the people are thicker than ants that surround these trees. Have you noticed, by the way, that one could not lean against one of these trees without carrying thousands of the pesky insects with him."

"Yes, Rabbi, I have frequently read of this, but had forgotten about it until now. I presume this maintains in all tropical countries, does it not?"

"I think so, Mordon. Just observe that in this intense heat, you find practically no one enjoying the shade. Just see this mob. I would not be surprised to see millions on millions assembled here tomorrow. Mr. Brigha told me as much."

"What is interesting me right now, Rabbi, is the mode of travel—elephants, camels, donkeys. I am think-

ing right now of the vast difference between this and my
country with its automobile traffic. You know, in my
country the horse has been practically eliminated from
the streets, and when one sees a condition like this, he
is constrained to wonder if he has gone back thousands
of years in history. This is intensely interesting to me."

The din of the human horde in one droll monotone
continued far into the night, so much that after the two
friends had arrived at their hotel, they sat for hours
listening to the rumble from the hundreds of camps
in the near distance.

Just after dawn the following morning, Mr. Brigha
aroused his guests, insisting that they make haste to
accompany him to the temple grounds, informing them
that he had obtained permission to show them the massive cars of the Juggernaut, together with the triad of
gods thereon. The privilege was gladly accepted, and in
a few minutes the three men were en route.

"By the way," began the priest, "what did you gentlemen think of the exterior of the temple? I hope
you were not disappointed but surprised at its great
dimensions, the quality of its architecture."

"To the contrary," replied Mordon, "we were amaz-
ingly surprised, for we had not the slightest idea that
such skill and fine artistry existed in India. We were
unable to form an idea of its great dimensions."

"Well, gentlemen, the main building is six hundred
thirty-five feet long by four hundred ten feet wide. You
observe, of course, that it required a vast sum of money
to erect it, and that means has not been spared. But
let us hasten on for I want you to witness the final arrangements for the festival cortege, besides, I shall be
obliged to leave you soon. It is a privilege seldom
granted a stranger to gain admittance to the great preparation scene, and were I not an official, the privilege would

not have been granted. I have explained your positions carefully to the management, so all has been arranged."

"We are indeed grateful to you, Mr. Brigha," returned the rabbi, "all of which we shall greatly enjoy, I assure you."

Even at this early hour, the street and open spaces were a jam of humanity and more especially as they neared the temple grounds were hundreds of thousands contending for strategic positions from which to witness the cortege. Had it not been that Mr. Brigha was a prelate of eminence, their admission had been a difficult one to procure.

Arriving at the scene, the priest began: "Behold, gentlemen, the three great cars of the Juggernaut. The gods you see, all robed in costly textures of silk and satin, are now about ready to begin their journey to their summer home. You will observe that there are three distinct cars, each supported by sixteen massive wheels, each wheel being about six feet high and around two feet in thickness. This is essential as each car weighs many tons. Krishna or the Juggernaut car is thirty-two feet square and sixty-five feet high; and, if you will observe, the features of this god are painted blue. His friends, Siva and Satrada, are painted white and yellow, respectively."

"By what power do these cars move?" asked Mr. Mordon, as he saw no outward evidence.

"You see," answered the priest, "those men attaching long ropes, six to each car. Each of these cords is fully five hundred feet long. Devotees by the thousands are eager to do homage to these gods, and at a given signal, will unitedly draw each of these cars to its destination."

An attendant delivered a message to the priest, who, in great emotion, bade adieu to his friends and withdrew, leaving them to make their exit alone.

Arm in arm, the American and Jew pushed their way through the vast crowd of pilgrims toward the vantage point suggested by Mr. Brigha. They were fully half an hour in gaining the heights, and had no more than arrived when came the deep gutteral sound of the oboes, as explained by the priest as the signal for the cortege to begin, which was followed by a rumbling din of thousands of voices in one weird monotone.

"Look," quickly spoke the American, "here comes a company of mounted English redcoats. I wonder what part, if any, they play in the Juggernaut cortege. They certainly cannot be so foolish as to participate in this absurdity."

"I wish it were possible to speak to them," suggested Ben Arden. "Do you think we dare do so?"

"Dare, yes. Dare anything, and why not?" With a motion of Mordon's hand, the company was brought to a halt, when the captain smilingly advanced, saying: "Good morning, gentlemen; you are, of course, strangers in the land, and especially to this sort of business."

"Yes," replied Mordon, "we have stopped over at Puri to witness the Juggernaut festivities."

"Which will be well worth your while, for you will experience what will be valuable to you. But, tell me, are you alone?"

"Today we are," returned Mordon, "otherwise we are guests of a Hindu priest, who is an official in the cortege."

"Well, well," answered the officer. "This will not do. I shall dispatch a bodyguard at once, for you might be glad of their protection before the parade is over. You must beware of what is known as stranglers or thugs, commonly called, for they are a murderous lot. I shall instruct your guard to give all necessary precaution, together with information that will be interesting to you."

Two mounted redcoats advanced, taking their places near the two men, and the company moved on.

"Why," asked the rabbi of the guards, "are your services essential in this celebration? You certainly do not participate, do you?"

"No, we do not, yet we play an important part. You see, these Hindus are so fanatical in their devotion to these idols that they have, in times past, actually thrown themselves under the massive wheels of the cars, only to be crushed to death, thinking that thereby they may extort from the gods divine favor as to passing to the Elysian fields of eternal bliss. The British government has forbidden the further practice of these gruesome deeds, and it is to this end that we are here to see that law and order be maintained."

"Do you mean to say," asked Mordon, "that men would really throw themselves beneath the great wheels?"

"That very thing, sir, and despite our efforts, there are occasionally a few that achieve death that way each year. Such a thing might happen today. I can take you along the road and show you bleached human bones of fanatics who have been crushed beneath the massive wheels, for they seem to go stark crazy when frenzy seizes them. Just wait and see for yourselves how emotionally crazy these Hindus can become."

"What an incessant monotone of shouts and other hideous noises," marveled John Mordon. "It does not seem possible that human beings could act thus. Now comes the signal. Just listen, a million fanatics screaming all at once, with the tom-toms or whatever they are called. Seems to me all the hideous noises of the jungles are turned loose at once in one deluge of vibration."

"Ah," quickly spoke the rabbi, "here comes the first car. It is the Juggernaut in lead. Observe how it

sways from side to side. Look also at the human horde
tugging at the ropes. There must be thousands of them
acting as human horses. I shall be glad when the car
draws nearer."

"And look," said the American interestedly, "cars
number two and three are now moving far in the rear.
Now all are en route."

The procession was headed by many drums and
other weird instruments, followed by chanting thousands singing more in a monotone than to any distinct
tune. Following them came large companies of priests
richly attired in brilliant colors. Then in turn, those
of respective castes came in order. Lastly, there swung
into view thousands of men stripped, with nothing other
than britch-clouts to cover their nakedness, all tugging
fanatically at the ropes.

"Watch carefully, gentlemen," spoke one of the
mounties. "See how carefully our boys ride close by
the cars. A mountie by the side of each wheel, lest
someone throw himself beneath and be crushed to death."

Turning to the rabbi, Mordon asked: "Mr. Ben
Arden, did you ever dream of such a spectacle as this?"

"Never, Mordon. I feel safe in saying that there
are millions of people in this moving mass. Just look
how the human horde is slowly descending from the
elevations, bent on falling into line with the parade.
Surely this mass marching hundreds abreast will require
hours to pass. Then, too, observe the elephants, camels,
and what not, seeming to clamor into line of march."

"Then," smiled Mordon, "everything in evidence
but clothes. It is little wonder the British government
has taken severe steps. If this is a sample of Brahmin
conduct, then I am mighty glad to be an American."

"Well said, Mordon, and I fear that Priest Brigha's
teachings will fall on stony ground so far as this Jew
is concerned. I have often heard of Brahminism being

a religion without a redeeming feature, and I am inclined to accept the statement."

The cars had passed, yet hundreds of thousands of Hindus, who had seemingly yelled themselves hoarse, were trudging along, nearly hidden in the dust that they had raised.

"Now, gentlemen," asked a mountie, "what think you of Juggernaut by this time?"

"From a standpoint of a human pandemonium," answered Mordon, "it is a gigantic affair, quite a spectacle that I would not have missed for anything. On the other hand, it is to me the limit of imbecility."

"Well said," interrupted Ben Arden, intently. "Yet I feel that allowance must be made for their ignorance. They are perhaps doing the best they know."

Turning to one of the soldiers, Mr. Mordon asked, intently: "Will you please indicate why it was necessary that you gentlemen be appointed as our bodyguard. Is there really any danger of our being alone in this human horde?"

"There may and there may not be," returned the soldier with austerity. "You may consider our presence advantageous to your safety at least, for these Hindus show respect to redcoats, knowing that it is best that they do."

"But the real risk?" inquired the American. "I thought the Hindus were quite law-abiding. In fact, I have seen nothing go wrong in this great festival."

"That may be. But there are a few remnants living of a once formidable band of murderers that are operative on occasions of this kind. I refer to the strangling thugs, of whom I have previously spoken. It appears that they do not operate for monetary gain, but, well, just to be destroying human life. It is a very old religious rite, a tradition from ages back."

"Yes," answered Mordon. "I have read of them, but thought the British government had long since subdued them."

"It is practically suppressed, sir. However, as you may conceive, the enforcing of a law among this frenzied human mass always has its problems. We do not even achieve that in our large centers of civilization. So it is here, these stranglers at times, even knowing it means death if detected by us, still resort to their damnable practices."

The rabbi was intensely interested in this conversation, and finally entered into the discussion. "What religious motive could prompt human beings to resort to such dastardly practices?"

"There is a legend," returned the soldier, "that accounts for its origin and practice. Long, long ago, the story runs, a giant demon infested the world, destroying mankind from the earth. A goddess named Kali attacked this giant and cut him down, but from each drop of blood sprang another demon, resulting in many millions of them like the former one. Then Kali concocted a scheme whereby she could destroy them without shedding blood. To this end she created two men to whom she gave handkerchiefs, instructing them secretly to seize and strangle the whole brood. When this had been successfully achieved, she ordered men strangled in a like manner to repay her for her service to humanity. From these two men, came the Hindu strangling thugs."

"Was this taught as a profession?" asked Mordon, wishing for more definite information.

"Yes, sir, even the handkerchiefs, and the tools used to dig shallow graves were considered by the priests as sacred, and tradition says that hundreds of thousands have fallen in this manner. The espionage that once maintained was most formidible."

"How long," asked Mordon, "has the British government been subduing this gruesome practice?"

"It was first discovered," the soldier replied, "at the beginning of the nineteenth century, and during the next twenty years two thousand stranglers were executed by the government. Despite this, they occasionally give way to this fanaticism. Just so fast as we discover these men and arrest them, they are at once executed."

"Perhaps I am egotistical," spoke Mordon, "but I doubt that one of these fellows could get his rag around my throat without my knowing it."

"Do you think," asked the rabbi, "that there is any use our remaining longer here?"

"Nothing more," replied a soldier complacently, "than to watch this mass of people at their feasting and evening ceremonies of singing, dancing, and what not, at which they are adepts, indeed. You will observe, however, that by dawn tomorrow, many thousands of them will have left the city for their remote homes. The weather is hot and dry, consequently they travel by night as much as possible."

Pointing up the road, the soldier exclaimed, "Look, here come the captain and his company. Our instructions are to meet him in the grove yonder, so we bid you adieu." With this, the soldiers departed.

"Well, Rabbi," began Mordon, "once more we are alone, and I know not how you feel, but now that the excitement is over, I feel pretty tired and hungry, for we have been here many hours. Shall we return to the hotel?"

"Agreed, Mordon, but for heaven's sake, let us take another route, if possible, for should I be compelled to gaze again at those horrid fakirs, my stomach would rebel at the sight of food."

"A good idea, so let us take a roundabout route

for I, like you, want no more of those nauseating scenes."

The return journey was interesting, for on every hand were scenes of Hindu life with ceremonies in the direct aftermath of the great festival. The two men soon reached their hotel, indulged in a good bath, then after dinner, spent the late evening on the veranda witnessing with intense interest the ceremonies under the glow of a full, clear moon.

"Rabbi," said the American, "today with all its absurdities and nonsense, has been better than a circus to me. I am certainly glad you had me stop over at Puri."

"Had you not been here, Mordon, I know not what would have become of me alone in this human jam. Some strangler perhaps would have had his noose around my neck. I shall be happy if your stopover has been worth your while."

"Man, I wouldn't have missed it for a fortune, and you may depend upon it that I shall have a story to relate to my American friends when I return home. By the way, I wonder what has become of our friend Brigha? You know, he promised to meet us at dusk, and now it is hours after that."

"He did make that promise, didn't he? Perhaps in his excitement, he has forgotten us. He seemed very emotional today."

"Rabbi, I am not in a position to judge, perhaps, but he appeared to me to have been very excited from the first time I met him."

"I admit that he has been emotional since you met him. But, because I have spent long days listening to his philosophy disclosed in the most cool manner possible, I have formed quite another opinion of him. He is a gentleman and a scholar, I assure you."

"Yes, yes, Rabbi. I have often observed this trait of human nature, how men of education can allow their emotions to overbalance them at times. I have seen men of learning do some of the strangest things imaginable, and I feel prepared to take almost anything that comes, charging it to human weakness. In some of our American political campaigns, for instance, I have seen aspirants from higher walks of life act so ridiculous that, to me at least, all they seemed to lack were the long ears and the bray of the barnyard quadruped." Mordon was suddenly amused as he watched the Jew seeming to withdraw within himself. He continued, "Well, Rabbi, why the meditation all at once?"

"I was just trying to fathom what you meant by the long ears and bray."

Mordon laughed heartily. "Well, upon my word, Rabbi. You from Jerusalem, the land of the ass, and don't know him when he is described to you!"

"How ludicrously stupid I am, Mr. Mordon. Truly, it requires a kick from an ass to awaken an antiquated Hebrew like me from his stupidity."

Again Mordon laughed heartily, eventually returning: "Good enough. I observe that you are getting Americanized already. You'll soon be a typical Yankee, to be sure. That was a dandy slap at me, wasn't it?"

The rabbi seemed stunned, wondering what he had done. "Slap at you, Mordon? What do you mean? What have I done this time?"

Again Mordon laughed. "Just a little unconscious wit that you do not seem to be conscious of. See how cleverly you called me an ass."

"I did nothing of the kind, Mr. Mordon. That was farthest from my mind."

Mordon poked the rabbi in the ribs. "Now, listen. Did you not say it took a kick from an ass to wake you up? And was it not a kick from me that did so?"

Ben Arden was instantly mortified. "Oh, a thousand pardons, Mordon. I really did not mean—"

"Now, Rabbi, stop that foolishness. It was a joke and a good one. Jokes, you know, go free with Americans. I wouldn't give a snap of my finger for a man so sanctimonious that he could not give and take a joke."

"Well, Mordon, perhaps it is as the Hindu says, that you have to rub up against a brass nail before you get a tarnish."

Mordon laughed heartier than ever, while the rabbi seemed to hold his breath lest he had made another slip of the tongue. "Listen, Rabbi, a minute ago I was an ass, now I am a brass nail. Guess I'll be a fakir next."

The abashed rabbi replied, "Mordon, understand me. O, shucks, I am an ass myself to the extent that when a joke escapes my lips unconsciously, I am too dense to detect it."

"Rabbi, you are naturally witty and don't know it. But some day you'll capitalize on your natural wit. Perhaps your rubbing up against a brass nail might, after all, have some good effects on you."

Ben Arden was disturbed, nonetheless. "But, tell me, Mordon, were you offended at my stupidity?"

Mordon slapped the Jew on the shoulder as he laughed. "Bless your soul, no. A good joke is medicine to me. By the way, Rabbi, don't you people joke in Jerusalem?"

"I should say not, Mordon. That would be the height of impropriety, especially among the rabbinical class with whom I had been associated."

"That being so, Rabbi, it is no wonder your people are antiquated. Now, pardon the implication, but it seems to me that many of your people must have come from the burial vaults, or some other place."

"True enough, and I feel like one of them, or like some hibernating dormouse, just awakening from some prolonged sleep."

"Well, Rabbi, just get away from that silly stuff, and make up your mind right now that from now on, you will convert your college education into more constructive channels of practical life. Just learn to bump up against each passing obstacle that comes—to give and take life with all its crises and if you'll do as I suggest, you will surprise yourself how you will get on in the world."

Ben Arden became very serious: "I appreciate those words, Mordon, the best advice I have had in years which sinks more deeply that you can imagine."

"Well, Rabbi, just try a dose of that medicine daily and watch yourself grow. But look at that man staggering up the walk yonder. Is not that our friend, Mr. Brigha?"

"Yes, yes, it is he I am sure, tired and worn out, poor fellow. I wish he would go right to bed, which he will not do, for you know, he promised to see us here, and you may depend upon it, he will keep his word."

A few minutes later the priest made his appearance on the veranda, and the sight of his newly made friends caused him to heave a sigh of relief. Gravely he exclaimed: "Gentlemen, I am glad to find you safely here, for I have been much concerned as to your welfare."

"Why, my dear Brigha," answered the rabbi, "we're here safely from an experience long to be remembered."

"But as to your safety, gentlemen?"

"All that could be expected, for we had the honor of having two British redcoats. But you seem dreadfully tired, Mr. Brigha."

"Almost exhausted, gentlemen, yet I dared not retire until I satisfied myself as to your safety."

"Now that you have found us safely home," interrupted Mordon, "you go and have a good night's sleep and rest, for we are about to do the same."

"Rabbi," said the American after Mr. Brigha had withdrawn, "I wouldn't be as tired as that man for a hundred dollars. I'll bet he sees ghosts before morning, or some mystic juggernaut or other in a continuity of successive nightmares."

"I shall be mighty fortunate, Mordon, if I do not see some horrid fakir or something, for I am just now realizing how very tired I am."

CHAPTER IX

AFTER bidding the Hindu priest adieu, Rabbi Ben Arden and John Mordon enjoyed a pleasant voyage to Calcutta, where they were met by Charles Johnson of the American consulate, who insisted that Mordon's friend, the rabbi, also be a guest at the Johnson home.

A few days elapsed in sight-seeing in the great city of Calcutta, a city of nearly a million and a half people. Although much of the city was quaint, there was quite a modern business air about the place, all of which was a great surprise to Mordon, and an altogether new adventure to Rabbi Ben Arden. Mr. Johnson was called by official business to leave his guests for several days. However, they managed to fit easily into the new environment, and with a little assistance from police and others who could give information, Mordon managed to move about in the great city and to see, with Ben Arden, the business section, the quaint residential and more modern districts, of this unusual city.

It was late one afternoon when Charles Johnson and John Mordon, after discussing various topics, turned their conversation to Rabbi Ben Arden who, to the consul, seemed somewhat of a paradox. For some time, Mordon spoke of his Jewish friend.

"Yes, Mordon, I have already observed that he is a man of learning, with a brilliant mind, together with a kind, affable spirit to the extent that one feels quite at ease in his company. I have often wondered, John, what he is doing in India, and have been going to ask when the occasion was opportune."

"Had you done so, Charlie, you would have received a ready answer, for he is an admirable character,
keeping nothing under cover. Besides he, being a Christian Jew, can outclass any man of the cloth I have ever
met."

"Do I understand you, John, that he is Christian?"

"Yes, he is an apostate from Judaism, and a true follower of Jesus Christ. He is here on a peculiar mission, in a noble quest for what he is pleased to name his
Priceless Pearl. What that is I shall not attempt to disclose, but rather leave that for him. In a word, Charlie,
he has taught me more real Christianity than I ever
dreamed of."

"That gives me an urge to hear his story."

"You are going to find him bubbling over with the
spirit of his mission, and you will discover no hallucina-
tion or emotion, mystery, or egotism in his demeanor. He
is a logical reasoner with profound knowledge. But here
he comes now."

"Good evening, gentlemen," spoke the rabbi as he
entered. "I hope I am not intruding upon your renewal
of friendship."

Mr. Johnson, grasping his hand warmly, replied:
"To the contrary, Rabbi, for you have been a subject of
our conversation, hence we are anticipating your arrival."

"How singular," replied the rabbi. "By the way, permit me to present a new acquaintance of mine, Mr.
Karuda, a priest of Buddhism, with whom I have had
quite a long and pleasant conference this afternoon."

"Mr. Johnson and I are already well acquainted,"
spoke the priest in very good English, "and it affords
me pleasure to meet you, Mr. Mordon, who I trust is
a whole souled American gentleman like my friend Mr.
Johnson has proved to be."

Addressing the priest, Mr. Johnson explained: "My old friend John Mordon has come all the way from the United States to pay me a long-promised visit, for we are friends of long years standing."

"Mr. Johnson," asked the rabbi inquiringly, "may I ask why you were anticipating my arrival? You have made me curious."

Mr. Johnson smiled. "Certainly. Mr. Mordon has been giving me a brief and interesting account of your mission in India, and has intimated that you would, perhaps, relate your story to us this evening, provided of course you have no reasons to make you feel indisposed to tell it."

"The pleasure will be mine," returned the rabbi kindly, "and that from a two-fold standpoint. I am eager to place my motive before you, Mr. Johnson, in view of perhaps getting some assistance. Then to bring my thoughts from the horrors of that abominable Juggernaut, and back to the real object of my quest."

"I shall be honored in being an attentive listener, Rabbi, and I am sure my friend Karuda will be equally interested. But first, let me call Mrs. Johnson and my daughter."

"My dears," began the consul after his wife and daughter had been comfortably seated, "our friend the rabbi seems to be in India on a very singular mission in which Mr. Mordon is intensely interested, and the rabbi has kindly consented to disclose what he is pleased to call his quest."

"How delightful," returned Mrs. Johnson. "I shall be delighted, for Mr. Mordon has told me of his fund of information and strength of character."

The rabbi seemed somewhat abashed: "Please do not flatter me, Mrs. Johnson, lest it arouse undue egotism. I shall feel delight to narrate in brief just why I am a world wanderer." Briefly, he again related his story.

Mrs. Johnson asked, "to give us a proper setting, will you please indicate what you mean by the supernatural element?"

"Simply this," returned the rabbi. "There is a spiritual and physical power of God, under the operation of which worlds are formed, solar system controlled, suns lighted, and men receive wondrous benedictions commensurate with their faith. In fact, whenever the Lord has had a people upon the earth worthy of recognition, this power has always been manifest. Conversely, in each epoch of apostasy, when men through transgression placed themselves out of harmony with the polarity of the heavens until there was no affinity between God and man, the power was lost, just as naturally as an electric dynamo would lose its power were the current disconnected."

Mr. Karuda now proposed a question, "Rabbi, this afternoon you spoke of priesthood, its workings on earth. Will you kindly clarify just what you meant by that?"

"To me," continued the rabbi, "it means not priestcraft, but the power and authority of God delegated to man to function and operate the higher laws of heaven on earth—laws of natural phenomena, not only for the spiritual but also for the temporal welfare of man."

"A very beautiful definition," interrupted John Mordon, "and there is, as you will learn, an abundance of evidence of its wondrous manifestation."

"A delegation of this authority," continued the rabbi, "was given to Moses and successive prophets. Under this power great miracles occurred. Then, until the dispensation of Christ, it was lost to the world. Under Jesus Christ another delegation of priesthood was given to men. The winds and waves obeyed divine mandate of the Master; miracles were performed; and finally the miracle of miracles was evidenced in the glorious resurrection of the Master. A continuity of this power of priesthood remained in the hands of the apostles after Christ's passing. This, friends, is what I have been pleased to designate the Priceless Pearl, this power of God unto salvation, and it is that for which I am making my world-wide quest."

"Since my acquaintance with Rabbi Ben Arden," interrupted John Mordon, "I have thought about the question profoundly, and the more I contemplate it, the more I am convinced that the rabbi is right. You will perhaps remember what John Wesley said in contemplation of this lost power: 'The real reason why the extraordinary gifts of the Holy Ghost were no longer found in the Christian Church, was because the Christians were turned heathen and had but a dead form left.' Moreover, a homily in the original Protestant church reads something like this as I recall: 'So that laity and clergy, learned and unlearned, all ages of men, women and children of all Christendom, a horrible and most dreadful thing to think, have at once been drowned in abominable idolatry, of all vices most detested of God and damnable men, and that for a space of eight hundred years and more. I could give you many confessions of this nature of honest divines of our day, but shall defer for the present."

For hours the rabbi held his listeners spellbound as he developed, step by step, the motives of his quest.

Silence maintained while the listeners meditated, until, breaking the silence, the consul, moved deeply, arose, offering his hand to the rabbi: "Mr. Ben Arden, here is my hand as a token of appreciation, for you have taught me more real, genuine Christianity tonight than I have ever before thought. We must admit your logic to be profound, reasonable, plausible, and we must also confess the loss of this power in modern Christendom. But what perplexes me is: why have we lost it?"

"May I," interrupted Mordon, "read a passage from Isaiah: 'Behold, the Lord's hand is not shortened that he can not save, neither his ear hardened that he can not hear, but your iniquities have separated between you and your God.' This could possibly have been the fundamental cause."

"Perhaps so," returned the consul. "At any rate, it is quite apparent that it is not to be found in modern Christianity as I understand it."

"May I ask," inquired Mrs. Johnson sincerely, "why our ministers do not have this power similar to those of olden times? Is it because they are all sinners?"

"Not necessarily so," returned the rabbi, "but when this power comes to earth again, if it is not already here somewhere, it will be given by direct revelation from God, comparable to the bestowal of it to the prophets in all ages who have been recipients of this benediction. They will be called and ordained by those having power to confer this authority to those worthy of receiving it. Now, friends, will you show me a Christian minister who does not teach that all revelation has ceased, even in face of the direct statement of Amos of old, that where there is no vision the people perish?"

"Well said," returned the consul. "From my experience, at least, I could point to none who would even tolerate the thought of divine revelation to man."

"This being so, my friends, I hope you will be somewhat sympathetic to my quest, and not think that I am chasing bubbles on a precipice, as it were. Already, I have searched Parseeism only to be disappointed; also, in Brahminism, where there seems not the slightest trace. My next move is to be a thorough search of Buddhism."

All eyes turned to Priest Karuda, the consul suggesting: "This, Mr. Karuda, is a task for you to deal with, and I think you are going to have your hands full to satisfy our Jewish friend."

"Be not too sure of your ground, Friend Johnson, for a religion that sways the thought of one third of the human race is not to be easily disposed of. I shall be pleased to have you spend a few hours with me, if only to learn of the great Gautama, the Enlightened One, the light of Asia and the founder of the great Buddhist religion."

All seemed eager to listen to the priest, even though the hour was already late, for, despite the fact that the consul had been in contact with the Buddhist people, he had learned little of their philosophy, tenets, and workings of the great religion. None could have been more eager to learn than Homer Ben Arden, who spoke his interest: "I have heard considerable and read much of Gautama, the Buddha, and I assure you that, from my part, I shall be gratified to learn of him and his teachings."

Priest Karuda began, speaking cautiously and with great care, with apparent emotion, but in a kind manner, expressing a profound conviction. "There is no character like Gautama, as there is no religion comparable to the one he founded that has sunk deeply into the hearts of millions, embracing as it does in its tremendous scope, the savage on the one hand and the most highly civilized on the other. It controls the destinies of hundreds of millions of souls, as it has done for twenty centuries."

"I confess," answered the Jew, "that you have a great, or the greatest oriental philosophy known, to me at least, and as to its following, it is unique in its magnitude. But even that might or might not be a criterion of measurement of its authenticity or divine appointment."

"Very true, Rabbi, but the fact that so vast a horde of human beings find therein a satisfying solace, implies

unquestionably that there must be a force of truth upon
which the structure stands. Moreover, the very fact that
the Supreme Power has been pleased to place at the
head, the greatest of all human beings, implies its
divinity."

"Which, of course, is a controversial subject," injected
the rabbi, kindly. "We Christians see the greatest of
all in Jesus Christ, who did for humanity what no other
has been able to do. I refer to the breaking of the bonds
of death in a glorious resurrection of souls. However,
I apologize for my interruption in your narration."

"To continue," spoke the priest, "about the sixth century before your Nazarene was born, a wise king reigned
in Kapila vatthu, about one hundred miles north of
Benares. His people were herdsmen, living on the prod-
ucts of their flocks and farms, and all were devotees
of Brahminism. The wife of this king, because of her
beauty, was named Maya, and was childless until her
fortieth year, when the little prince Siddartha, was born,
and was named Skya-muni, but by his clan he was
known as Gautama. Numerous histories and traditions
of his remarkable birth and personality have descended
to our day. At his birth, we are told, ten thousand
worlds were filled with light. The blind saw, lame
walked, trees burst forth into bloom, the air filled with
singing birds, and even the fires of hell were temporarily quenched. Five days after his birth, one hundred
eighty wise Brahmin priests met to select for him a
name, and one wiser than the others predicted that the
child would become a Buddha, and would yet remove
the veils of sin and iniquity from the world."

Consul Johnson interrupted: "Will you kindly explain what you mean by the word 'Buddha'?"

"With pleasure. It signifies the Enlightened One.
To us, it signifies as much or more than the word Christ

or Messiah does to you Christians. His whole life was devoted to teaching the arts, sciences, philosophies, for he was wisdom personified. Frequently, he has accused by his kin of neglecting that which goes to build the physical part of man. On one occasion, provoked at their incessant tauntings, he challenged all comers to meet him in athletic contest. He surpassed all in archery, horsemanship, and numerous other tests, that they forever held their peace. In his twenty-ninth year he devoted himself entirely to religion and philosophy."

"And this," suggested the rabbi, "was where his profound teachings had their birth. Am I right?"

"Yes, Rabbi, and from this time on he led the intellectual thought of all time in everything that was aesthetic and beautiful. Among other things he taught that nothing on earth or in the universe was stable, nothing real, that even life was a spark engendered by the friction of worlds, lighted only to shed an effulgent ray comparable to a passing meteor, then to be extinguished, that men knew not whence they came or whither they go, like the strain of music that comes and goes, none knowing where."

"Mr. Karuda," said the consul, "there must be some continuity of life."

"Gautama asked himself that question in the following: 'There must be some intelligence where the soul can find repose. If I can attain it, I will bring light to men, and free myself and them—in a word, I can deliver the world.' To this end, he became austere in his solitude as he launched his quest for truth. To pursue a hermit life of complete isolation to him was essential. Herein came his test of strength, courage, and love when it came to his bidding farewell to his devoted wife, Ysodhara, and his little son, Rahula.

"It was midnight as he came to bid farewell to his

wife and child. She was sleeping softly with the child in her arms, and as he watched them his bosom swelled within him with grief such as none before or since have experienced. He dared not awaken them, so, touching their feet with his lips, he turned to wipe away his tears. Thrice, he passed around his sleeping loved ones, when at length he said softly: 'Never lie I there again.' With the last fond look, he nearly swooned. His parting words to his servant were: 'I quit this prison where my heart is caged. Henceforth, my life is given to the emancipation of man.' "

"He must have been a remarkable character," suggested Mrs. Johnson, with a degree of emotion. "A parallel to this would be hard to find in human experience."

"There is no parallel," quickly injected the priest with firmness. "But to continue with the story. Then he became an ascetic, changed his clothes with an unfortunate mendicant, and became homeless, a begging hermit, his sole retreat being a mountain cave. Here, he became attached to a Brahmin philosopher, under whose guidance he sought to gain control over the supernatural. Then he went to the jungles, where he spent six years in fasting and self-denial. His achieved self-control gained for him fame, in that disciples flocked to him in humble obeisance. Came then the severest test, when he returned to his native village and sat beneath a tree, that since that day has been known as the 'Bo Tree,' or the tree of wisdom. Here, in his temptation, his philosophy seemed to fail him, the penance and self-denial he had trusted seemed to mock him. As evening dawned, however, the inner-side of his nature dispelled all doubt. Faith had triumphed, and he was once more emancipated from sorrow and doubt. This test was all that was required to make of him the Great

Buddha. The solution of all care, grief, and sorrow had been reached, and the nectar to alleviate the sorrows of men were well within his grasp."

"Such a life sounds much like a fairy tale," said Mr. Mordon, calmly. "Too much fairylike to be real."

"Believe it or not," retorted the priest, "it is true, nonetheless. There and then he renounced all thought of penance as faulty, for he had learned achievement through self-control, declaring that man, of his own strength, could save his soul, independent of the gods. In his super-ultra confidence, he said: 'I shall set rolling the chariot of a universal empire of truth and righteousness.' Friends flocked to him, even his deserted wife, Ysodhara, became his devoted follower. At the age of eighty-four years, he died, and was buried in a humble grave."

"Gautama, the Buddha," said the rabbi, in his admiration of such a character, "must have been a wonderful personality—an intellectual giant, indeed."

"Yes, yes, friends," contested the priest, quickly. "You Christians see much in your Nazarene, but we see far more in Buddha. Advisedly, I affirm that had Jesus lived to old age, he, too, might have become a Buddha. However, so far, the only personality to have achieved that eminence is Gautama Buddha, the Enlightened One, the Light of Asia."

John Mordon ventured with: "A wonderful man, to be sure. He must have been born a thousand years before his time."

"Aye," returned the priest, "ten thousand times ten thousand years, if you measure him by modern standards, for ages unborn will never know his equal."

"Friends," Rabbi Ben Arden said, "the one thing that appeals to me at this time as we have listened to the story of this remarkable life, is where I see the first glimmer of hope, for he seemed to possess, to a degree, at least, some power wherein the higher laws of heaven were manifest. He must have attuned his soul to the polarity of the spirit world."

Mr. Karuda smiled in his satisfaction. "I felt sure you would grasp that, Rabbi, and I am free to affirm that all knowledge you Christians possess along this line came originally from Buddha. In fact, you Christians have nothing that we have not had since Buddha flourished centuries before Jesus Christ was born." The priest looked at his watch, then arose. "Friends, it is past the midnight hour, hence time for all good people to be sleeping. However, if you will grant me another interview, I shall be happy to disclose the doctrines of Buddhism."

"Agreed," responded the consul, "and let it be here at our home." All agreed as they bade the priest good-night, with thanks for the narration of that remarkable life.

CHAPTER X

AT the appointed hour, all were comfortably seated on Consul Johnson's veranda, eager to listen to Priest Karuda's disclosure of Buddhism.

Waiving all preliminaries, the priest began: "Friends, I sincerely trust you are here this evening with open, unprejudiced minds as I discuss the principles and practices of Buddhism, of which I have the honor to be a member of that great religion. Should I, however, allude to Christianity at times as being subordinate to Buddhism, or even subservient thereto, please take no offense."

"For my part," spoke Rabbi Ben Arden, "I am eager to have you freely disclose candidly your convictions which I shall fully respect, and I feel that I am expressing the thoughts of all here." To which all present acquiesced.

"To begin then," continued the priest, calmly, "there was a devout Christian scholar, Max Muller, who studied Buddhism perhaps as no other of your people have. Of our religion, he had this to say: 'There is in Buddhism that which is intelligible to the poor and suffering, which has endeared Buddhism to the hearts of millions. Not the silly phantasmagorias of worlds of gods and worlds of Brahma, of the final dissolution of the soul in Nirvana. No, the beautiful, the tender, the humanly true which, like pure gold, is buried in all religions, even in the sand of the Buddhist canon.' Buddha taught this perfectly framed religion over a period of fifty years, during which time his fundamental teachings became

thoroughly established. In the interval between his
death and the reign of the first Buddhist king, Asoka,
many stories of Buddha's miraculous deeds and teachings were written. The wise king called a council to
consider which of the many writings were orthodox,
and which were to be considered apocryphal. The canon
of these books selected by this body is known as the
'Tripitka' or three baskets. To us, these are all or even
more than your Bible can mean to you Christians, for
therein we find the sublimity of Buddhist belief. The
first of these baskets is the 'Vinara.' Its teachings are
based entirely upon the ethical. Next is the basket called
'Sutras,' containing in general the sermons of Buddha.
Then, lastly, comes the 'Abhidrama,' containing philosophy and metaphysics. The second and third 'pitikas'
taken together are known as the 'Drahma,' or the law.
The first and second 'pitikas' contain five separate works,
while the third one contains seven. Following this
standard canon, we have numerous other books, such
as commentaries, and parables that were written by the
famous Buddhist missionary, Buddaghosa, which, to us
are invaluable. Finally, we have the great Drahma-
Pada—Footsteps of the Law, which contains the codes of
morals and ethics."

"Can English versions of these records be purchased?" inquired the rabbi, earnestly.

"Oh, indeed, Rabbi. I have some of them with me.
Besides, you may procure them in the leading bookstores
of this city."

"Now, friends, as to doctrine," continued the priest,
"I shall begin with man. We believe that just so long
as he is bound by bodily existence in this material world,
he is liable to grief, sorrow, decay and death. So long
as he allows unholy desires to remain with him, there
will be unsatisfied longings, useless weariness and care.

To attempt to purify himself, like a Brahmin, by wasting his body and thus oppressing his vitality, were nothing more than futile effort. As a result of gross evil in his heart, man is a slave to bodily life, which makes and keeps him material. Virtue added to his badness may relieve him temporarily, yet only the complete eradication of evil will set him free from the bondage of existence where he is tossed about on the waves of transmigration."

"That being so," suggested the consul, "you teach the transmigration of souls from one form of life to another."

"Decidedly so, as we have done from the beginning, upon which hinges the fundamental cause of existence, embracing, as it does, all flora and fauna."

"I am somewhat confused," confided the rabbi, earnestly, "as to distinguishing marks between your doctrine and that of Brahminism, for I observe they have a similar doctrine. Am I to understand that you are an offshoot of that religion?"

"Not an offshoot, Rabbi, but a reformation of it. Our having come from that religion is readily conceded; but under Buddha it took a radical transition and transformation, for he purged that religion of the absurd doctrine of extortion through suffering, the dogma of the 'suttee' and numerous other rites contrary to the logical aspect of human life and nature. Such foolish practices as you gentlemen witnessed at the Juggernaut festivities, is to us the height of absurdity, having nothing whatever to do with the emancipation of the soul. Man triumphs as fast as he overcomes and purifies his life through mental effort and self-denial. There lies the fundamentals of earth progression, and his freedom from mortal bondage. To us, material existence is but a negation and violation of fundamental law."

"You imply then," suggested the rabbi, "that mortal existence is brought about by violation of some law?"

"Indeed, Rabbi, and so do you Christians, which is implied in your doctrine of paradise lost in Eden."

Mrs. Johnson, amused at the strange thought, asked: "Am I to understand, Mr. Karuda, you to infer that had man not at some time sinned before his earth life, he would never have had mortal existence?"

"That is right, Mrs. Johnson, and he lost this paradise through sin or the violation of law, which implies that his mortal task is to gain, rather regain through mortal effort, the status he once possessed, then lost. We have four great truths which teach: First, that misery always accompanies existence; second, all existence is a result of passion and vain desire; third, the only escape from the unrefined quality of mortality is through the destruction of desire; and fourth, the great goal is gained by following the paths which lead to Nirvana."

"If," inquired the rabbi, "mortal existence is a negation or freak of nature, what must man do in order to rid himself of that negation, and what becomes of his identity when thus freed?"

"A very timely question," answered the priest. "As he realizes his dilemma, the scales fall by degrees from his eyes, and he begins to realize the mystery of sorrow; that pain and existence are inseparably connected; that earth abode leads to the vexation of spirit. When, like Buddha, he turns to the Enlightened One for relief to the extent that he becomes awake, he can be considered as taking the first step. When he has banished all desire, hatred, revenge, he takes the second step. When he is freed from all these negations, and rises above them, he is considered as having taken the third step. This condition of true enlightenment implies great kindness

and charity, love unfeigned, and until these are achieved
his mortal bondage is continued. But when these are
gained, he has power within himself to throw off the
material shell forever and enter the Elysian fields of
bliss."

"Your inference suggests," queried the consul, "that
he requires no assistance other than his own achieved
power to usher him into this condition of absolute
freedom. Am I right?"

"Decidedly so. You Christians seem to place a ban
on the powers of man by insisting upon the necessity
of a divine hand to lead man to his goal. To us, it
belittles man, who naturally should possess innately
the powers of his emancipation."

"Now, as to man's destiny after he has been freed
from his mortal encumbrance, after having achieved, he
has power to unlock the binding chains of mortality
and is fully qualified to enter the realm of bliss known
as Nirvana. In a word, he is absorbed into Deity. As a
distinct identity, he is no more, for he is now dissolved
back into Deity from which he came, and of which
Buddha explained: 'Those only who have arrived at
Nirvana have achieved eternal rest.'"

"May I ask you," inquired the rabbi eagerly, "if
this doctrine of Nirvana is in any way comparable to the
Moksha of Braminism? My reason for asking is that
Mr. Brigha taught it to me, and I see little difference."

"I confess, Rabbi, that the doctrine antedates
Buddhism by thousands of years. In fact, it existed before human history was written."

"Then," asked the Jew, "am I to glean the thought
or concept that man is an abstraction of a principle,
rather than being begotten of a divine parentage?"

The priest smiled as he returned somewhat ostenta-
tiously, "You still are inclined to force your Christian

conceptions. It is true, of course, that the human body comes through the law of procreation into this struggling life into which he is imprisoned, his ego coming from the all-pervading essence of Deity, with his final state, the reversion of destiny back to his source."

"Is it possible," inquired Mr. Johnson, after a prolonged silence, "that your hundreds of millions are led to live their ethical lives as a product of these teachings alone?"

"Not altogether, for we have numerous codes of morals that regulate soul and character building."

"So I have been informed," answered the consul, "but which is the most potential in swaying and guiding the mind of Buddhist laity—the doctrine of Nirvana on the one hand, or your ethics on the other?"

"The more educated of us place explicit confidence in Nirvana; but there are millions who know little of it. With this class it is ethics that guides them to standards of citizenship. Our laws are clear, fascinating, and easily understandable; our morals sublime and inviting, sufficient to allure the most mediocre among us."

"I have read somewhat regarding your teachings," interrupted the rabbi, "and I am free to express my belief that they must be more potent to the average Buddhist than could be your metaphysical philosophies."

"Yes, for the masses, at least. Buddha possibly envisioned that very thing when he gave the world the most beautiful teachings which are contained in the Drahma-Pada. Many of them are, in a way, comparable to those taught by Christ. They are gems of great wisdom as you will observe from the following which I read: 'There is no fire like passion, or no shark like hatred. . . . A man is not learned because he talks much. . . . Hatred is never overcome by hatred but by love alone. . . . As rain breaks through an unthatched roof, so passion breaks through the unreflecting mind. . . . A virtuous man will always be happy. . . . The fragrance of flowers travels not against the wind, but the aroma of good people is all-pervading. . . . The fool who knows his foolishness is wise, but the fool who thinks himself wise is a fool indeed. . . . A word of common sense is superior to a sermon of senseless words. . . . He who conquers self is greater than he who conquers millions. . . . A wise man controls his appetite, body and mind. He who indulges in intoxicating liquors digs up his own root.'

"The foregoing, my friends, are but a sample of what is contained in the Drahma-Pada. Then we have the very inspiring beatitudes, analogies, and innumerable stories based on history and fiction, all of which are powerful mediums for the uplift of humanity, and upon which the superstructure of Buddhism is founded."

"Pardon me," asked the rabbi, "but I fail to see a significant line of demarkation between Brahminism and Buddhism, especially regarding the sum of doctrinal principles. I wish you would kindly clarify this for my information."

"In the first place, Rabbi, Buddha did not aim to do more than reform Brahminism. This, I wish to make very impressive."

"How is it then," continued the rabbi, "that you are now two great religions?"

"Largely by Buddha's organization of the Sanga or brotherhood, which to us implies all that the church does for you Christians. Under him the Sanga grew rapidly until it contained millions of adherents. On the other hand, laws governing the prosyletes and members were so elevating in nature that hordes came to the fold. In passing, permit me to state that scarcely a trace of this exists in Brahminism. For instance, before being

admitted, the candidate for Buddhism must comply with
the following requirements: 'I take the vow not to
destroy life. I take the vow not to steal. I take the
vow to abstain from impurity. I take the vow not to
lie. I take the vow to abstain from intoxicating drinks,
which impeach progress and virtue. I take the vow to
abstain from dancing, singing, and the stage. I take
the vow not to lust for gold and silver.' These few
tenets with many of a kindred nature instill in the
Buddhist clean living through sane thinking. What
this has done for humanity is strikingly reflected in
Japan, China, Siam, Ceylon, and India. I suggest advisedly that it is the greatest known building force in the
world."

"The teachings are beautiful," said John Mordon
after a long silence. "But in the nations you mention,
and especially in India, one must find millions who
are not of Buddhistic persuasion."

"Just as you have millions in Christian countries
who are not Christians," retorted the priest, kindly.
"The super-observance of Buddhism, of course, is found
among the Jains, yet we have converts who cannot measure up to their high standards."

"That is a new word to me, Mr. Karuda," spoke
the rabbi with interest. "Will you kindly tell us something of them?"

"With pleasure. In English, the word Jains signifies conquering saints. To a large degree, they have
overcome the allurements of mortal weakness. We point
to two great cycles that defy human calculation. The
first Jaina of the second cycle lived nine thousand four
hundred years, but each succeeding Jaina lived shorter
periods than his immediate predecessor, down to the
present age of man. This was brought about by the
infusion of wrong living, moral weakness, and kindred

negatives. At one time the Jains would not kill or in-
jure any living thing. Water was even strained before
drinking. They would sweep the ground lest some
minute life be crushed beneath their feet. They refrained
from eating seeds lest some life germ be destroyed, and
would not touch dead flesh with their fingers, much less
eat it. In a word, they were pure in thought, deed and
action."

"In this," smiled the consul, "I see both the sublime and the ridiculous. I cannot conceive of man's ever
having lived such a life."

"Which privilege," returned the priest, confidingly,
"is yours, of course. What a boon it is that thinking
men can differ and still remain friends."

"One more question," asked the rabbi, "what other
marks of differentiation can you give between Buddhism
and Brahminism?"

"This further: The Brahmin would extort through
bodily torture to be emancipated from lower transmigrations, such as you saw with the fakirs at Puri, the suttee
and other nonsense. The Buddhist disclaims all this,
claiming that it is through self-denial, mastery of self,
that man's superlative achievements are realized."

"Another question," asked the rabbi, "what do you
teach regarding such records as the Zend Avesta, the
Vedas, the Manus?"

"In a word, Rabbi, we condemn them as being
apocryphal, hence untrustworthy. The Vedas and
Manus especially to us are nonsensical and foolish, in
that they disclose the false doctrine of castes, the thought
of which is damnable to us in the extreme, while their
doctrine of torture through bodily suffering is equally
idiotic. Hence, we repudiate these books and their
teachings."

The rabbi looked at his watch. "It is already late,

Mr. Karuda, but I wish to make a brief comparison before we separate. You people aspire to a time when your individualities as tangible beings will finally become dissolved into Nirvana, in a word when your light is blown out. On the other hand, I always hope to be Homer Ben Arden in eternity, just as tangible as I am today. I long for the time when I can meet my dear old father and mother as actual beings and shake their hands and sense their touch and they mine. I do not believe we shall be dissolved into some metaphysical abstraction. You know, Mr. Karuda, the dearest thing to me is the hope of a continuity of life beyond the grave, and to me at least, when we depart from that logical, rational concept, life would be shorn of its real meaning."

"I admit, Rabbi, that your philosophy has a pleasant ring to it, and it might be more tangible than it appears. However, you are Christians. I am a Buddhist, born one, and I expect to die one."

CHAPTER XI

IT had been a long and tiresome week for Homer Ben Arden, who had busied himself as best he could seeing the sights of the famous old city, studying its architecture, mannerisms of the people, libraries, and conditions in general. The consul and John Mordon having taken a business trip to Benares, gave him sufficient time to meditate upon the diversified philosophies that had come up for his consideration. Several long evenings had been employed in his study of his newly-acquired copy of the Tripitaka.

One morning as he was strolling along a narrow street, he met Mr. Karuda, who, in a very courteous manner extended his hand, saying kindly: "I hardly knew, Rabbi, how you would be feeling by this time; whether you would have turned against me, or have decided to turn Buddhist." He laughed as the latter words fell from his lips.

"Well, Mr. Karuda," returned the rabbi, pleasantly, "I am happy to inform you that it is neither one. I have the greatest respect for you, to whom I am indebted more than you, perhaps, realize. Yet I am of the same opinion as to your religion and its philosophy."

"Which, of course, is all I should expect. By the way, Rabbi, have you had the privilege of seeing the great Mohammedan mosque that stands near the river Hugli?"

"No, I haven't," returned the Jew. "Where is it located?"

"If you will join me I shall be delighted to escort

you to the residence of the caliph of Calcutta, where you will meet a charming personality, affable and kind, educated and wealthy."

The caliph's mansion stood in the center of a cluster of ornamental foliage, quite a distance from the outer gate, and as the two men gazed through the iron bars, the beautiful statuary, flowers, and foliage were first to greet their gaze. Finally the priest began, "You see, Rabbi, a sample of Mohammedan extravagance. It seems to me that these people have no conception, rather I should say no concern, how they lavishly spend money in buildings and surroundings."

"It is remarkable," returned the rabbi in his amazement, "and no doubt worth the expenditure. The caliph must enjoy this haven of beauty."

A servant came to the gate in answer to the bell, returning again a few minutes later with an invitation to the visitors to enter. The caliph met them at the front portal, extending formal recognition, when Mr. Karuda said: "Your Highness, I present my friend Homer Ben Arden, a Christian Jew from the Holy City. This, Rabbi, is Mr. Akbar Koutaj, the Mohammedan caliph of Calcutta. Now, I beg your leave, for I know the rabbi will be in good hands, and will be well entertained." So saying the priest bowed graciously and withdrew.

Ben Arden seemed enraptured with the beauty of design and symmetry, the luxurious furnishings, blendings, marble statuary, richly designed mosiacs, gold trimmed curtains, expensive rugs of Persian design, in the palace.

"So," began the Caliph, after the formalities of acquaintance were over, "you are a Christian Jew, direct from Jerusalem. You know, I thought the people of that city were affiliated either to Judaism, or Mohammedism. It seems to me very queer for a Jew to be of Christian persuasion."

Homer Ben Arden was really amazed how perfectly
the caliph spoke English, for he spoke with a remarkable accent with enunciation seemingly perfect. "It is,
your Highness," returned the rabbi. "Generally speaking, you are right. I was born and reared a Jew and
had been sufficiently educated to have been ordained a
rabbi. However, I now am most happy to announce
myself a Christian, a neophyte."

"It is much to your honor, Rabbi, and I congratulate you upon your being a follower of the Nazarene,
for we look upon him as having been a great and powerful man in his day. But, of course, you will admit that
there is but one God, which eliminates Jesus as being
another."

The rabbi smiled as he replied candidly: "Which
I take in good part, Mr. Koutaj, and, of course, you will
allow me to differ with you as to my own convictions.
I am a seeker for truth. In fact, I am making a world
tour in quest of truth, and shall be gratified to have you
disclose the philosophy and beliefs of Mohammedanism.
My call upon you was suggested by my friend Karuda,
who informed me that your kindness might be extended
to the extent of showing me some of your wonderful
buildings, and especially the mosque that stands adjacent
to this great city."

"Nothing could give me greater pleasure, Mr. Ben
Arden, and after we have dined, we shall motor out to
the edifice."

"In your automobile?" returned the rabbi in his astonishment. "You mean to tell me you drive a car?"

"No, no, not myself. Yet, I do much traveling by
car. I was in the United States last year, and became so
infatuated with that mode of travel that I purchased an
automobile, and more than that, I brought a young
American chauffeur with me to Calcutta, quite an

adept driver, as well as being well able to repair the car."

The caliph pressed a button which brought the young American into the room.

"Jamison," said the caliph, "I want to introduce Mister Ben Arden; perhaps I should say Rabbi Ben Arden, from Jerusalem."

"I am pleased, indeed," replied young Jamison, "to make your acquaintance."

"You are far from your native land, are you not?" asked the rabbi.

"Oh, yes. However, I thought a few years in old India might be a good experience, and too good a privilege to pass up, and I'm mighty glad I'm here; besides, the caliph seems to need my assistance."

"I assure you," interposed the caliph, intently, "that he is indispensable to me, for he is an adept with my car, so much so that it seems to mind him as if it were human." Turing to his chauffeur, the caliph continued. "Have the car here in an hour to take the rabbi and me to the mosque."

"It seems queer to me," said the rabbi after Jamison had withdrawn, "that a mere youth like him should leave his home for this remote land. Moreover, that in his tender years he should be skilled as you indicate."

"True, Rabbi, he is a stripling, but remember that boys in the United States are often comparable to men of mature years in our country. When I purchased my car in New York, I engaged him at a tempting salary, and in truth, I would double his salary rather than lose him."

At the appointed time, the car halted in front of the caliph's mansion, and soon the caliph and Ben Arden were en route.

It was obvious to the caliph that the Jew was not accustomed to automobile riding, and in his amusement, he asked: "Well, Rabbi, how are you enjoying the ride?"

"I hardly know, Caliph, whether I am enjoying it or not. It is all so new to me, especially at this speed."

"Speed," laughed the Caliph, "why we are not going twenty-five miles an hour. What would you say if we were to go fifty?"

"Not for me," returned the rabbi, feverishly. "I had rather walk."

Overhearing the conversation, young Jamison was itching for a stretch of clear road when he could step on the accelerator. The occasion came, when the lad said, smilingly, "Now for a touch of high life. Just watch me step on her." The car seemed nearly to jump from under them, while Ben Arden hung to the seat as though flying through space on some wild meteor. "Thirty, forty, fifty," shouted young Jamison. "How do you like that, Rabbi?"

Ben Arden did not speak until the car slowed down, when he replied, "I hardly know, for it took me all my time to hold on and keep breathing."

Bringing the car down to ten miles an hour, the lad continued: "Gee, Rabbi, I wish I had you on a good stretch of American pavement for awhile, just to show you what this boat will do when opened up. Why, I'd give you your breakfast in Calcutta and your lunch in Bagdad."

"Yes," answered the rabbi ironically, not yet having learned to enjoy the experience, "and my sleep in kingdom come. This speed was not meant for human beings."

The lad laughed in his enjoyment. "I guess then I am not human, for, by golly, it feels just right when I am cutting the air at fifty miles per."

"Perhaps so, but you do not seem to realize the danger of such recklessness."

"Oh, but I do, Rabbi. I have the car under perfect control, so equipped with hydraulic brakes on all four wheels that I can stop mighty quick."

"Should you go to America," said the caliph smiling, "you would see that whole nation going at a pace that would make your hair stand straight up, for it all seems to be a perpetual buzz of traffic. Really, one needs go there just to learn that he is alive, or perhaps I should say, to learn that we in these old countries are scarcely alive."

"I am astonished, Caliph, and can easily believe you. This is the second American I have met. The other one is my traveling companion, a John Mordon, whom I want you to meet, for he is a remarkable character. It seems to me he gets more out of life than I ever could."

"You know, Rabbi, I found that the American people enjoy life much more abundantly than we do, for the reason they seem to understand human nature more deeply. They certainly keep abreast with progress. Rather, I should say, ahead in progress. You know, my association with this lad has been educational to me. He is thrifty, and shrewd as a judge, amusing as a box of monkeys, congenial as a mother, a good mixer to the extent that were I downcast he would soon dispel the gloom."

"The thing that amuses me is how cool he seems as he manipulates the machine."

"Cool as a cucumber," laughed the caliph. "Nothing seems to bother him, and under his manipulation I feel perfectly composed and at ease." The caliph looked the rabbi in the eyes. "Now that we have slowed down, Rabbi, how do you enjoy it?"

"Why, it's great, Caliph."

The caliph laughed aloud. "Say, Ben Arden, where

did you get that Yankee slang. Certainly you do not have it in Jerusalem."

"Certainly not. I borrowed it from my friend, John Mordon. But, returning to the car, how different this from the old camel mode of transportation, and the donkey. Of course, we have some automobiles in Jerusalem, but I have always steered clear of them."

The caliph had been much amused, when, changing the subject, he asked: "By the way, Rabbi, what think you of the scenery along this route?"

"Grand and serene, Caliph. This placid, tranquil stream with its foliage mirrored in the water is all that any landscape artist could desire for a setting for his canvas for a masterpiece."

"Now, Rabbi, it comes to view. Behold the beautiful mosque yonder—the famed mosque of Calcutta, standing as it does eminently elevated and surrounded at its base with a frieze or rare ornamental shrubbery. What think you of this first vista?"

"Palatial, indeed, Caliph. I had no idea there was so wonderful an edifice in India."

"But you have a mosque in Jerusalem which is considered one of the best in the world."

"True, the mosque of Omer which, by the way, is a credit to your people."

The automobile came to a stop. "Now, as to the mosque, Rabbi. Look closely at those rare architectural designs of intricate skill, the general stone-cutting, and symmetry. It is estimated that the edifice cost in excess of six hundred thousand pounds sterling. Even this building is insignificant as compared to the mosque of Delhi on the Ganges River, the very entrance to which cost more than this entire edifice. It is known as the temple of Jummah-Musjid. Its construction is of rare sandstone and is entirely of Hindu-Mohammedan

design. In all, it is considered one of the rarest buildings of India. Speaking of this mosque, one of your
Christian writers, Bishop Heber, said: 'This spotless
sanctuary showing such a pure spirit of devotion made
me, a Christian, feel humbled when I considered that
no architecture of our religion has ever been able to
produce anything equal to this temple of Allah!'"

"You have given me an urge—an inspiration, Caliph,
to visit Delhi. Even this one we behold is a masterpiece
that is baffling as a product of human skill."

They drove back toward the caliph's palace.

"Wherever you go in Mohammedan domain, Rabbi,
you will find that we lead in the massiveness and beauty
of our edifices. Near Agra, between here and Delhi,
there is the famed tower of Kotub, then at Agra stands
the famed Taj Mahal or Jewel Tower, described by another of your Christian writers: 'The Jewel Tower of
India—the kohinor of beauty is the Taj Mahal.' The
tomb was built by Emperor Shah-Jehan, the grandson
of Akbar, constructed for his wife, whom he loved profoundly. While she lay on her deathbed, he promised
her to rear to her memory such a mausoleum as had
never before been erected. To this end, he gathered
architects from far and wide who rivalled each other in
extravagance of design, resulting in a structure of fabulous cost. On it some twenty thousand artisans were
employed over a period of many years. The cost was
met by the contribution of the entire Mohammedan
populace. The edifice is one of the most famous in the
world, of which enthusiastic travelers frequently assert
that to see it is worth a trip around the world. We admit that there are larger and more massive buildings,
but this one distinguishes itself from all others in symmetry, majesty, grace, and beauty. Another of your
Christian writers wrote: 'They built like titans and
finished like jewelers.'"

"Such an edifice," replied the Jew, "must be almost beyond description. I certainly must see it."

"And remember, Rabbi, it is the insignia of magnificence, not a church, or sanctuary, but a tomb, a poem, a dream of paradise."

"Well," said the rabbi, as the automobile halted before the caliph's palace, "we have had an interesting time together, invaluable to me, I assure you."

The caliph returned: "Yes, Rabbi, and I observe that in our return trip you seem to have gained confidence in motoring. Perhaps you are now almost ready to relieve Jamison at the wheel."

"Not on your life," quickly returned the rabbi. "Were I to do so, there would be a wrecked machine, and three souls ushered suddenly into eternity. Oh, no, Jamison can do all the manipulating."

"You just bet your socks," interrupted the lad. "I wouldn't feel safe with even the caliph at the wheel. When it comes to driving this boat, I know my onions, you bet."

At the honk of the horn the great gates swung open, and soon the car halted at the palace portal.

Turning to Jamison, the rabbi said earnestly: "My young friend, you have no idea how much I have appreciated your acquaintance, together with my initial experience riding an automobile."

"Well," smiled the youth complacently, "if this has added joy to your life, I hope you have many similar experiences. Believe me, I have got a kick out of giving you your first ride in an auto."

The rabbi seemed abashed: "I confess, young man, that I must have appeared to you as some curious animal you might see in a zoo. However, your amusement has been educational to me."

When the caliph and the Jew were comfortably

seated in the palatial audience room, the host said, earnestly: "Now, Rabbi, I want you to consider yourself my guest, and after dinner, I shall be pleased to have a dispassionate discussion with you on Mohammedanism."

CHAPTER XII

THE setting sun had left rays crimson, amethyst, and golden, the beauty and grandeur of which were commented upon by both the caliph and the rabbi as they sat on the veranda that overlooked the landscape gardening below them. Breaking the silence, the rabbi said: "My dear caliph, who designs the artistry of these beautiful gardens with their perfectly balanced symmetry and winding walks? To me, it is exquisite and novel."

"I have an elderly gentleman who has made a life study of his art at which he is an adept. He has full charge of developing his own designs."

"So far as I am able to judge, Caliph, he could have few rivals."

"No, Rabbi, you may travel far and wide to find his equal. You are not by any means the first tourist to be amazed at his skill. And more, I venture to affirm that you will find many things to startle you as a result of our wonderful religion regarding practical life and beautification."

"That is not unlikely, Caliph," as he looked at the flowers, foliage, and statuary. Then another thought seized him: "About what is the total following of Mohammedanism, Caliph?"

"I would estimate, Rabbi, that there are about two hundred ninety millions of Mohammedans, or Mussulmans, as we are crudely called. We are scattered widely over Asia, Africa, and in some parts of Europe. Starting as we did with but a handful of adherents under Mo-

hammed, we began to grow until we now embrace about
one tenth of the world's inhabitants.

"For centuries our slogan has been, 'God is God,
and Mohammed is his prophet.' In the early days of
our building, much was achieved by the sword, but since
that time we have developed into a gigantic missionary
system. For instance, in Cairo alone, we have nearly
seven thousand young men training for the ministry.
Just think of it, two acres of Mussulmans in one university that is more than nine hundred years old. These
students are being schooled in the teaching of the Koran,
having gathered from the lands of Morocco, Zanzibar,
Nubia, Soudan, Turkey, Arabia, Bokhara, Turkistan,
Afghanistan, and China. When graduated, they return
to their peoples whom they instruct in the teachings of
Mohammedanism."

"That is remarkable," answered the rabbi. "I have
read much of Mohammed, and I appreciate immeasurably this opportunity of learning more authoritatively
as you disclose your story."

"Which I shall be glad to do, Rabbi, a little later
on, for I wish first to refer to our genealogy. We are
direct descendants of Abraham through the loins of Ishmael, and for all these centuries we have occupied the
lands adjacent to the Red Sea, Indian Ocean, Persian
Gulf, Euphrates Valley, and Syria. Generally, we have
been quite a nomadic people, traveling great plains and
deserts, principally in caravan fashion. The archives of
heaven have been our roof, with the phenomena of nature our perennial privilege. This has made of us a
strong, progressive people who have grown without
models or masters into the world's greatest philosophy.
In early days, we were inclined to worship the sun and
other planetary orbs, with adoration of holy angels, but
later the fundamentals of our religion evolved into what

we are today. We are taught that a Stone of Paradise fell to the earth with Adam, and was taken back in the days of the deluge; but later restored to Abraham when he and Ishmael built Kaaba. The Stone was placed in charge of the family, descending down through the ages, wondrously preserved."

"To what family do you refer, Caliph, as having been possessors of the stone of which you speak?"

"The legal heirs of Abraham, and of his lineage, and in the year five hundred seventy A.D. was born a son named Mohammed, a master spirit destined to revolutionize the religious life of the entire seed of Abraham. For many years the boy kept his calling from even his mother, until he finally became subject to something like trances. At twelve years of age an event occurred that influenced his entire life. He journeyed to Palestine, where he met with both Jews and Christians, gleaning knowledge of the Bible that was helpful to him in future years."

"Do I understand you to indicate that he spent some time in the Holy Land?" asked the rabbi.

"Yes. There he found the Jews in their idolatry, as he termed it, as being repulsive to his spirit, with the Christians little better than the Jews. At the age of twenty-five, he entered the service of one Khadijah, a rich widow of Mecca, who appointed him her camel driver. Charmed with his manliness, she sought to marry him, which marriage was a happy one that continued to her death. When the world turned against him, she would not forsake him, for, despite the scorn he endured, she saw in him a prophet of God. Frequently the twain retired to a secret cave to pray, and here he received visions and revelations."

"You imply that he had attuned his soul to the spirit world. Am I right?"

"Exactly so, Rabbi, he was in touch with the heavens. When forty years of age, he spent much time in solitary confinement within his mountain recess, and it was here that one night a personage, holding a silken scroll in his hands, stood before him, announcing himself as Gabriel, bidding Mohammed to read. Then the personage disappeared."

"You state," asked the rabbi with an air of doubt, "that Gabriel of old, who lived and died, appeared in actual revelation to Mohammed?"

"The same, Rabbi, and this divine being never failed him in time of need. Often when doubt seized him, Gabriel would shout from the heavens: 'O Mohammed, why dost thou doubt, for thou art a prophet of God, and I am Gabriel.' This commission from the heavens was made known to him, then to his wife, and later to his immediate friends and resulted in his gaining forty converts. Gabriel came again, saying: 'O, Prophet, arise and preach, and magnify the Lord. Clean thy garments and flee every abomination.' In the face of opposition and persecution, he remained steadfast, and before long had eleven valiant missionaries in Abyssinia. Viewing the idolatry of his people, he exclaimed: 'Your intercession may be hoped for with God. Your idols are empty shells which ye have made to be your gods.' Spurned and ostracized, he was cut off from their friendship, and to escape mob violence he fled from the city and dwelt with the pilgrims of other lands, finally arriving at Mecca. Here his wife Khadijah, died, and while he mourned this great loss, many pilgrims came to him. Hundreds in Medina were converted to his teachings, and his fame and doctrines spread to every household in the land. Upon the lips of tens of thousands came the universal shout, 'God is God, and Mohammed is his Prophet.' "

"This is indeed interesting," said the rabbi, who had listened with undivided attention. The rabbi continued: "Quite like other great minds that seemed to be born centuries before his day."

"Yes," quickly spoke the caliph, "but none have been so great and received divine appointment as did Mohammed. But to continue, in June, six hundred twenty-two A.D., his hegira, or flight, occurred, and from this we date our era of constant progression. Eight days later he made his triumphal entry into the city of Medina where he was officially recognized a prophet of God. To defend and establish his calling necessitated a series of religious wars. The battle of Bedar ensued when troops of Meccans came to destroy him, and would have done so had not three thousand angels come to his defense. Conflict after conflict followed, during which a remarkable gain was realized, too often at the point of the sword. Finally Mecca was subdued, and later on, Arabia fell to his conquest. At the age of sixty he contracted a severe fever, and realizing that his passing was at hand, he lisped: 'Oh, to depart—to be near the Lord and eternity—pardon,' and the greatest of all prophets was gone."

"A wonderful personality," remarked the rabbi, "whose passing needs no monument to mark the place, and his death must have been the seed of his church."

"A wise statement that," answered the caliph. "A very strong character, Mohammed's friend, Abu Behr, was elected his successor, who received the name of caliph, which is the highest ecclesiastical calling known to Mohammedans. A succeeding caliph was Omer, under whose administration we spread northward to Damascus, and later to all Palestine and Syria. In the year six hundred thirty-six, came the triumphal march into Jerusalem, and on the site of Solomon's temple was erected, in his honor, the mosque of Omer."

"Yes," returned the rabbi, "and a beautiful edifice it is, standing as it does on a plateau called the 'Harem Area,' and is one of the important edifices of the city."

"Following these conquests, Rabbi, Persia and Egypt soon yielded, which extended his empire from Syria on the north, to Arabia on the south. As years passed, there came a succession of caliphs down to seven hundred thirty-two A. D., when Haroun-al Raschid was made caliph, establishing his headquarters at Bagdad. Then came the Christian crusades with its page of history written in blood and human suffering. It was at this time that Pope Urban the Second, aided by Peter the Hermit, a disciple of Christian intrigue, was the cause of deplorable bloodshed in which multitudes of Christians and Moslems were slain. In the year seven hundred forty-eight came another Christian crusade under Saint Bernard, with the view of repossessing Palestine. But the Christians met a terrific defeat. Again, in the year twelve hundred twelve, on the supposition that the former crusades failed because of Christian impurity, the idiotic Childrens' Crusade was launched under Stephen and Nicholas. Fifty thousand children under the name of the 'Militia of Jesus,' marched unarmed against our forces in Palestine, the result of which were better unmentioned."

"Yes," answered the rabbi sadly, "the crusade of children was a tremendous blemish on Christianity, so-called, that time can hardly efface. Those were certainly dark pages of history."

"These were indeed, Rabbi, yet remember that Christians were the sole aggressors in their successive incursions."

"That I concede, Caliph, yet after all said and done, those days of indiscriminate slaughter of human beings, was little less than religious fanaticism. I see no justification for it."

"Yes, Rabbi, I agree with you, for while we possessed territory that aforetime was not ours, yet it was God's request that we hold it at all costs which led us to triumphant victory."

"May I suggest, Caliph, that we eliminate discussion of those scenes of blood and carnage and come to the teachings of your Koran, together with the tenets of your faith?"

"It is well," returned the caliph kindly. "So now to the source of the Koran. It is composed almost in its entirety of the revelations of Mohammed, which please understand did not come from his pen, for his wives and friends wrote it from memory. Then we come to numerous doctrines that Mohammed wrote on the shoulder-blades of camels, sheep, etc. We also have many suras, or chapters, on various subjects written by his scribes as God would inspire them, until when compiled into one volume, they constitute our present Koran."

"Which, I take it, Caliph, differs widely from the message and compilation of our Christian Bible?"

"In many ways, yes, and in others there is quite a semblance. We, like you, believe in God and that he has revealed his will in former ages, also that he has inspired men in all ages and epochs."

"You recognize then, Caliph, the dispensation under Abraham, Isaac, Jacob, and Moses."

"Indeed, Abraham, especially. Yet I wish to impress upon you that of the prophets of all time, none was comparable to Mohammed."

"For argument's sake, Mr. Koutaj, let us accede that you may be right, and pass on to your faith."

"Agreed. To begin with, Rabbi, the fundamentals of Mohammedanism, are faith in God, and Islam, which means full submission to his will. Then comes what is known to us as the Creed, which teaches that there is but one God and that Mohammed is his prophet, which implies in the fullest sense that we are in no wise idolaters, but like you Christians, that we recognize the supremacy of an All-wise Creator, and our rule of faith, is the Koran."

"Now, Caliph, to what extent do you recognize priesthood or divine authority? I mean by that the power of God delegated to man to officiate in his stead."

"Rabbi, there is no such absurdity in Mohammedanism to burden the spirit of Islam, for man deals individually with his God. Even the Prophet Mohammed confessed that he was a sinful man, and was ever imploring forgiveness. Salvation is promised to the believer, but to obtain it he must live a life of self-denial, good works, and observance of the requirements of Islam, all of which comprehends the daily life of the Moslems."

"But these principles and ordinances, if such you call them—will you kindly indicate of what they consist?"

"Certainly, Rabbi. Each day opens with prayer at dawn, and prayers are repeated at intervals during the day, closing with one at vesper time. Each prayer consists of two or more prostrations in which are recited special gems from the Koran. We like to meet in thousands at a time to offer en messe these vesper prayers. Then there are tithes, alms, and fasting, especially during the month of Romodham."

Seizing another thought, the inquisitive rabbi asked, "I have heard that you people believe in predestination, which I shall be glad to have you clarify if you will, please."

"We are decidedly advocates of that doctrine, Rabbi. To us the fate of man is fixed innately, as you may learn from the Koran which I quote: 'God misleadeth whom he pleaseth and guideth whom he will aright. He created man upright and then caused him to be the vilest of the vile. The fate of every man is bound around his neck.'

We believe, however, that prayer modifies those decrees
of fate, hence our praying continuously. We exhort men
to believe and do good works lest they be cast into perdition, as salvation is contingent upon faith in God, and
man may, to an extent at least, achieve paradise on the
one hand, or the consequences of hell and damnation on
the other. Moreover, there is no vicarious work with
us as with you Christians. The burdened shall not bear
the sin of another, there being no taint upon the human
family by reason of Eden's fall. Man sins naturally, but
his sinning is in no manner the result of any antecedent
act of his progenitors."

"Then" asked the rabbi earnestly, "will you kindly
indicate your attitude as regards Jesus Christ, the Son of
God?"

"Of course, Jesus Christ was not the son of God as
you Christians are pleased to state. But again, I quote
from the Koran: 'The Jews say Ezra is the son of God,
and the Christians say Christ is the Son of God; this is
their sayings in their mouths they imitate the sayings
who were believers in former times. But God resist them.
How they are infatuated. They take their priests and
their monks for lords; and Christ the son of Mary as God,
while they are commanded to worship one God only.
There is no God but God.'

"To us, Rabbi, the very thought of Christ as God
is sacrilege, but again from the Koran: 'Verily, the idols
which ye invoke besides God can never create a single
fly, though they were all assembled for that purpose, and
if a fly-catcher snatched anything from them, they can
not recover the same.' I am bold, Mr. Ben Arden, to
assert that there is but one God, and Jesus Christ was
more impostor than prophet."

Smiling at the inference so emphatically declared,
the rabbi returned calmly: "Of course, Mr. Koutaj, I, a
Christian, take it all good naturedly. However, I might

indicate my views later on. I wish you would enlighten me as to your conception of paradise or eternal life."

"The answer to your request must, as usual, come from the Koran, which I quote: 'There are many who shall approach near unto God; they shall dwell in the gardens of delight, reposing on couches adorned with gold and precious stones. Youths shall continue in their bloom forever, and maidens shall go around to attend them with goblets of wine; their heads shall not ache by drinking, neither shall their reason be disturbed. The flesh of birds shall be their desire. Within they shall not bear any vain discourse, or any sin, but only salutation— peace—peace. They shall have their abode among the lotus-trees, free from thorns, and laden with produce. Verily we have created the damsels of paradise by special creation, and have made virgins beloved of their husbands.' The foregoing, Rabbi, discloses briefly our conception of beautiful paradise."

"And is this the goal to which you aspire?" asked the rabbi.

"And pray," answered the caliph with an air of sophistication, "what more could you ask that such a haven of love?"

"Well," returned the Jew thoughtfully, "the heaven to which I aspire is more tangible by far than that, for I anticipate continuing to be a progressive being in eternity as I am here, and my happiness shall be to be my brother's keeper, and to execute the design and will of my Creator. This, of course, is where we differ. Now, this brings up the consideration of your views of resurrection and the final destiny of the human soul. Will you please disclose your beliefs in a tangible resurrection?"

The caliph was somewhat reticent. "As to this, Rabbi, there is but little taught in the Koran. In several of its suras, Gabriel made reference to it, hence we affirm it. As to its tangibility, all that is written is in one sura, where Gabriel said he could even bring the fingerbones together, and when Mohammed asked as to when it would occur, the query was left unanswered. To us, it must be far remote, to occur when the sun shall fold up, the sea boil, the stars fall, and when the very elements will melt."

"Apparently, dear Caliph, resurrection to you means a very mystic and uncertain thing. I understand you do not take it very seriously."

"No, not to the extent that you Christians do. In fact, we seldom mention it as a possibility."

"After all this," spoke the rabbi, "what then is to be the ultimate or final analysis of man as an entity? Will he be tangible, or will he be dissolved into some metaphysical, incomprehensible essence?"

"I am not prepared to answer authoritatively, for while we believe in some form of life continuity, still no man has ever had a vain conception or even thinkable inference of what the condition might be. To us, such is sinful to speculate upon."

The rabbi smiled. A flood of thoughts seemed to pass through his mind, as he looked over the landscape to observe the crimson clouds meet the horizon, perhaps seeing little, for his thoughts were elsewhere. Eventually he turned to the caliph, saying: "Caliph, you will, I hope, pardon my frankness when I say that your narration has been clear and concise, for which I am grateful. I am, however, free to confess that your disclosure does not impress me deeply. Of course, remember, I am not here to find fault, but to gather information, all of which will add potentially to my quest."

The caliph seemed to wonder, then asked with interest: "You know, my rabbi friend, I wonder what you mean by what you call your quest, for I have been at my wit's end to know just why you are here in India. Have you some special mission here?"

"I have, indeed, Caliph," replied the Jew, with interest. "I am in quest of the true Church of God with its power and salvation. That Priceless Pearl which has characterized the Lord's work in different ages of history."

At once, the caliph registered interest, as he asked: "I fail to fathom your meaning, Rabbi. Will you, therefore, be more explicit?"

"It is my pleasure to do so," returned the rabbi, calmly. And he related again his reasons for having become a Christian and setting out on his journey.

"Your logic, Rabbi, has a pretty ring to it and might be plausible. However, I am sure your search will be a futile one, and you will go down into history as one who has followed a will-o-the-wisp, or chased bubbles on a precipice. As for me, I am a Mohammedan, as such have lived, and as such hope to die. You are a Christian entitled to your persuasion, and as such, I honor and respect you."

"What a blessing, my dear Caliph, that God has given the propensity to differ and take exception in weighty matters, and still keep within the bounds of friendship. It is majestic, is it not?"

"I have often made that same observation, Rabbi. Even in our most radical views, I feel even warmer toward you than ever. So I suggest that we retire, wishing you sweet sleep and pleasant dreams. On the morrow, I shall deliver you safely at the consulate."

CHAPTER XIII

THE cold winter months in the Himalaya Mountains offered an experience new to the rabbi, but as began the dawn of spring he set out for his eastward journey en route for Peking, China, and at Calcutta he bade adieu to his friend, John Mordon, who had spent the winter with his friend, the consul. The parting was a sad one, for the two men had developed a warm friendship, yet there was an understanding that when the rabbi came to America, the Mordon home was to be his headquarters.

The voyage from Singapore to Hong Kong was a long and rather tiresome one, even though scenes new were entrancing, and friends anew were made en route. The quaint peoples, manners, and customs he contacted on the ship were valuable. Then the country in general as viewed from the shores as he passed, all bedecked in the blush of spring, seemed to mean much to the deeply spiritual Ben Arden. His reception among these orientals was satisfying, for he met on every hand courtesies that he had not anticipated.

The day following his arrival in Peking found the rabbi wandering through the streets, until at last he came to the great historical stone bridge that spans the Lotus River. While he had read much of this rare piece of massive architecture, the realization that he actually stood upon it seemed too strange to be a reality. The rare foliage that overhung the placid water; ducks, geese, and other species of waterfowl, made the spring morning glorious.

En route to his hotel, he often stopped to smile amusingly at some of the actions of the people. The bustle of marketing, chatter of passing throngs in so queer a language, not one word of which was intelligible to him, not even the phonics translated anything to his previous experience but nonetheless fascinated him.

Arriving at his hotel, he was agreeably surprised to make the acquaintance of Clara Banks, an American woman representing a large United States publishing house, who was in China in the interest of her company. Her clear voice, freedom of speech, altogether so affable a nature, perfect deportment, and yet typical freedom of an American, caused the rabbi at once to feel at home in her presence, and for hours they conversed of lands and climes that had come under their experiences, each having an interesting story to relate. Finally, the drift of conversation was turned to their being in the celestial empire.

Miss Banks disclosed her interest in the study of the life and mannerisms of the Chinese people. She presented scores of interesting photographs she had taken in China, all of which gave the Jew an additional urge to visit many of those rare regions.

In turn, Ben Arden related his story of life in Jerusalem, and the object of his journey.

"Rabbi, your quest is a noble one, indeed, for I see but a disabled Christianity today. But what availeth it to make a search with so little encouragement of success? To me, the demagoguery of Christianity in today's pandemonium of religions, is sufficient to discourage one from taking any part therein." She hesitated momentarily. "In fact, I am free to state that I am disgusted with the paradoxical admixture that seems to characterize the Christianity of the present."

"Perhaps you are right, Miss Banks, yet somehow

I have an intuition, seemingly innate within me, that impels me to make the world-wide quest with the assurance that somewhere I may yet find the true church of Jehovah in which shall be manifested the very fruits that have characterized the Lord's work in different dispensations of his dealings with the more righteous of his people. Don't you think this possible, Miss Banks?"

"Well, Mr. Ben Arden, you may live to do so, but I confess that such has never come into my experience, and I have met many, many peoples of the nations."

"Even that, Miss Banks, could not discourage me, for I feel quite sure that I, sooner or later, shall find it, and who knows but that I may find it in your own cherished America."

Miss Banks thought deeply, and she replied: "It seems to me, Rabbi, that such faith is sufficient to move a mountain, and I hope you will not be disappointed in your quest."

The conversation continued until lunchtime, following which, Miss Banks suggested walking to the city wall. As they looked at it, Miss Banks spoke about the famous old Chinese wall, saying it was fifteen hundred miles long with an average height of forty-two feet, and wide enough for heavy-laden wagons to drive on its summit. She said she had traveled to see it on several occasions since her arrival in China. "It is estimated," she said, "that there is as much material in this wall as in all the buildings in the United States together. Just think, this massive thing being fifteen hundred miles long. What an army of millions must have been employed in its construction, and goodness only knows how many years were required in its building."

"The wonder of it all, Miss Banks, "is that it seems to antedate history as we know it."

Returning from the wall, the rabbi and Miss Banks

made their way through the busy and narrow thorough-
fares, Miss Banks acting as guide. "This," she explained,
"is what is known as the Forbidden City, and is much
revered by the celestials. Now, we are are approaching
what is known as the 'Gate of Heaven,' through which
we enter. Kindly observe the elaborate ornamentation
in exquisite porcelain and marble, for nothing has been
spared to make it a rare sanctuary of beauty."

"It certainly is a masterpiece of architecture, Miss
Banks. I never dreamed these celestials had so enriched
a sense of the arts."

Following a brisk walk, the rabbi exclaimed: "Well,
this is certainly an Eden, to be sure, beautiful beyond
my language to express."

"Rare, indeed," returned Miss Banks. "This is
known as the 'Altar of Heaven.' The Chinese claim
with great emphasis that right here is the center of the
universe. The Chinese emperor, under the old regime,
at least, accompanied by the Royal Guard, would come
here annually, and upon the tile in the center of the
huge circle yonder, pray to the gods."

"How calm and serene it all seems," answered the
rabbi. "This place implies its sacredness."

"The Chinese boast of its being the most sacred
spot in the universe, and consequently challenge all the
world to furnish its rival. Moreover, I have my doubts
that their challenge will be accepted. In this celestial
center you observe other buildings, among which is the
imperial palace yonder, which has been the residence of
the royal family for ages, but is now occupied by the
president of the republic, and other prominent government officials."

"You know, Miss Banks, I was astounded at the
magnificence of Mohammedan architecture, but in this
I see many things that equally match it, unless, of course,

it is the Taj Mahal or jewel tower, that stands unique in all the world for its rarity of design and jeweled value."

It was late when they arrived at their hotel, and as they were looking at the passing people, Miss Banks burst into a hearty laugh, characteristic of her jovial nature. The rabbi asked the reason for her merriment.

"Didn't you see those two Chinese shaking hands with themselves? It is too funny for words."

Ben Arden admitted that he had noticed nothing out of the ordinary, as the girl continued: "You see, Rabbi, when we meet a friend we each shake the other's hand. Not so here, for when friends meet, each shakes his own hands."

"How ridiculous," returned the rabbi.

"Not altogether, Rabbi."

"An idiotic custom, I would say, that to me connotes nothing of friendship's warmth."

"Not to them, Rabbi. It means to them what a handshake means to us. Yet they have other customs that are ethical to them though absurd to us. For instance, we uncover our heads as a mark of respect, while for the same reason the Chinaman keeps his covered. We black our shoes; the Chinese whiten theirs. We reserve the place of honor on the right; the celestials place it on the left. We say the magnetic pole is in the north; they say it is in the south. We locate the seat of reason in the brain, they locate it in the bowels, and thus it goes that their customs, so at variance with our policy of politeness, are perfection to them. Moreover, their written language is equally queer, so unlike the alphabet of the Japanese that is built on phonic sounds, but to the contrary it is constructed similar to what we stenographers call 'word signs,' by which I mean that they seem to have a character for each word of their language."

"Then, Miss Banks, what an endless task it must be for a stranger to acquire it."

"Indeed it is, Mister Ben Arden, for it is estimated that they have forty-three thousand characters. However, it is estimated that the average Chinaman gets by with the use of less than one thousand, and manages to go through life to his satisfaction."

"Have you made much study of their religion?" asked the rabbi, deeply earnest. "You know, that is what will interest me above all else."

"To quite an extent, Rabbi. I have conversed frequently with a Chinese sage, quite an adept and ardent student of the great religions of China. But please do not ask me to enlighten you on the subject. The friend of whom I speak is a deep philosopher. He is really an inspirational character, well educated, speaking a perfect English, and besides this, he is a very artful entertainer. Tomorrow, if you are agreed, I shall be pleased to escort you to his palace, where I am sure you will be an avid listener to his eloquence and information, for he is a veritable encyclopedia, and as kind as a father."

"Which pleasure shall be mine, Miss Banks, but I hope I will not be intruding upon your valuable time, if I ask you to remain for the interview."

"I should regret to be deprived of the privilege, Rabbi, for I know the conference will be an intellectual treat, and the information will add to my story of life among the Chinese orientals."

"Just like you Americans," returned the rabbi admiringly. "You people seem an inspiration from a standpoint of real living. You know, I have a warm-hearted friend whom I left in Calcutta. He is jovial, profound, and comical. Then I met a young American chauffeur to the caliph of Calcutta, whose personality seemed nearly as cheerful as your own. You all seem to have a something of natural pleasure that makes you different from other people of my knowledge—jovial, graceful, brilliant, and entertaining."

Miss Banks was embarrassed. "Please do not endow me with all those attributes. I have learned in practical life that the source of true happiness is in doing things that need to be done, in being a brother's keeper and friend, when possible, in a word, to be a useful cog in the great wheel of life."

"Such lives," returned the rabbi, more amazed than ever, "certainly will require no monument to mark the place."

CHAPTER XIV

EN ROUTE to the palace of the Chinese sage, Miss Banks and the rabbi freely chatted as to the delightful evening that was in store for them.

"I observe," noticed the rabbi, thoughtfully, "that you have a new notebook, which implies that the old one must be about filled up."

Miss Banks smiled. "Yes, Rabbi, and when we leave this interview, be not too sure that this one will not be filled to overflowing. You have little conception of what is in the offing for you, but I have had interviews with him to my great joy and satisfaction."

At the great vestibule, the visitors were met by a youthful page, who, taking their card, disappeared, only to return, ushering them into a palatial room decorated with most exquisite Chinese art. They were no more than comfortably seated, when an elderly gentleman appeared, robed in a beautiful black gown covered with golden medallions. In a joyful manner, he addressed Miss Banks: "How charming of you to do me the honor, and your friend is—?"

"Mr. Homer Ben Arden. Perhaps I should say Rabbi Ben Arden, a Christian Jew from old Jerusalem."

"For the first time in my life," returned the sage, "I have the honor of greeting one from old Jerusalem."

"Oh, a thousand pardons," faltered Miss Banks. "This, Rabbi, is my friend, Mr. Klang-Ho-Tsche, a gentleman of deep learning and eloquence."

"I presume," laughed the old sage, "that to fraternize and bid you welcome to my palace, I must forego

Chinese customs and meet you on your own ground by shaking hands as you Christians do." So saying, the sage extended his hand and a hearty handshake followed.

"Yesterday," began Miss Banks, "I was talking with the rabbi relative to your knowledge of Chinese philosophy and religion, and I took the liberty of stating that you would be pleased to disclose what he is so eager to learn."

Like all great men, the sage was modest, so he replied, "I fear you have built up a false premise, Miss Banks. However, nothing could give me greater joy than to tell the rabbi what little I know."

"How kind of you," answered the rabbi; "this, I assure you, will be greatly appreciated. You see, I am touring the world in quest of a religion that was aforetime among men, but now seems lost. It is that which I search. Therefore, if you feel to disclose your philosophy and beliefs, religious, et cetera, I shall indeed be grateful."

"That would be a long, long story, Rabbi, yet time is not too long for me when I feel that I am doing a good turn, and especially when it comes to preparing sincere men for life."

"Such splendid spirit," returned the rabbi, "coupled with your sense of the ethical life, is a gem seldom found among men."

"No, no, not that, Rabbi," quickly answered the sage. "You are wrong, I fear, for it is no uncommon thing among men in this celestial empire to find the spirit of true brotherhood maintained. The converse is the exception and not the rule."

Homer Ben Arden seemed somewhat confused before he replied, "I am happy to learn that, Mr. Klang-

Ho-Tsche. I am ashamed of myself for not knowing more of your people than I do."

"You are no exception to the rule, Rabbi, for through prejudice and gross ignorance, the world looks upon us with a disdainful eye, even ignoring our wonderful ancestry and history. This reminds me of a saying of one of your illustrious philosophers, Herbert Spencer, who wrote, 'There is a principle in life that is a bar to all progress, and will keep man in everlasting ignorance, and that principle is contempt prior to investigation.' Christians are prone to ridicule our education and skill, classing us with the illiterate and ignorant, semi-civilized, and what not, simultaneously forgetting how very much they owe to China for much of their vaunted knowledge, ingenuity, and invention."

Miss Banks seemed to miss not a single word of the conversation.

"I confess," answered the rabbi, "that you have an exceeding ancient history, together with existing monuments that point to long ages past, when your ancestors wrought wonderful works—"

"Just as we do today," interrupted the sage with a smile, "hence the source, cause, and effect of our commonwealth."

"May I ask you, Mr. Klang-Ho-Tsche, to what you attribute your success as nation builders?"

"To religion, Rabbi—it is the cornerstone of existence, that moulds into symmetry the mandates of the gods. Besides, as another of your Christian writers disclosed beautifully: 'It is religion that produces the nectar that God places in every sorrow.'"

"Very true," answered the Jew. "A man could not think in such terms without becoming great and noble to the extent, at least, that thoughts become constructive."

"Just so, Rabbi, and it is that which has made China

what she is today. It is really wonderful what the great religions of China have done as soul and nation builders."

This gave Ben Arden a thought. "You speak of religion in the plural," asked the rabbi with sincerity. "Am I to understand that you have more than one recognized religion?"

"Certainly, Rabbi, and why not? Is a man supposed to be one-sided—half-developed? Or is it better that all corners of his nature be moulded into symmetry to prepare him to withstand attack from all conceivable angles? Yes, we have three great religions. First, we have Confucianism, that teaches the moral nature of man, disclosing a strict line of demarkation between vice and virtue, duty and compliance with all the aesthetic and practical, with a base of sympathy, pity and filial love. Secondly, we have what is known as Taoism, which is quite largely materialistic. Its notion of the soul is physical, composed of finer element or substance than is discernable to human intelligence. By it, immortality is gained only through a process of physical discipline—a sort of chemical process, if you will, which transmutes element into more refined structures. Thirdly, we have Buddhism, which is entirely metaphysical in nature. It teaches that the world of sense is totally unreal. Its gods are personalized ideas. It denies matter entirely, concerning itself only with the operations of mental reaction."

"Do you imply, Mr. Klang-Ho-Tsche, that these three religions, each in itself distinct, can be practical and collectively applied?"

"Why not?" inquired the sage candidly. "The moral, the material, and the metaphysical all combine into a complete triune to build super-manhood."

"With your indulgence," asked the rabbi, "how do

you manage to reconcile this with the peculiar doctrine of Confucius?"

"In this manner, Confucius knew God, but did not honor him as God, which left the way open for polytheism. He built more upon morality than religion. Hence, we found that the combination of the three great systems automatically adjust themselves into one symmetric whole."

"Mr. Klang-Ho-Tsche," interrupted Miss Banks for the first time during the interview, "I am sure the rabbi would much appreciate your narrating the story of Lao Tsze, as you did to me a few days since, and I assure you that I should like very much to have embodied in my notes."

The sage smiled, seeming to appreciate her confidence in him. He began: "This illustrious personage flourished, according to Christian reckoning, about six hundred four years before Christ. From his birth, he appeared to have the intelligence of a man, hence his name, Lao Tsze, which means 'Old Boy.' It is said that on one occasion he mounted into the air, saying: 'In heaven and earth, Tao alone is worthy of honor.' His complexion was white and yellow, ears large; he had ten toes on each foot, together with several irregularities sufficient to render him different from other men, which implied his uniqueness. He possessed wonderful power to accomplish miraculous works, even to ascending into the clouds at will. He was master of the talisman of life, which power he also gave to his servant, Seneka, but, being displeased with the servant's demeanor, he withdrew that power from him, and Seneka immediately was reduced to a heap of bones. At the pleading of Yin-He, however, Seneka was brought back to life. Following this, Lao Tsze bade farewell to the world, and, mounting a cloud, disappeared into space.

On leaving he gave Yin-He a book of five hundred characters that contained a resume of his eventful life of meditation and sacrifice. From this record the greater part of Taoism has been extracted. The first chapter tells of the nameless-latent space. Tao, produced of the First Great Cause, two natures, male and female, that resulted in all that heaven and earth contains."

"This seems to smack of Gnosticism," interrupted the rabbi.

"Perhaps so, but don't lose sight of the fact that our religion existed millenniums before Gnosticism was conceived of. Hence all they possess came directly or indirectly from us. They copied much of our philosophy, just as you Christians have done," answered the sage.

The rabbi and Miss Banks smiled. Yet Homer was determined to extract the concrete as he asked: "If all things had their beginning through the operation of this male and female principle, what is to be the ultimate or final solution of existence?"

"A good question that, Rabbi. All things material are destined to endure for a set time, then perish. Together, they came into being, and to each is allotted a period for development to maturity. But when the apex is reached, all returns to its root. This is known to us as the reversion of destiny."

"In other words," interrupted the rabbi, "it is practically the same, or has the same significance as the Moksha or Brahminism, or the Nirvana of Buddhism. Am I right in my deduction?"

"To an extent, yes, for remember that in the final analysis, emptiness is the only reality of existence, hence the superlative of all. Let me explain. The space between heaven and earth may be likened unto a bellows which though empty never collapses, and the more it is exercised, the more it brings forth. You will agree that in each case it is the non-existing or empty part that had the greater potentiality. The walls of an earthen vessel, the spokes of a wheel are all advantageous, yet each depends entirely upon the space between them. Existence then may be said to correspond to gain, but non-existence to use. A thing cannot be weakened until it has first been straightened. It cannot be brought low until it has been first raised up. That which is taken away must first be given. In this superiority or superlative of non-existence over existence is the principle from Tao, that Lao Tsze sought to teach mankind."

The rabbi did not seem to fathom the philosophy to his satisfaction. "To me, Sage, that is very complicated. Can you give me a more simple example that I might grasp your doctrine?"

"It is very simple, Rabbi. For instance: You may name the sunshine and rain that raises a tree to its apex, the grace of God, if you will, even the grass, the flowers, embracing all flora and fauna. Then you are forced to admit that the same grace of God that produced them will, when they have reached their apex, rot and disintegrate back into the emptiness from which they originally came. There is no denying this, Rabbi. Apply it to all physical existence. The emptiness that first produced it will ultimately dissolve it back to its root—emptiness from which it came. In life, man has been prone to seek things of the body and forget the inner man. To seek after the urge of passion and overlook the within part of him. Colors that delight the eyes may produce blindness. Sounds that enchant the ear may produce deafness. The palate that receives the sense of taste may lose the sense of flavor. The pursuit of pleasure and ambition has its deception. Hence, it goes after all, the mission of life is not to gratify man't external passions. I am sure, Rabbi, that all existence in its root is emptiness from which all material worlds have at some time evolved, and will never be in a state of perfection until reverted back into emptiness from which they originally came."

Homer Ben Arden sat deeply thoughtful, at length answering: "Your philosophy, Mr. Klang-Ho-Tsche, seems to have quite a fascinating ring to it, but please be not disappointed if it fall on non-fertile soil. In me, the philosophy may have little germination."

"Nor can I expect it," quickly and kindly retorted the sage. "It would require years for you to assimilate even the elementary principles."

"That might be," smiled the rabbi, politely. "You know I am a Jew, but I am not a follower of Judaism. To the contrary, I am pleased to be known as a Christian catechuman."

"Which is much to your credit, Rabbi, and I am happy in greeting you as such, much more, in fact than were you of Jewish persuasion. However, kindly remember this, that the truth found in Christianity came from China, where it was taught long centuries before your Nazarene was born. In all due respect to you and your faith, I am free, without mental reservation, to express my opinion that, while Christianity has much truth, still it is so buried beneath the rubbish of distorted tradition and gross superstition as to render it largely unrecognizable, especially when compared to our philosophy."

"Of course, Mr. Klang-Ho-Tsche, you do not believe that I take that with seriousness, do you?"

"Perhaps not," returned the celestial with a smile. "But remember, you teach of Jesus Christ, but we present a much greater character in Lao Tsze. You boast of your sacred Bible, but we produce a greater volume in our Tao-Te-Ching—book of rewards and punishments.

Permit me to read briefly from its sacred pages, and I
invite you to compare them to your beatitudes. 'Advance along the right way and never retreat. Do not
betray the secrets of a household. Be humane to ani-
mals. Rectify yourself so you can convert men. Show
compassion for widows and orphans. Rejoice in the
success of others, and sympathize with their misfor-
tunes as though you were in their place. Expose not
the faults of others. Bestow favor without expecting
recompense. A man who does good is called virtuous
whom all respect, providence protects him, god-like
spirits guard him, he succeeds in all he lays his hands
to do. A handsome figure may excite the admiration
of the world, but cannot deceive heaven.' From the
foregoing, Rabbi, you observe that Christians have no
monopoly on sublime scripture."

Ben Arden had listened with intense interest to the
reading, and when the sage had finished, he asked:
"Have you much of such teachings, Mr. Klang-Ho-
Tsche?"

Placing his hand upon a volume, the sage returned
with emphasis: "Yes, this entire volume, and much
more. This being an English edition, I take great
pleasure in presenting it to you, on condition, of course,
that you promise me to read it with an open mind."

The rabbi was touched with such kindness extended to him: "I promise you, my friend, that I shall
do so, for my life aim is to glean from all peoples their
conceptions of life and its continuity. I thank you
sincerely."

"It is well," answered the sage as he took his foun-
tain pen from his pocket and autographed the book,
first in English and then in Chinese.

After the rabbi had more fully expressed his appreciation for the gift, he spoke touchingly: "We have

been highly edified, Sage, yet in my eagerness, I would like to learn more of Confucius and the part he played in Chinese philosophy. In asking this, I hope I will not be deemed selfish."

"Quite to the contrary, Rabbi, for if I can say anything of this great character who has so embellished the moral and ethical status of China, the pleasure will be mine." Turning to Miss Banks, the sage asked: "And, you, kind lady, will your strength and patience endure more of this conversation? You must be already fatigued."

Miss Banks smiled. "Why, Mr. Klang-Ho-Tsche, I have been too fascinated to be fatigued. Perhaps I am as eager to learn the beauties of China as is the rabbi."

"Well, friends," began the sage, "my story begins with a noted character named Hein. It is said that at the age of seventy-five he married Chin-Tsai, an estimable lady of about his own age. Of this union a son was born whom they named, translated into Latin and hence into your language, Confucius. While born under the most humble conditions, in a cave on Mount Ne, his birth was heralded by innumerable incidents, which I shall not take time to narrate here. His childhood was wonderful, and at the age of fifteen he became a student. At nineteen he married, but this marriage was of short duration. At twenty, he became a teacher of advanced students. His policy was, as often explained by him: 'I do not open the truth to one that has no capacity and urge for knowledge; nor do I assist any who are not anxious to explain. When I present one corner of a lesson to a student, and that student cannot discover the other three, I do not repeat the lesson.' At thirty, he took up the study of music under a great instructor named Saing, who assigned to him a hymn composed by the illustrious Wan Wang, sage of ancient days.

At the end of five days Saing would again teach him, but Confucius replied: 'Not yet, my master, for I must first seize the thought that lies buried in the tune.' When the next five days had elapsed, he said to Saing: 'I see the thought, but dimly; I pray thee, give me another five days, then if I have not learned the great lesson contained therein, I shall leave music as beyond my power.' When the time had elapsed, Confucius stood before Saing and cried in his ecstasy: 'The mists flee, the shadows are gone, and I am as one standing upon a cliff gazing into the wide open world, for I have mastered the secret of thought. I see a noble face, his voice is deep and full, his very self-inspiring love the virtue. I know that I behold the very sage of ancient days, even the great Wan Wang, the Just.'

"In deepest emotion and with moistened eyes, Saing replied: 'Confucius, thou art my master, for though I have played the sacred tune during long years of striving to know its mystery, yet thou hast reached it at a single bound. Henceforth, the gods alone can teach thee tune.'

"From this time on Confucius became famous. Students and nobles flocked to him for instruction. It was at this period of his career that he first visited the illustrious Lao Tsze and was further instructed by him. On and on he advanced, collecting the Book of Odes, and many volumes of historical information. Then he became magistrate to Ching-Too; later, a philosopher and philanthropist, superintendent of public works and minister of crime. On one occasion, as recorded, a father brought accusation against his son, anticipating judgment in his favor. But to his disappointment, as also to the onlookers, the man and his son were both cast into prison. To the remonstrances of the Ke-Clan's appeal, Confucius replied: 'Am I to punish for a breach of filial piety, one who has never been taught to be filial minded? Is he not that neglects to teach his son filial duties, equally guilty with his son who fails in them? Crime is not inherent in human nature, therefore the father in the family, and the government in the state are responsible for the crimes of filial piety in public laws. If a king is careless about publishing laws, punishing in accordance with the strict letter of them, he acts the part of a swindler. Should he collect taxes without giving due warning, he is an oppressor, and should he put people to death without having first instructed them, he is the greater criminal.'

"Confucius went from state to state, and from power to power, until at the age of seventy, being the year four hundred seventy-nine B.C. according to your way of reckoning, he walked before the door, saying: 'Great mountains must crumble, the stormy beam must break, and the wise wither like a plant.'

"Then Confucius passed in death. No man met greater contempt than he, and none have received greater veneration after death.

"The teachings of Confucius are contained in the record known as Lun-Yu, the Ta-Hich, and the Chung-Yung. He derided the spiritual, and seemed to have little or no concern as to future life, saying but little about the gods. He was not concerned as to the origin, and destiny of man, for to him man was the master of his own destiny. He was a statesman and reformer, rather than teacher. He taught: 'It is not virtue to feel discomposure when men take no notice of him. Learning without thought is labor lost, while thought without learning is perilous. To see the right and then not do right is a lack of courage. I am not concerned that I have no place, but I am concerned how I fit into one. I am not concerned that I am not known, but I seek to be worthily known. A man should guard well his words, lest his acts fail to measure up to them. Rotten wood cannot be carved, nor can dirty earth receive a trowel. Do not unto others that you would not wish done to yourself. Is not respectability the main word of life? They who simply know the truth are not the equals of those who love it, and they who love it are equals of those who delight in it.' The foregoing, my friends, are but a few of Confucius' sublime teachings, and I am sure you sense deeply their sublimity."

"Most beautiful," replied Ben Arden, who had listened to the rather long narration with intense interest. "He was a philosopher certainly born before his time."

The celestial continued: "In conclusion, I wish emphatically to impress upon your minds this one thing: That what I have told you today may be considered the superstructure of Chinese philosophy. Yet, from this, many base rites, schemes, superstitions, and gross misrepresentations maintain among the less informed classes. Some are monothetists, while others champion polytheism. Some adore planets, while others pay devotion to images of sages who flourished in earlier dynasties. Yet, withal, to some extent the fundamentals are more or less manifest."

"I am indeed grateful to you, Mr. Klang-Ho-Tsche, for your patience and kindness," spoke the rabbi, with great sincerity. "I trust that you feel how very much I appreciate this information."

"Be assured, Rabbi, that I have not been unmindful of your interest in my narration, and more, what is pleasing to me is to observe that our stenographic friend has pretty well filled her notebook."

Miss Banks smiled: "Yes, just about full, and I think I have not missed a single word of this interview.

What a store of interest I shall take back to America with me."

"Wonderful," answered the sage. "What can I do to obtain a copy of this conversation? Kindly name your price."

"Don't mention price," stated Miss Banks, "for I am more than repaid for my trouble. I shall present you and Mister Ben Arden with typed copies not later than tomorrow afternoon."

After the sage and the rabbi had freely expressed their gratitude to Miss Banks for her service, the sage continued: "Before we part, Rabbi, I want to ask you something that has been troubling my mind since first we met this morning. That is why you, a Jew, are a proselyte to Christianity, the religion to which your people are so antagonistically opposed? Again, why are you here in Peking and so intensely interested in world religions? May I hope that your having left your people to become a Christian, you find yourself still in error, and have come to China to learn the truth?"

"No, Mr. Klang-Ho-Tsche, it is not that I am searching a different source of truth from that of the original Christianity that maintained with the apostles of old. On the other hand, I am in your beautiful country to see if I can find a continuity of that truth, of which I shall be pleased to explain if you desire."

The sage, open-minded in the search of truth, seemed elated at the suggestion: "I shall be delighted to be an ardent listener, Rabbi," as he rolled his thumbs as was his wont.

"To begin with then," continued Ben Arden, "I am free to confess that I might seem to you somewhat of a paradox, and you will probably conclude that I am pretty much of a nomadic wanderer. Be that as it may, I am here in a quest of a deep-rooted desire. A search, if you please, for that which once existed among men and now seems lost. So, to make myself clearly understood, I beg your indulgence by listening to my story." Again, the rabbi told the object of his quest.

The celestial had listened with profound attention, at length faltering sincerely: "Kind Rabbi, have you found anything to your satisfaction here? I really tremble for your reply, for I, to be honest with myself, must confess that I know of no such powers among us as you claim to have maintained."

The rabbi continued: "Candidly, Mr. Klang-Ho-Tsche, I have found in the sincere narrating of your philosophy a most wonderful code of life rules and regulations, together with sublime teachings, and beatitudes that have had tremendous power, evidently, in making you people what you are, to the extent that you are a kind, loving people. However, I must confess that I have not found the least trace of that power of which I seek, hence, as you may realize, I am once more disappointed."

The sage seemed spellbound, eventually exclaiming dispassionately: "My dear rabbi, you almost persuade me to your belief. May I ask you one last favor?"

Ben Arden looked the sage in the eye as he replied: "I hope I can answer it to your satisfaction, Mr. Klang-Ho-Tsche."

"It is this, Rabbi. When you have found that Priceless Pearl of yours, will you promise to advise me of it, for really, for the first time in my life a living faith seems engendered."

Ben Arden leaned forward, seizing the elderly sage's hands in his own, saying with deep interest: "I assure you with my promise that when I shall have found the object of my quest, you shall not be forgotten."

"I know, Rabbi, you will keep your promise, hence I shall hope for greater light."

The interview coming to an end, the rabbi continued: "Now, my dear Mr. Klang-Ho-Tsche, I bid you farewell, and in doing so, I present you with a copy of the English Bible. Read it, I pray you, with an open mind, keeping in mind always the power of God delegated to man, of which I have told you, and I promise you that your declining years shall bring you great joy and contentment."

The rabbi and Miss Banks, following a warm farewell from the softened sage, left for their hotel.

CHAPTER XV

A warm friendship had developed between Homer
Ben Arden and Clara Banks, and it was with regret
that the time of their parting had at length arrived.
She chose to remain in Peking, writing her history of
Chinese manners and customs. Ben Arden, as winter
approached, made his way southward, visiting the Philip-
pines, New Zealand, Australia, thence on to Honolulu,
where he remained an ardent student until the following May. He had rented a comfortable apartment that
overlooked the sea. Here, day after day, he delved
into his now treasured library, as well as purchased
writings of the diversified Christian cults. However, in
all his research, he seemed to meet discouragement, for,
in creed after creed, his research proved futile, for no
sign of his quest was he privileged to find. He had
studied the Baptists, Presbyterians, Methodists, Unitari-
ans, Seventh Day Adventists, Episcopalians, and Catholics, with many other churches available to him. In
all, he found but a confusion or melange of doctrine
that impressed him as being, in their final analysis,
man-made and not of God. Protestants were outstandingly antagonistic to Catholics, despite the fact that they
had nothing by way of reformation to offer. So, all
in all, his winter sojourn in the lovely Hawaiian Islands
resulted only in a rich store of information as to the
beliefs and tenets of the contending cults. Grieved with
his findings, he was impelled to exclaim: "Oh, you
gentiles, how you have departed from the way of the
Lord. The Master took the olive vine and grafted it

into you, and the power of God took root for a time. But now, how clearly I see the name written on the wall. How very truly did Isaiah write: 'Behold, the hand of the Lord is not shortened that he cannot save; neither is his ear heavy that he cannot hear; but your iniquities have separated between you and your God, and your sins have hid his face from you, that he will not hear.' "

It was late in August when the rabbi, having scores of notebooks well filled with his masterly research, set sail for America, and during September the great ocean liner entered the Golden Gate, docking at San Francisco, where Homer Ben Arden at length realized his fond ambition to set foot on American soil.

The bustle and din of American traffic, as formerly explained to him by his friend, John Mordon, was at length experienced, yet it was far beyond anything he had been able to visualize. In the bustle of the traffic, he was really afraid to cross an intersection. "Is it possible," said he to himself, "that civilization is thus advanced? It is little wonder that the United States leads the world's industry."

Ben Arden spent many days visiting San Francisco, together with side trips to Oakland, Palo Alto, Angel Island, Berkeley, even as far as Monterey, Long Beach, and Los Angeles. Finally feeling somewhat familiarized with American procedure, he prepared to leave for Indianapolis, the home of John Mordon, where he was assured a warm welcome.

Daylight the following morning found the rabbi comfortably seated in a Pullman east-bound through the Sierra Madras. The railroad accommodations, so complete in detail, caused him to marvel. The day passed with his viewing the splendid scenery of the Feather River and other passing vistas, and the following morning brought him to Ogden, Utah.

As he was passing the scenery of Weber Canyon, a companion voyager, seemingly interested in the rabbi's strict attention to the Devil's Gate, took a seat by him, asking: "Pardon me, friend, I have been watching you for some time, and I conclude that such scenery as this must be somewhat unfamiliar to you."

Thanking the gentleman for the courtesy, Ben Arden answered kindly: "Oh, no, I have seen very much rugged scenery, but this peculiar formation, for some reason, seems to have an unusual appeal to me."

"Are you new in the United States?" asked the stranger.

The rabbi smiled. "Yes, very new, indeed, and quite inexperienced with American life and environment. However, I am learning American ways quite beyond my anticipation."

Looking the rabbi in the eye, the gentleman inquired: "May I ask your nationality, my friend?"

Ben Arden smiled as he turned to the stranger: "My very face is indicative of my racial origin. You will agree I need no other identity, surely."

The stranger seemed somewhat abashed, thinking that perhaps he had been rather insistent, as he faltered: "I have already observed that you are Jewish, yet you know there is no nation under heaven in which your people are not generously represented."

"That might be true, my friend," returned the rabbi. Then he said: "My name is Homer Ben Arden of Jerusalem, Palestine."

"You really mean to tell me you hail from the Holy City?"

"The same. I was born and reared within a stone's throw of the great Mosque of Omer," answered the rabbi genially. "And your name is?"

The stranger in turn told him his name: "I am Bishop H. D. Meldon, Chicago, Illinois."

The rabbi studied for a moment, but eventually he asked, "Am I to understand that you are a divine of the Catholic church?"

"I have the honor," returned the bishop, "to present myself as one possessing divine authority by which one acts officially in the name of the Lord. Of course, this might have little appeal to you, a follower of Judaism."

Ben Arden was foremost with his reply: "I beg your pardon, Bishop Meldon, for while I am Jewish, I am not affiliated with Judaism. To the contrary, I am a Christian."

The bishop seemed amazed: "What, a Christian Jew? How singular that sounds. May I ask with what church you are about to cast your lot?"

"With none of them," quickly returned Ben Arden with emphasis. "I am a devotee of Jesus Christ and the power he and his apostles held on earth, whereby the very elements bowed in humble obeisance to priesthood mandate. When I find the church that can satisfy me of the acquisition of that power, then I shall have found the church of God. In a word, I shall without delay become a communicant of that church. But thus far, I fail to find it in the many contending Christian churches so discordant, each ready at all times to fly at the other's throats, if you will, all claiming to be the church of Christ. Thus, I fear I shall go very slow, indeed, in reaching my decision."

The bishop seemed impressed with the thought that here was, indeed, fertile soil for the Catholic church, as very confidently he returned: "My dear rabbi, there never has been but one church of the Master. This he organized himself, conferring divine authority upon his apostles. It is that authority that has come down in an unbroken chain from Saint Peter to our day, fighting its way as it has done through adversity and genealogical descent to more than three hundred popes. Through that power and by virtue of that authority, I am proud to present myself as one ordained of God, and fully prepared to present to you the fulness of the gospel of Jesus Christ."

Looking Bishop Meldon in the eye, the rabbi asked with great earnestness, "How am I to know you are one possessed of divine authority to officiate fully in the name of the Master?"

The bishop, more zealous than ever, replied positively. "There are several ways, Rabbi. First, credentials such as these." The prelate presented his certificate of ordination. "Second, the spirit of the individual possessing that authority; third, testimony of true doctrine; and fourth, the great unbroken chain of priesthood that has come down from the days of Saint Peter to our day, with an unbroken succession of divine appointment."

"Your points are well defined," replied the rabbi, "yet am I not entitled to require the evidence, or criterion of measurement, that the power of which you speak is comparable to that in the days of Jesus and the apostles?"

The bishop was positive in his query. "And should I satisfy you, Rabbi, with our exactness?"

"Then," answered the rabbi quickly, "I, of course, shall present myself a convert to Catholicism. However, bear this in mind, that the church of Jesus Christ must be flawless in organization, doctrine, and power. Anything short of this will have little appeal to me."

Bishop Meldon hesitated momentarily, at length replying assuredly, "You are very exacting, Rabbi. However, I know you will not be disappointed in the Catholic church."

Ben Arden was unflinching as he answered: "And why should I not be exacting in this great pandemonium of Christian strife?"

"Well, Rabbi," replied the bishop, with an assured air, "I affirm that our authority to officiate in the name of Jesus, has descended through an unbroken succession from Saint Peter to this day. Moreover, no sect of assumed Christendom dare lay claim to such a condition, for they are apostate, hence have no communication with the heavens. I am sure you will agree with me that no man can exercise authority without having been ordained to that calling, and who has power in turn to impart by ordination that authority to others."

"Decidedly so," returned the rabbi in full acquisition. "This is, of course, an indispensable requisite. One must receive this authority before he attempts to officiate in the name of the Master."

The bishop, seeming more assured than ever that he had the Jew thinking along with him, answered: "Then, Rabbi, you admit the necessity of possessing divine authority before one can officiate in the name of the Lord?"

"I concede that, Mr. Meldon, but I am not ready to admit that the Catholic church possesses that authority. I shall, with propriety, require more proof than a mere assertion that such is the case, or even that your certificate of ordination may not, in the final analysis, be spurious. You know, in two thousand years there may have been many chances that there were breaks in that lineage, schisms, breeches, and sin that might have grieved heaven sufficiently to have caused a rupture in priesthood continuity."

The bishop was becoming annoyed, and it could be seen that he was losing his equilibrium. "That might work in theory or assumption, Rabbi, but in reality, there is no possibility of such a thing happening, for God will not allow his church to partake of corruption."

"Now, Mr. Meldon, in all kindness, suppose I were to question your personal priesthood, and demand your genealogical linking back to Peter. What then?"

"Of course, Rabbi, I am not prepared to give it. Nor do I think it at all necessary that I should do so. All I need to do is to point to the workings of Catholicism as evidence of our being acknowledged of heaven, which certainly is more potent and assuring than all thought of genealogical lineage."

Ben Arden, dissatisfied with the reply, insisted: "Am I to understand that you evade my fair question, Mr. Meldon?" Ben Arden looked into the bishop's eyes.

Bishop Meldon, somewhat evasive, and to make the best of a bad situation, returned: "My answer is that through the eye of faith and through my experience with the Spirit of the Lord, I have not the slightest doubt as to the authority that maintains in our church. I have a list of all popes from Saint Peter to our day, and while I may not be able to give the details of ordination through the ages, yet, I am candid in stating that these holy men were heaven approved."

Ben Arden was calm as he asked dispassionately: "Does the fact of that printed list establish the efficacy of their heaven approved lineage in righteous authority?"

"To us that goes unquestioned, Rabbi. In fact, I have never met with this kind of questioning before. Do I take that as a challenge?"

The rabbi was quick to detect the rising ire of the prelate, yet he was calm in his answer: "Certainly not, yet I anticipated a more conclusive answer than you have given. Really, I think I am entitled to something more satisfying, do you not think so?"

"The thing is that I cannot stand to have my priesthood questioned."

Ben Arden was amazed at the bishop's sudden turn, as he answered quietly: "Please, Mr. Meldon, be composed and considerate, for am I not fully justified in demanding something more than a mere inference, and especially in the face of your past history, which records so many schisms and variations of priesthood descent?"

This was too much for the prelate, who retorted with determination, "Well, if you are a professed student of history, I challenge you to refute this statement: We have a chain of divine authority coming in unbroken continuity from Saint Peter to the present ruling Pope of Rome."

The rabbi was not to be easily bluffed, for he had been a careful student of secular as well as ecclesiastical history. "A pretty definite challenge, Bishop Meldon, and while I am not aggressive in nature, yet I feel that your challenge should not go uncalled. However, I want you to consider that this discussion is to be in all kindness and dispassionateness. I pray you to recall the criterion of measurement you gave me of the evidence of your calling. I mean what you said of the spirit of the prelate."

Bishop Meldon seemed suddenly ashamed as he said, "Rabbi, I take the rebuke with apologies, so now I am ready to listen to, and meet your charge."

"Very well, Bishop Meldon. Who was Saint Peter's successor?"

"His name was Linus," returned the bishop, "and he was ordained at Rome under the hands of Peter himself."

"Which, of course, I must question, for the best evidence in history claims that this was not the case. How very indiscreet Paul must have been when writ-

ing to the Romans to mention him nowhere. Now,
if Linus were Saint Peter's successor, I must ask you
what you will do with John, the beloved apostle of our
Lord, still living at that time who, sixty years later,
rather sixty years after the crucifixion, thundered his
praise and denunciation against the seven churches then
existing, never once mentioning the church of Rome.
Moreover, may I ask as to Saint Peter's priesthood calling at the time you claim he ordained Linus?"

"Certainly, Rabbi, he was bishop of Rome."

The rabbi retorted kindly, "Peter was never a bishop
of Rome or elsewhere. To the contrary, he was head
of the apostolate, with James and John as his counselors.
These men in the outlying churches ordained bishops
in various churches, at Antioch, and perhaps Rome, but
history denies that Peter was ever a bishop."

"You might and might not have such history at
your fingers' ends, Rabbi. Are you sure that is not
merely an inference?"

"As you choose, Mr. Meldon. However, let us proceed. Your church claims that Cletus was ordained
pope in A.D. ninety, and that Clement was ordained pope
in A.D. ninety-three. Mind you, the Apostle John still
living who, according to your history, says John died in
A. D. ninety-six. During all the time previous, and sixteen
years after Peter's death, he was the remaining apostle.
In John's writings reviewing the seven then existing
churches in Asia, he began his review with this statement: 'The Revelation of Jesus Christ which God gave
unto him to shew his servants things which must shortly
come to pass; and he sent and signified it by an angel
to his servant John, who bare record of the word of
God, and the testimony of Jesus Christ.' Now, Bishop
Meldon, I ask you in all fairness: What are you going
to do with John? For, until you can move him from

the picture, Catholic authority certainly falls to pieces. Again, why did not John acknowledge Popes Linus, Cletus, and Clement? Your church claims quite definitely that Cletus was Linus' successor; if so, you must have had two popes reigning at the same time."

The bishop was still angered, so he retorted: "That is something neither you nor I know anything about. I agree that there are writings to that effect, but the source is not authentic."

The rabbi was not easily silenced. "Bishop Meldon, there is not in your church the slightest historical evidence in written scripture or otherwise, other than tradition, the only thing you have to stand on. I speak advisedly in this, Mr. Meldon. Can you refute my statement?"

"I have not that information, Rabbi."

"No, nor has anyone else in your church, for it does not exist, for never has the evidence been forthcoming."

"That might be, Rabbi, yet I doubt it very much." The bishop was disturbed, for he now saw that the rabbi seemed to be well informed.

"Now, Bishop Meldon," the rabbi was intensely sincere, yet firm, "in face of the evidence, there remains no premise whatever to substantiate any authentic link or continuity of priesthood as coming from Saint Peter. Next, I referred to variations during the successive history of your church."

"Which, of course, Rabbi, you will find clean and worthy in all cases."

"I would to heaven it were so, Bishop Meldon. But it is not so, by any means. I have been years in my search of history, the reason for which I shall disclose later on." The rabbi drew a notebook from his suitcase. "Now, to begin, Bishop Meldon. In the year A.D. three fifty-five, Liberius was pope. He was banished, and Phelix was ordained to the papal chair, which caused a sanguinary war in which Phelix was overthrown and the banished pope, by force of arms, regained the throne. In face of all this bloodshed, it is surprising how these two bloodthirsty popes could have been sainted. Again, Bishop, in A.D. five hundred thirty-six, Vegilus and Silverus simultaneously held the papal chair. This you cannot deny, your people having only explained it by silence.

"We come now to the year A.D. seven hundred fifty-seven when, at the death of Paul the First, the Duke of Nepi compelled some bishops to consecrate his brother Constantine pope. Later, Stephen the Fourth was elected, and the unseated Constantine had his eyes burned out.

"Next comes the year eight hundred seventy-two, finding John the Eighth pope, when one Formosus conspired against him and murdered him, for which foul deed, Formosus was excommunicated. But a few years later this murderer, Formosus, was elected pope. Then Stephen the Eighth was made pope, who began by having the body of Formosus exhumed, propped in a chair, tried, and convicted, and his dead body thrown into a river."

The bishop sat motionless, unwilling to listen to the history being thrown into his teeth, and yet helpless to stem the tide.

The rabbi turned more pages of his notebook, beginning: "In the year nine hundred five, Sergius the Third gained the papal chair by military force, which was followed by his lewd life with the prostitute Theodora, and her daughter Morioza, both of the underworld. Theodora caused one of her paramours, John the Tenth, to be made pope. Fourteen years later he was succeeded by John the Eleventh, whose life of immorality was no better than that of his predecessor. Then came the boy pope, John Twelfth, whose lewd, immoral life incited the German clergy to protest. He was tried and convicted of adultery, concubinage, and turning the Lateran palace into a bawdy house, putting out the eyes of one prelate, and sterilizing another. He was finally deposed. And, Bishop, I could go on further, but, I am giving this undeniable history in all kindness to you, which I never would have mentioned had you not hurled at me such a defiant challenge to refute your claim as to priesthood of your church in the past, of which I cannot but believe that you are somewhat familiar. But I am not yet through with history. Now, the rabbi turned more leaves in his notebook, "In the year a. d. ten hundred thirty-three, Benedict and Sylvester were contending popes. Benedict eventually won out, then sold the papal chair to one John for fifteen hundred pounds, equivalent. John sold the papal chair at auction, and Gregory Sixth bought it. Then came the schism between the popes at Rome and Constantinople, each holding equal authority. In this strife, each pope excommunicated the other. The very singular thing is that the church has had no answer except silence. Next, in the year thirteen hundred seventy-eight, Urban and Clement were contending popes. Clement was supported by Scotland, France, Spain, Italy, and Sicily, while Urban's supporters were Portugal, Germany, England, Denmark, Sweden, and Norway. This abyss that, according to ecclesiastical history, has never been bridged over.

"Now, the last schism I shall mention maintained in the year fourteen hundred thirty-one, when Surgius and Felix were contending popes. This divided Europe for fourteen years, which eventually resulted in inter-excommunications.

"I must not refrain from mentioning the awful deeds

under Opeda, in which the French Parliament acquiesced. Then the horrible slaughter of the Albigenses—
one of the blackest pages of history. Then in the year
twelve hundred thirty-nine, Dominic was appointed
inquisitor general, and his emissaries were known as the
'Militia of Jesus,' resulting in such tortures as the rack,
cutting chains, screw-clamps, and many, many kindred
tortures worse than one might expect among the grossest
barbarians. Anything to stamp out those who differed
in faith from Catholics came under this torture. In the
church's determination to stamp out Lutheranism, the
mandate was to exterminate them even by applying fire.
The French historian puts it: *'Se servir de remedes plus
violens et de servir de feu!'* Think of the fate of Joan
of Arc, falling under mandate, being burned at the
stake. Next, think of those horrid crusades waged in
the name of 'Christ and the Cross,' each one failing.
Thinking it was attributable to the impurity of the cru-
saders, the children's crusade was inaugurated, sallying
forth unarmed. The fatal result is too pathetic for
words.

"Now, Bishop Meldon, in the face of all this, can
you consistently and dispassionately conceive of such
a muddy stream producing a rivulet of ministerial purity
under the guise of divine authority?"

Father Meldon sat motionless, seeming to weigh
proper words with which to reply sagaicously. At length
he said honestly. "Rabbi, I am not altogether ignorant
of the history you have narrated. Yet, withal, I cannot
but feel that in some manner the Lord would not allow
divine authority to go from the earth, for he said that
the gates of hell should not prevail against it."

Despite the tenseness of the occasion, the two men
were big enough to meet the issue in a friendly manner.

Turning to Bishop Meldon, the rabbi said calmly:

"Now, Bishop Meldon, it is really too bad that you forced me to such a stern measure which, but for your challenge, I again repeat, had never occurred. Now, to make myself clear and understood. I am touring the world in quest of the Church of Jesus Christ as it existed in the days of the Master, of which I shall be happy to give you details at the proper time. To this end, I have listened to the prelates of Parseeism, Brahminism, Buddhism, Mohammedanism, the religions of China, together with many Christian churches. So I consider myself fortunate in having the privilege of your telling the fundamentals of Catholicism. You have already referred to the criterion of true doctrine, and it is that about which I wish you to inform me. First, may I ask that you disclose your doctrine of the Holy Trinity —the Father, the Son, and the Holy Ghost? I shall listen attentively. However, at its conclusion, I might make some comparisons should I detect differences or what I consider departures from the church in the days of the Master."

"That is very fair, Rabbi, and I feel assured you will find complete harmony as the story is told. In the first place, we believe in God, the maker of the heavens and earth, and all things that in them are. Then we teach of the Son of God in Jesus Christ, and lastly the Holy Ghost, each one a God in himself and all combining into the Holy Trinity."

"Very good," replied the rabbi. "However, please tell me of their natures, by which I mean the corporal or uncorporal nature of God the Father, then of the Son."

Following such a historical tirade that at best was disconcerting to him, the bishop now felt at last somewhat at ease in disclosing Catholic belief. "To begin with, Rabbi, we disclaim any thought of a corporal God, but we affirm that God is a spirit, rather a spiritual es-

sence, and although perhaps incomprehensible, we point
to him as being a universal essence of intelligence manifested in his everywhereness. Next, we point to the
Son, originally of universal substance, that was made
flesh for a divine purpose, lived according to the sacred
story as a mortal being, was crucified, arose from the
dead and ascended into heaven whence he came. The
Holy Ghost is also an essence of universal intelligence."

"Permit me, while the thought is opportune, to ask
you: What of Jesus Christ right now, two thousand years
after his ascension?"

The prelate eventually affirmed his belief and the
doctrine of the church. "It might not be palatable to
your fertile mind when I state that he must have been
dissolved, if you will, back into his everywhereness."

"Indeed," returned the rabbi, as he drew a volume
from his suitcase. "I know of this doctrine. Allow me
to read from the works of the Abbe L. Bataille, who
wrote in nineteen thirty-two, a course in Catholicism.
Of Jesus Christ, he poses a query, 'What has become of
Jesus Christ. Where is he right now.' He answered
'Jesus est partout comme Dieu.' Everywhere like God."

"Yes, Rabbi, the abbe was right, for that is our
belief."

"Yet Christ was the first fruits of resurrection, was
he not?"

"Yes, indeed he was, for none before him had experienced the gift."

"Or, such as the Nirvana of Buddhism, the unthinkable doctrine of the Chinese that emptiness is the in-
evitable solution of existence?" suggested the rabbi.

"Scripture and tradition, Rabbi, tell us so little in
detail of conditions after death other than that we must
pray for souls to be delivered from purgatory to be
ushered into paradise, that I confess I have never been
able to satisfy myself as to the actual condition."

The rabbi sat quietly, at length giving words to thoughts that were chasing through his mind: "That being the case, Bishop Meldon, I am wondering if it is worth while for saints to have faith in a glorious eternal life, unless they can have some tangible faith in what that eternal life really consists of? For me, and I speak candidly, is not this a fundamental cause of infidelity, if not atheism?"

"Perhaps in your way of looking at it. But to us, there is a hope of eternal life."

CHAPTER XVI

FOR fully an hour Homer Ben Arden and Bishop Meldon sat in the observation car enjoying the passing scenery, narrating experiences both in Jerusalem and America, according to their respective versions. The rabbi was intensely interested in the account of American life, while the bishop seemed equally interested in descriptions of life in the Holy Land, also of the many places in the orient the rabbi had visited, the manners and peculiarities of the different peoples. But what seemed to perplex the bishop was why the rabbi had made his world-wide pilgrimage to so much of the world at such tremendous expense.

Turning to Ben Arden, the prelate asked: "Rabbi, if it is not impertinent on my part, I ask why you are making this world tour? Surely, I take it, there must be some motive other than that of a casual traveler?"

Ben Arden, who always enjoyed telling of his mission and quest, seemed to hesitate. "Bishop, I am not touring the world merely as a traveler, not by any means. To the contrary, my wandering has a very definite motive, for I am on a very urgent and particular quest. However, with your indulgence, I wish to hold that in abeyance for the present, with the promise that when the proper time arrives, I shall relate my mission fully, and I feel sure it will be to your gratification. Will you accede to this with due forbearance?"

Although the bishop was curious, he answered: "Certainly, Rabbi, for I take it that you have some justification unknown to me, so I shall patiently await your pleasure. However, I take it that your motive has a religious aspect. Am I right?"

Ben Arden smiled: "Exactly, and with that let it suffice for now. My story, I assure you, is an interesting one, and I think it will surprise you as it has other prelates of the religions I have contacted, each time having brought me warm sympathy from strangers who have become my friends, interested and sympathetic to my quest."

"It seems to me, Rabbi, that with great zeal you are applying your search of the fundamentals of religion, or religions, as it were."

"Exactly so, Bishop Meldon. It is fundamental in my life quest, all of which will come later on. However, let us resume our conversation relative to the workings of your great church. In the first place, I wish you would tell me candidly, the conception and teaching of the atonement—just why Christ should atone and allow himself to be sacrificed at Calvary."

"To begin with, Rabbi, Jesus Christ came into the world to effect redemption, that is to deliver men from the grasp of demons that overpower mankind, to open the heavens as a celestial heritage, to this end he suffered on the cross, leaving in the hearts of men the sublime thought of redemption, the mystery of love, the splendors of heaven. He came also to save us from the majority of life's vicissitudes, wherein he became the incarnation of all that is divine. To this end God gave his only begotten Son to be the mediator between earth and heaven. Without blemishing his divinity, he took upon himself mortality. However, in it all, it was not absolutely necessary that Christ should suffer death, for the least of his acts could redeem the world. Yet he became a humble supplicant for his love for our souls, to teach us patience in our sufferings. He died for men, for he would that all men be saved."

Ben Arden, as was his wont, was taking notes for his information, and while he would have questioned the prelate relative to the atonement, he held that in reserve. He continued: "Thanks, Bishop Meldon, for your explanation. Now, next, may I ask that you explain baptism as observed in your church? Why baptism, and its efficacy? Who may baptize ordinarily, and even in an emergency? These you understand are to me procedures that I desire exceedingly to know. Surely you will have no objection to my taking careful notes as we proceed?"

"No objection at all, Rabbi, for I take it that it will be useful to you when the time comes for your induction into the Catholic church. Ah, yes, I seem to read your thoughts, 'if that time ever comes.' Such would not surprise me in the least, for the history of Catholic experience is that men of all walks of life eventually become communicants. But to answer your question: We baptize with one sole view and that is fundamentally, besides an outward sign of inward grace, to eradicate from the soul the stain of Eden. This is baptism's true efficacy, to this end we baptize infants who, like all humanity come into the world under the ban of Eden's transgression. Now as to your other query, 'Who may baptize.' Naturally, it is the duty of the priests. Yet should emergency arise communicants may baptize, and in extreme cases even in the absence of a priest, the father or mother may baptize with full efficacy."

Rabbi Ben Arden, suppressing his feelings with dignity, cautiously enscribed essential notes. Then turning to the bishop, he asked: "Now, Father Meldon, will you please enlighten me as to your holy communion in what you call transubstantiation? I have read of it but wish to get this first-hand from you."

With this thought in view, being exceedingly sacred

to the Catholics, the bishop crossed himself, then taking a book from his valise, he began: "Perhaps, Rabbi,
there can be no better answer than what the church
recently published in one of its parochial calendars under the caption, 'The Real Presence of Christ in the
Eucharist.' I quote from it: 'This doctrine of the Catholic Church is one which has been much misrepresented.
It has been held up to scorn by many opponents of
Catholicism, and therefore all non-Catholics should be
glad to have an authentic statement of it, and of the
reasons for believing in it. The Council of Trent de-
clares that the Catholic Church teaches, and always has
taught, that in the Blessed Eucharist that which was
originally bread and wine is, by the consecration,
changed to the body and blood of our Lord together—
in other words, his entire person; which change is properly called Transubstantiation. How incomprehensible, nay, how repugnant this doctrine seems to many!
Yet to us it is the most consoling, the most cheering and
in every way the most blessed portion of our creed.'
This article, Rabbi, was abridged from Cardinal Wise-
man's Lectures."

Rabbi Ben Arden sat motionless as thoughts flooded
his mind. Although he emphatically resented such
dogma, he held his peace. He, however, asked: "Father
Meldon, do Catholics in general believe this doctrine?"

"Indeed," returned the bishop. "Were it otherwise,
they could not be considered worthy communicants. Of
course, this is too deep for you to fathom at once in all
its spiritual beauty."

"Perhaps it is well that I do not possess that degree
of spirituality, Bishop Meldon. I cannot but resent the
doctrine and practice as being an utter impossibility.
However, may I now ask that you explain your doctrine
of supererogation of which I have read somewhat?"

Bishop Meldon took a book from his collection and, after turning page after page, looked into the rabbi's face. "Mr. Ben Arden, I prefer to give you the written word as to the doctrine of supererogation as believed by the Catholics. Here it is: 'That there actually exists an immense treasure of merit, composed of pious deeds and various actions which the saints have performed beyond what is necessary for their salvation, and which are therefore applicable to the benefit of others; that the guardian and dispenser of this precious treasure is the Roman pontiff, and that of consequence he is empowered to assign to such as he deems proper a portion of this inexhaustible source of merit, suitable to respective guilt, and sufficient to deliver them from the punishment due to their crimes.' While this was written by one not of our faith, still it rings quite true to our conception of it."

"That is about as I have understood it, Bishop Meldon, and I thank you for your elucidation of it. Next, I wish you to have the kindness to explain your doctrine and practice of what are known to you as indulgences, for I have read much regarding the procedure, and consequently shall be glad to have some firsthand information relative to them."

The bishop unhesitatingly responded, saying: "Rabbi, in the first place, Jesus Christ has given to the church—that is to the Pope and bishops—the absolute authority and power to pardon and forgive sins of any nature whatsoever, be they individual or collective. Such a boon to communicants is certainly worth their paying for the same by a contribution, voluntary or specified, for the maintenance of the church. This has prevailed from the early centuries. Even penance for insignificant transgressions are worth the price of pardon. And why, I ask you, should it not be? One has said, 'As we pay others, we are paid; life gives us back just what we give.' It is the great law of recompense, of which Emerson wrote: 'To receive something for nothing is receiving without merit.' Therefore the church has very advisedly, from the early centuries, established the system of paid indulgences, whereby the sins, misgivings, and transgressions may receive, under the hands of delegated authority, a remission that is bound in the very heavens. Who is there, I ask, who would not gladly pay a specified price for such a pardon, to stand before God fully forgiven, knowing that in this fee he is adding to the treasury of the church? In the past, collective indulgences have been issued under papal authority, and surely has moved the very heavens. Even though this might seem unreasonable to you, Rabbi, yet were you to delve with sufficient depth into the procedure, you would, I am sure, be fully in accord with the sacred unction."

Taking a volume from his suitcase, the rabbi asked: "Do you read French, Bishop?" The bishop admitted that he was not familiar with the language, and the rabbi returned: "Then I shall interpret something from the French *Brief History of Switzerland*. It tells of one Baron John de Stein, a military chieftain among the Helvetians. The hawker of Catholic indulgences coveted a dappled-gray horse John possessed, and for acquisition of the animal he offered John absolution for his sins for life. When John refused, the offer covered his family. Later his officers, and finally all his soldiers were absolved from any sin they might have committed or would commit through life. And here is another: A French cobbler secretly buried his wife, for which he was brought before the Catholic bishop for condemnation or excommunication for not having had her given supreme unction. The unabashed cobbler then and there presented a certificate, for which he had paid considerable, guaranteeing that he and his wife had been absolved for the full duration of their lives and in eternity. I am wondering, Bishop, if there could be a limit to indulgences, for most certainly the procedure has been shamefully abused."

Bishop Meldon sat motionless for a spell, when eventually he said: "No doubt the procedure might have been overdone through people's being overzealous. This, at times, is a fault of human nature, Rabbi. However, none can overstep divine appointment and remain free from ministerial censure."

"But, my dear bishop, please remember that perhaps John Tetzel was the one in your church who unscrupulously sold indulgences at the sacrifice of all honor, and the pathetic thing is that in all his scheming to raise money for the church, he received papal sanction. This is undeniable history, Bishop Meldon, that none, even the pope can deny. However, pardon me, as I have other desires for information."

"And they are?" asked the bishop.

"I wish you to inform me as to Mary, the mother of Jesus, and why you saint her as a holy one, even worshiping her and praying to her in your rituals."

"Yes, yes, indeed, Rabbi. Gabriel announced Mary as being choice above all women, she being vouchsafed the motherhood of our Lord Jesus Christ. She holds the lofty position in heaven as being the intercessor between mortals and God. She has power to save struggling souls at death from entering into purgatory, the Benign Assumption, if you will, whereby Mary became the mighty benefactor of the race. That virgin who after the birth of Jesus remained ever after a blessed virgin incarnate, until God, in his great mercy, as an act of divine will, brought about her resurrection, when she is, as I have said, now the intercessor, our advocate with the Father for us miserable sinners. Why, Rabbi, should we not adore her with devoted worship?"

Homer Ben Arden had been taking careful notes. At length he replied, "Thanks, Bishop, for this information. Yes, yes, I have seen, in many of your cathedrals, very artistic paintings of the ascension of Mary, to which you have referred." Ben Arden looked out at the passing scenery, his elbow on the window sill and his hand supporting his chin. Evidently he was thinking more than viewing the passing vistas. Eventually, he asked: "So much for that, Bishop. Next, will you please inform me as to the organization of your church? This, you know, must be a criterion of measurement that must characterize the true Church of God."

Bishop Meldon was anxious to disclose the varied authority that officers this great church numerically. "In the first place, Rabbi, we have the pope — the vice-regent of God, who represents Jesus Christ on earth to the fullest degree. He it is who has all power in his hands to forgive sins, to bless or to curse. As such, he is the one divinely approved of God on earth, invested with the power of God and godliness. Then we have the College of Cardinals, in whose hands reposes the authority of electing and ordaining a new pope to succeed the former one. Then come the bishops, who hold authority over the various dioceses throughout the world, and under them come the priests. Both bishops and priests, under ordination by or under direction of the pope, have been given authority to pardon and remit sins, or conversely to refuse to remit them, as they see fit. Of course, we have monks, and what the world crudely calls nuns, in charge of monasteries and convents, respectively. This, Rabbi, briefly outlines our organization as to official personnel."

"My next request, Bishop Meldon, is that you in-

form me as to why you believe in celibacy for the clergy.
Just why it is that such should remain unmarried
through life? I wish to know why this very unnatural
thing to human life maintains?"

"First, Rabbi, those ordained represent Jesus Christ
on earth, and as he never married, purposely, of course,
that he could devote all his time and attention to the
salvation of men. Even so, must those who represent
him on earth remain unmarried that their minds,
thoughts, and work in the ministry be not hampered
with marital affairs. This might seem repugnant to
you as it does to many, yet it is God's order and procedure in his church. You know, marriage is not the
superlative act of human life, rather, it is the great
sanctity of men devoting their entire lives to saving the
souls of men, functioning under authority that is not of
earth. Why, I ask, should such become so mundane as
to divide their efforts spiritual with mortal vicissitudes?
I feel sure you see the beauty of what we are pleased to
name celibacy. It is God-given, hence, who dare challenge the divine injunction?" The bishop could plainly
detect by the rabbi's countenance that he seemed to resent the doctrine, yet he felt that he had sufficiently
covered the question.

Determined to understand the actual workings of
Catholicism, the rabbi pressed another query: "Next,
Bishop, will you inform me as to the inner workings of
the great masses of your people? I would know of the
sincerity of their worship. You know, I have often witnessed people in your great cathedrals, coming and going, kneeling on low chairs that face the Holy Shrine,
offering some silent prayer, then passing to a bowl of
water, having been consecrated, dipping a finger in the
water, crossing themselves, then leaving. And I have
wondered if this is not more form than deep-rooted

faith and devotion, for I have seen them leave as un-
concerned as though they had done some ordinary act.
It appears to me that it is part of the great mechaniza-
tion of your church." Ben Arden was intensely serious
in this request, for he had formed quite an adverse opinion as to the sincerity of the worship.

Bishop Meldon thought a moment before he replied,
wondering how best to present the matter, for he was
aware that after all was said and done, it was only too
often more formal than of deep-rooted devotion. "Rabbi,
we begin with our children when very young, training
the tiny, tender twigs until Catholicism comes second
nature to them. You know we have the adage: 'Give
us a child to train in infancy, and when he is grown
he will always remain a Catholic.' Yes, it becomes
second nature, for we teach them prayerful devotion as
soon as they can lisp a prayer. Then after the communion, they proudly become devoted participants in
reciting formal prayers. Formal prayers, I stress, for
who, like the originator of these under divine inspiration, can word the prayer that should be said on specific
occasions, the sum of which covers every divine thought
that can occupy the human heart. Perhaps you understand that each bead of the rosary is the insignia of a
certain prayer, and it is the sum of all these prayers that
inspire our people to lives of spirituality. Now, when
our communicants enter our sanctuaries, they know
their inmost desires, and at once inspiration brings to
their hearts the prayer that should be fervently said.
When this is done, they bow to the Holy Shrine, then
pass to the bowl of holy water and with wet fingers
cross themselves, with the thought in the crossmarks,
the Father, the Son, and the Holy Ghost. Rabbi, in
all sincerity, this is true devotion."

A little time elapsed while each one seemed to appreciate the quietude. At length, the rabbi, continuing the thought with which the bishop closed, said sincerely: "You know, Bishop, you speak of true devotion, yet you will agree that that might or might not be indicative of the Church of God. I know of no deeper devotion than I have witnessed in some of the oriental religions. Really, in some ways they can shame Christians in the depth of their sincerity in prayer. I speak especially of prayer among the Mohammedans. Truly, some of their devotion is touching so much as to promote reverence to those who witness it."

Bishop Meldon at length said, "Rabbi, I wish I had enjoyed the privilege of seeing the world as you seem to have done, and witnessed the religious customs of the peoples you have been privileged to encounter. It must be a rare opportunity."

The rabbi replied promptly: "Very true, Bishop. Yet, on the other hand, to meet discouragement on every hand as to satisfying my quest, had not been so pleasurable as you might think. For, despite it all, I left each time with disappointment. On the other hand, the experience was valuable beyond words I have to express."

Bishop Meldon would sincerely know more of the rabbi's quest, but essayed to appease his curiosity until that "proper time" the rabbi had spoken of.

The colored porter was already pulling down the beds, seeing which, Homer Ben Arden returned his books to his suitcase, suggesting: "Bishop, suppose we close our discussion for today. Let us go to the observation car while the beds are made up."

CHAPTER XVII

THE eastbound overland train had arrived at Omaha, and during the forty-minute wait, Rabbi Ben Arden and Bishop Meldon availed themselves of a brisk walk in the near vicinity of the depot. It was a real relaxation after the long trip from the coast thus far on their eastward journey. The bishop being somewhat familiar with the city, pointed out places of interest, together with some interesting facts of history. Soon, however, they were again in their Pullman, and the train was rolling along in its course.

Rabbi Ben Arden was so eager to finish his review of Catholicism, that he felt no opportunity should be missed, so he asked kindly: "Bishop, I need very much more information relative to your great church, and I hope you will not think me overinquisitive or overbearing in asking much further information."

Bishop Meldon took this more as a compliment than a task, as he answered, "To the contrary, Rabbi, the explanation of the beauties and graces of the Church of God come first in my life, hence I am free and happy to concede to your request. However, as usual, I shall expect that you indicate largely your desires in parts of doctrine and procedure of which you might be unfamiliar."

"That is exceedingly kind of you, Bishop. So, to begin, I wish to ask some things that came into my mind this morning long before daybreak. They are, your conception of what is known to you as paradise, purgatory, and hell."

Bishop Meldon smiled as he turned to the rabbi. "Quite a large order that, Rabbi, yet, nonetheless, a very important thread of thought. I could spend many hours in elucidation of these great subjects, but perhaps a brief review will suffice. In the first place—as to paradise. We point to it as the superlative beatific beatitude, where the perfect, redeemed soul soars on majestically beyond the limits, if you will, of the vast infinitude, even beyond the brilliancy of the stars. Such are now beyond all thought or necessity of repentance or expiation, for they have been exalted above all wrong, hence are heirs of perfection in God. There will be no more tears or grief, for all that has been overcome as they have vanquished the many vicissitudes of mortality, hence the soul returns to that God who gave it, and where they learn to know and appreciate God in his omnipresent and omnipotent essence through the beatific vision that is theirs. Their illuminated intelligence enables them to see God as he is. We explain it as the light of intelligence exceeding the brilliancy of the sun, comparable to the glory of Jesus Christ. Such are empowered to fly through space with the speed of thought, even like Christ, able to pass through opaque objects with no resistance. Spiritual beings as they are, all nourishment such as food is nonessential. Such is the boon of the elect. It is their divine beatitude. To gain this condition one must overcome all sin and transgression to obtain celestial grace. One small sin would disqualify a person, for he would be an enemy to God. Moreover, placed as they are beyond temptation, they are in a position where no further forgiveness is necessary. Know this, that the least negative life condition would disqualify the aspirant from this celestial beatitude."

The rabbi looked off into space, eventually saying: "Bishop, I take it that you have very briefly and beautifully covered your church's conception. Such a glory is, of course, beyond my conception."

"Quite naturally, Rabbi, for as a stranger to Catholicism, one could not expect you to absorb the aesthetic beauty of this celestial benediction with a single bound. However, with my brief explanation, let us pass on to what is known to us as purgatory, which is a place of purification where the souls unworthy for paradise must overcome the vicissitudes of life through being purged and purified before they can enter that haven of bliss in paradise. We teach as a basis of faith in purgatory that one must believe in its actuality. Then that within that realm they are powerless to do much for themselves, but on the other hand, the prayers of the righteous in mortality, also those of the righteous departed avail much. The superlative, of course, is the majestic intervention on the part of the Virgin Mary, who, in her unbounded love for the wayward soul, is a constant supplicant in behalf of these unfortunates. In purgatory, there are two kinds of punishments. First, the deprivation of the beatific vision they might have enjoyed had they merited it. Second, the tauntings of conscience that is ever burning as a seemingly inextinguishable fire. These sufferings, of course, are much less than those endured by the people who are consigned to hell. The duration of one in purgatory is contingent upon the guilt, each soul remaining therein until the exacting demands of stern justice be satisfied.

"And now, Rabbi, as to hell. It is the eternal from which there is no relief. Separated from God forever, theirs being the suffering of the damned with demons, they, too, are enemies of God and must suffer his wrath. We teach, not however with certainty, that hell is in the womb of the earth. Of the extent of this condition of souls in hell, we know little, yet it is our candid belief that the torture of the soul's mentality could not be conceived to compare to it. To experience it is beyond mortal conception."

The rabbi, who had been taking careful notes of the disclosure, seemed deeply appreciative of the bishop's explanations. He said, sincerely: "Bishop, I greatly appreciate your explanation of these tenets of your faith, for while I had a hazy conception of this part of Catholic doctrine, I now have much more enlightenment as to the church's belief in this regard."

"It is too bad, Rabbi, that this vast condition of souls beyond the grave could not have been given in more detail. However, you have a cross-section, if you will, of what we believe and teach in this regard."

"For which I thank you, Bishop Meldon. Now, may I ask that you give me your reaction on some knotty problems that naturally arise. I am going to refer to conditions before Catholicism existed. Some of them are: What is to be the fate of the unbelieving world now living? Of those master minds who died many centuries before Jesus of Nazareth was born—such great souls as Aeschylus, Homer, Socrates, Plato, and many, many other great people who lived great and died noble. In a word, what, in your teachings, is the fate of a hundred generations of people? To what extent are these worthy and unworthy souls of men from Adam down to Christ, also those who have lived, died, and had their being since he established his gospel, covered in salvation powers according to the Catholic church?"

Bishop Meldon hesitated before he ventured a reply. At length, he said: "Rabbi, you are forcing me into pretty deep water. I hardly know how to answer you and keep within the limit of Catholic teachings."

"But, surely, Bishop Meldon, there must be an answer. These noble people must not be forgotten. If so,

God would cease to be just, and would be a respecter of persons."

Bishop Meldon hesitated, finally admitting regretfully: "Rabbi, I confess that I do not know, nor do we have teachings that I know of that cover the problem. We are taught to 'seek no crop where 'twas not planted, nor the day where reigns the night.' The Catholic church teaches that there is no salvation except it be in the Catholic church, and under the authority of Christ's gift of priesthood to us. We teach that such as you mention do not even have the privilege of paradise. Hence, they must be in hell, subject to perhaps some divine intervention in their behalf. I am free to admit as the master minds that whom you have mentioned. All I can say is that they are in the hands of their Creator, but the Catholic Church is powerless in their behalf, nor does she have a doctrine to cover it."

The rabbi might have been startled at the disclosure, yet his mind was rapidly being prepared for almost anything. Finally, the rabbi ventured another thought: "Then, Bishop, in face of what you have explained, rather have not explained, please allow me to quote the words of Jesus." The rabbi took from his valise the New Testament and read: "'Marvel not at this; for the hour is coming, in which all that are in their graves shall hear his voice, and come forth; they that have done good in the resurrection of life; and they that have done evil to the resurrection of damnation.' Again I read: 'For Christ also hath once suffered for sins, the just for the unjust, that he might bring us to God, being put to death in the flesh, but quickened by the spirit: By which also he went and preached to the spirits in prison; which sometime were disobedient in the days of Noah, while the ark was preparing, wherein, eight souls were saved by water.' This means, Bishop, that Christ announced that the dead were about to hear his words and live, and come forward in a resurrection. The passage from St. Peter tells of him, between death and resurrection, actually preaching the gospel to spirits, even those who had lived in the days of Noah. And in connection with this, let me again read from Peter, telling why Christ went into the spirit world, 'For this cause was the gospel preached to them that are dead, that they might be judged according to men in the flesh, but live according to God in the spirit.' The foregoing, Bishop Meldon, implies that there is a salvation for those who died without gospel privileges, whether the problem is covered in Catholicism or not."

Bishop Meldon did not expect this reaction on the part of the rabbi, who had been such an attentive listener. But he said, calmly: "Rabbi, naturally, there must be some medium of grace for these souls, but it has not come to my understanding. Have you, in your researches, found a solution?"

"Not in my experience, Bishop, but in my Biblical research. I read of the existence of baptism, that you admit is positively essential to salvation, having been administered in the days of the apostles. I mean by this that by proxy, those living, and worthy, were baptized for those who were dead. Listen to the Apostle Paul to the Corinthian saints. He was stressing the resurrection of Christ, and as one of his arguments, he asked: 'Else what shall they do which are baptized for the dead, if the dead rise not at all? Why, then are they baptized for the dead?'"

"Be that as it may, Rabbi, it might have maintained in the days of the apostles, but I confess it has no place in Catholicism."

Rabbi Ben Arden drew a book from his suitcase. "Perhaps I can give you a reason for your having excluded it from your creed. I shall read from your Doctor Milner's Catholic Belief, for it is an honest and humble confession: 'She (meaning the church) does not dictate an exposition of the whole Bible, because she has lost tradition concerning a very great portion of it. For instance, concerning baptism of the dead of which Paul speaks, and the prophecy of Enoch, of which Jude speaks.' The thought is this, Bishop Meldon, will your church be satisfied and stand blameless in allowing the dead of ninety generations to perish, just because you have not tradition sufficient to explain and clarify the doctrine? While it is plain in sacred writ, still profane history speaks of its prevalence with the apostles."

Bishop Meldon was uneasy, and somewhat angry, as he looked out at the passing scenery, perhaps seeing little. His face registered his mingled feelings.

Rabbi Ben Arden smiled, not the smile of achievement, for he felt deep sympathy for the bishop's situation. Slapping the bishop on the shoulder, he said with a laugh: "Come, don't take it all so seriously. Let's get away from our strenuous religious discussion, and go back into the observation car."

CHAPTER XVIII

IT was late in the afternoon, and after having talked for an hour or two of things in general, both the rabbi and the bishop having enjoyed pleasant cigars in the observation car, they returned to their Pullman to resume their conversation. Especially was Ben Arden eager to close his investigation. He began: "Now, Bishop, so far as I am concerned, the investigation of Catholicism is nearing its close. However, there remains one very important matter I wish you to clarify. It is the very thing that, perhaps more than anything else, has driven men to atheism, Bible students, in particular. They have charged God as having failed to bring about his promises, hence their estimation of Christianity or the belief in God and his works, has been abandoned."

"And that is?" asked the bishop, with interest, wondering what the rabbi was driving at.

"Simply this, Bishop: The children of Abraham— they who were to become so numerous as to be compared to number to the stars of heaven or the sands of the seashore, had become so absorbed in idolatry that a purging was necessary that, as Paul puts it, they might be schooled to faith. They were scattered over all the world, in every nation, in all parts of the earth, while many, seven hundred years before Christ, were taken captive in Assyria, and this body became lost to history, but not to God. Now, my question is, Bishop Meldon: God promised to restore these lost tribes named after the sons of Jacob, to their own lands, to bring them from all parts of the earth in full restoration. Because God has not done as I said, many great thinkers have been driven into atheism on the pretext or assumption that God had failed in his promises. Now, I wish you to disclose to what extent the Catholic church looks forward to this great culminating event in world history when the dispersed and lost of Israel shall be returned. By this, I do not refer to the Jews alone, for they were but one of the twelve tribes, but to Israel in its fullest sense. What are the teachings of your church in this regard, Bishop?"

Bishop Meldon had not expected a problem so strange to be presented. At length, he began: "Rabbi, why go into ancient history that had its culmination in the gospel of Jesus Christ?"

The rabbi registered disappointment. "Are you evasive of this mighty event, Bishop? It is an event to discuss or God would certainly fail in his purposes as has been charged by atheists. It is a matter that cannot be lightly passed by. Do not claim it was finished in the advent of Christ's majestic gospel, for it was part of his culminating work before he returns to earth to rule and reign."

Again, the bishop was hesitant, knowing not what or how to answer the rabbi. At length, he said: "Rabbi, in all my studies of Catholicism, and I have grown in knowledge of Catholicism until I have been ordained a bishop in this great church, I confess that it has never come so vividly to my attention. In fact, the church gives little thought or credence to such future events as being other than perhaps misplaced prophecy that may never materialize. And why should it, when what is most essential is that, under divine authority, the souls of men are freed from sin and saved in the kingdom of Christ?"

The rabbi closed his book and returned it to his

suitcase, and, taking out another, began: "Now, dear bishop, this that you claim of little import, or perhaps non-essential to the great scheme of events as prescribed by God in his *modus operandi,* are to me of vast importance. So, with your indulgence, I shall refer to some of the things that are weighty in God's kingdom. Listen to some of this from the mouth of inspired prophets who spoke denouncing the strayed posterity of Abraham. And, by the way, had you and I endured nearly four hundred years of Egyptian idolatry, becoming steeped in that condition, we, too, might eventually, or our children, or great-great grandchildren, have become just as idolatrous as was Israel. The mercy of God was too far-reaching to allow the race to perish— the race to whom the promises were made. In his mercy, he chastised them, purged them by scattering them world-wide. Listen to the words of the prophets: 'They were to be scattered from one end of the earth to another'—this from Moses, as recorded in Deuteronomy; again, 'The Lord would scatter them among the heathen' —this is recorded in Leviticus; 'Sift the whole house of Israel like corn is sifted'—this is from Amos; 'Cast them out of my sight, even the whole house of Ephriam'— this from Jeremiah; 'Disperse them among the heathen and among the countries'—this from Ezekiel, with numerous other chronicled events to befall the idolatrous Israelites. Please remember, I am giving these thoughts paraphrased for brevity. Should you wish, I shall read the full context. But I take it that you are conversant with the scripture in this regard.

"Next, Bishop, the word of God as to the gathering of these hosts of Israel from all over the earth where they had been dispersed. Perhaps the Prophet Jeremiah had more to say than other holy men. Among other things, he wrote. Again I paraphrase: 'The Lord promised to restore the house of Jacob, and the house of Israel' and, again, 'Will bring every man into his own land.' Jeremiah again: 'I will bring the captivity of my people Israel and Judah, saith the Lord; and I will cause them to return to the land that I gave to their fathers.' Says Isaiah: 'The Lord will lift up an ensign to the nations from afar, and will hiss unto them from the end of the earth; and behold they shall come swiftly.' Again, Isaiah: 'The ransomed of the Lord shall return and come to Zion.' And now the prophet Ezekiel: 'I will even gather you from the people, and assemble you out of the countries where ye have been scattered.' Now, listen again to Jeremiah, speaking of the mighty event that would eclipse the coming of the children out of Egypt: 'Therefore, behold, the days come, saith the Lord, that it shall no more be said, the Lord liveth that brought the children of Israel out of Egypt; But the Lord liveth that brought the children of Israel from the land of the north, and from the lands whither I have driven them, and I will bring them again into their own land that I gave unto their fathers. Behold, I will send many fishers, saith the Lord, and they shall fish them; and after I will send many hunters, and they shall hunt them from every mountain, and from every hill, and out of the holes of the rocks.'

"Now, Bishop, let me read from Isaiah: 'And it shall come to pass in the last days, that the mountain of the Lord's house shall be established in the top of the mountains, and shall be exalted above the hills; and all nations shall flow into it. And many people shall go and say, Come ye, and let us go up to the mountain of the Lord, to the house of the God of Jacob; and he will teach us of his ways, and we will walk in his paths: for out of Zion shall go forth the law, and the word of God from Jerusalem.'

"So, Bishop Meldon, any Christian religion that

eliminates this most outstanding catalogue of events to come from its creed and procedure, may understand why it is that ecclesiastical students refuse to affiliate with such organizations.

"Now," continued the rabbi, "I have come, I think, to the full investigation of Catholicism unless you have other things you wish to present for our consideration."

The bishop seemed glad that the medicine meted out to him was at an end. However, he asked: "Friend Rabbi, I wish you would give me fully and freely your candid reaction as to just what you think of Catholicism. And in this, I ask that you give me your unbiased and honest opinion. Following this, I shall ask that you give me your promised story as to your world-wide mission. Are you agreed?"

The rabbi hesitated, for he feared lest his review of his findings might wound the feelings of the bishop. He asked: "But, my dear bishop, will you promise me that in it all you will not feel hard against me if I rigidly come to points in your doctrine that I claim to be in direct opposition to the gospel of Jesus Christ, for I see very many points that are diametrically out of line?"

The bishop glanced at his watch. "I take it that your review is going to be lengthy; therefore, I suggest that we go to the diner, after which I shall be an ardent listener, profiting, I am sure, by your findings, for I am an earnest searcher of truth, and the lessons I have learned during our discussions are greatly elevating."

CHAPTER XIX

ONE might think that Bishop Meldon would hesitate in having the rabbi make a review of his findings in Catholicism, being assured that the review would not, and could not be other than somewhat severe. In the investigation, the bishop had met many defeats to the extent that he was very much less sure of himself than before. Hence, he rather courted than resented what might come. Turning to the rabbi, he said, candidly and dispassionately: "Now, Rabbi, I shall hold myself an ardent listener to your review even though it might be severe. I can expect nothing less, following your kind, yet very inquisitive investigation. I have an open mind, Rabbi, and desire to learn."

Homer Ben Arden was much touched by the humility of his friend, and wondered if he should make his review as contemplated. On the other hand, knowing the sincerity of the bishop, and believing in his candor, he felt free to make a kind, yet critical review.

"Bishop," began the rabbi, "I hesitate, lest I might say something to hurt your feelings, for I am an ardent believer in freedom and liberty, allowing all men to think, do, and worship with their full free agency in the true spirit of that democracy upon which the Church of Christ is founded. One of the greatest blessings to men is the right to differ, and it is meritorious when men can differ rigidly and still remain friends. So, with this in mind, I am willing to divulge my findings in your church as I have ofttimes done in reviewing the great religions of the orient."

From his suitcase, the rabbi selected a particular notebook, which he opened, then closed as he began: "Bishop, as a premise, let us consider the Lord's calling of his apostles when he said, 'You have not called, but I have called you and ordained you.' Giving his apostles instructions, he said to them, 'Heal the sick, cleanse the lepers, raise the dead; freely you have received, freely give,' and you know, as recorded in the fifth chapter of the Acts of the Apostles, how the very heavens were moved under their priesthood, very similar to the works of the Master. Think of Peter and John as they were entering the church at the Gate Beautiful. 'Silver and gold have I none,' said Peter, 'but such as I have give I unto you, in the name of Jesus of Nazareth, arise and walk.' You know the story, Bishop.

"Now, when the apostles passed, their priesthood passed with them, and man-made cults followed in the wake, those marvelous fruits of the gospel at once ceasing. The arrogant usurpation of priesthood, with its cold, clammy pretense, was a poor excuse for the gospel of our Lord with its marvelous workings.

"Next, Bishop, I come to the faulty claims of priesthood your church claims to hold, from Saint Peter down through a long purported succession of popes, and the shameful lives of those supposed to be God's vicegerents on earth. You must know that such pretense is as untasteful and unreal as that which I found in Judaism, that caused me to depart therefrom."

The rabbi turned to a page in his notebook. "Now, as to your doctrine of Deity. The assumption that God is an all-pervading essence, formless, incorporal, invisible, yet able to think, act, and guide the affairs of his universe, is unthinkable. Next, we come to Jesus Christ and his rising a resurrected personage of flesh and bone, being handled by his apostles, eating with them, living with them during forty days, then finally ascending into heaven, with the angel's assurance, as the awe-stricken apostles had witnessed his ascension, that he would in a like manner descend to earth. Then, in face of this, your church teaches that Christ has been dissolved into an all-pervading essence. He had been the first fruits of resurrection. He was the very prototype of it; then, as you teach, to become dissolved into everywhereness in space. After his passing, the graves were opened and many who slept arose, living, tangible beings, and appeared unto many. Mothers received their dead raised to life again; others, deferring the boon, that they might merit better resurrections. The thought is, Bishop, that if Jesus was dissolved as the true type of resurrection, then they who were resurrected must meet the same dissolution. This being the implied axiom, what more has your church to offer the soul struggling for salvation, than that offered by Buddhism, or other oriental religions, especially the Taoists of China who claim that emptiness is the only reality of existence?

"Next, Bishop Meldon, I come to the atonement of our Lord, and why it was. First, Adam fell, not through disobedience, as your church affirms. But he transgressed the laws of his immortality to become mortal in order to obey God's first commandment to him to multiply and replenish the earth and subdue it. Down through the ages holy men believed, hoped, and prayed for the time when the Shiloh—the Messiah—would come to be a ransom for that transgression. The great expiation was made in which the demands of stern justice was fully paid in that atonement, as voiced by Paul in the following: 'But now is Christ risen from the dead, and became the first fruits of them that slept, For since by man came death, by man also came the resurrection of the dead. For as in Adam all die, even so in Christ shall all be made alive.' Bishop Meldon, when your church baptizes a child with the sole view, as you teach, to remove from it the stain of Eden, in that very act the majestic atonement of our Lord is denied. Baptism, Bishop Meldon, was never instituted for that reason, but for altogether another purpose. Listen to what Peter said to those who had assisted in the crucifixion following Peter's stern accusation, when they asked what they should do: 'Repent and be baptized every one of you, for the remission of sins, and ye shall receive the Holy Ghost. For the promise is unto you, and to your children, and to all that are afar off, even as many as the Lord your God shall call.' How is it, Bishop, that your church would so radically depart from the factual in this awful misconception of the Lord's atonement and the necessity and salutary effect of baptism? Moreover, by what authority did your church depart from the mode of baptism Christ instituted, that of immersion? By what authority, I ask, was it done? Not by scripture, nor was it by tradition. But it was, of course, by the arrogance of an assumed priesthood claiming power to change the very fundamentals established by the Lord himself.

"Next, I come to your worship of the Virgin Mary, and your purported doctrine of her having always remained a virgin, that after Christ's resurrection, came her glorious resurrection, which, of course, is a gross error, for which you have not the slightest authority. According to the sacred writ, Mary was the mother of a large family of children after Jesus was born of her. Listen to this scripture by writers of the gospels: This is from Matthew, 'Is not this the carpenter's son? Is not his mother called Mary? And his brethren James, Joses, Simon, and Judas? And his sisters, are not they all with us, whence hath this man all these things?" This was the occasion when the Jews marvelled at Christ's miracles. Here we have four brothers and at least two sisters, six in all besides our Lord, Mary's first-born.

"Now, Mark writing of the same event, says: 'Is not this the carpenter, the son of Mary, the brother of James, and Joses, and of Judas, and Simon? and are not his sisters with us? And they were offended at him.'

"Next, when Paul returned from Damascus to Jerusalem, he wrote: 'Then after three days I went to Jerusalem to see Peter, and abode with him for fifteen days. But other of the apostles saw I not, save James, the brother of our Lord.' This is from Galatians.

"John says: 'For neither did his brethren believe in him.'

"Eusebius, the ecclesiastical historian, writing of James, says that he was called the Just because he came from the blessed womb of Mary. Then he tells of his righteous life and martyrdom.

"Do you not really think, Bishop Meldon, that Catholic claims of Mary, after the birth of Jesus, being gloriously resurrected, and in her saintly exaltation, intercessor for the unfortunates in purgatory, falls to pieces in face of that which is a factual narration by the Lord's apostles?"

Bishop Meldon said: "Rabbi Ben Arden, what I have to say, I prefer to say after you have finished your analysis. I prefer, really, not to interrupt you."

Ben Arden took another notebook from his suitcase, hastily turning some leaves. "My next point, Bishop Meldon, is a review of your doctrine of transubstantiation, that corruption of the simple, sacred administration of the holy sacrament by Christ, when he said, 'This do in remembrance of me.' The underlying thought and fact of it were symbolic of that great atonement. True, he said, 'This is my body, and this is my blood,' which must still be taken symbolically, as evidenced in the composite of the synoptic gospels.

"Now, Bishop, the un-Christian doctrines of celibacy, supererogation, perversion of baptism by immersion, indulgences for money, and numerous radical and arrogant departures from the Church of Jesus Christ, have but one answer, and that was voiced by the Prophet Isaiah who, speaking of the far future, said, and that truly: 'The earth also is defiled under the inhabitants thereof; because they have transgressed the laws, changed the ordinances and broken the everlasting covenant.' I read this from Isaiah. That he was writing of the future is axiomatic, for until Christ came, there had never been an everlasting covenant to be broken. How very true Catholicism falls under this defilement.

"Your having lost God—the God of Abraham, Isaac, Jacob, and the apostles, that he is a corporal being in whose image man was made, even having been seen by Moses, Jacob, and many others who bore solemn testimonies that they had seen and talked to him face to face, your worship of an all-pervading immanence in its everywhereness, could be nothing more than comparable to the sun's rays semophored to the earth, or the fragrance of a flower that pervades the room. Even God in his everywhereness can be nothing more or less that that divine radiation emanating from God to pervade all space. So you see how Catholicism has lost God.

"My last point will be Catholic indifference to that majestic gathering of the tribes of Israel from every part of the earth, even the restoration of the Lost Tribes. The fact that your church, as I have said, having made many, many infidels on the ground that God had failed. This, I state advisedly, is a terrible reflection upon the Catholic church.

"While this review could be extended further with equal evidences factual, I feel that this must conclude it, so far as I am concerned at this time. So, Bishop, you understand that I could not under any condition accept Catholicism as being the successor of the church established by Jesus Christ, and perpetuated by the apostles after his passing, until the church with all its gifts, miracles, blessings under the Holy Priesthood was supplemented by man-made creeds, since which time the very connection between heaven and earth has been severed. No more revelation from heaven, no more healing the sick, the lame, the blind, raising the dead— all of which would be impossible in a Christianity that had been thus paganized."

Homer Ben Arden looked at his watch, startled to find it was time to retire. He suggested: "Bishop, I suggest we retire. Then tomorrow morning, with your indulgence, I shall narrate, as I have frequently promised, just why I am making this world quest."

Bishop Meldon seemed gloomy and disturbed by the rabbi's critical review of the Catholic Church. Finally, as he arose, he said: "Rabbi Ben Arden, please do not think I have resented your review. To the contrary. Yes, let us retire, for I shall look forward with greater anticipation than you can, perhaps, imagine, to our continuance of this conversation."

CHAPTER XX

HOMER BEN ARDEN enjoyed a peaceful sleep. Not so with Bishop Meldon, who had lain awake for hours thinking of his experience with the rabbi, who, with truth as his shield, had startled the bishop into an evaluation of the church in which he had been, from the days of his youth, a communicant, being advanced step by step in priesthood until eventually he had been ordained a bishop.

Following breakfast the next morning, the two men had taken comfortable seats in their Pullman, the rabbi eager to tell his promised story, while the bishop was more eager than ever to listen.

In the spirit of a modest suppliant, the bishop asked: "Now, Rabbi, in a few hours we will be in Chicago, where we are to part, and I feel that all too short period should be given to you for your dispassionate story as promised by you, and honestly anticipated by me. So, now I shall listen to you carefully."

Rabbi Ben Arden was quick to observe the seeming change that had come over the bishop, once so bombastic and arrogant, but now of humble sincerity. "Well, Bishop, really I am sorry that our time together is so short, and as promised, it shall be my joy to disclose what and who I am, and the full and complete object of my world-wide search for what I have been pleased to advisedly name the Priceless Pearl."

"Which, of course, you will define later on."

Ben Arden smiled. "Oh, certainly, for my story without that name, would lose much." Simply, with quiet dignity, the rabbi again told his story, relating the experiences not only of his youth, but also of his travels and his long residence in various countries while he had studied carefully the many oriental religions.

"Again, Bishop Meldon, as in former religions of the orient, I found not the slightest trace of the Priceless Pearl. I will not say I was much disappointed, however, for I was by this time quite accustomed to failure.

"Following these experiences in the orient, I spent much time in Australia, then the winter at Honolulu, at which place I rented a bungalow that overlooked the ocean. It was here that I had the privilege of investigating Protestant churches in which I thought I might perhaps discover something encouraging. However, to my dismay, I found little more than I had found in the orient which would evidence a working priesthood power existing between heaven and earth. In fact, the thought of priesthood potentially between God and man as in the days of the Master, was ridiculed, as was also the very thought of revelation from God to man, so essential to the existence of Christ's church on earth. So, Bishop Meldon, once more I was disappointed. Yet, I was undaunted, for somehow there seemed to be an innate something within me that impelled me on and on in my research, for I felt and still feel sure I shall yet find it.

"Now, Bishop Meldon, I am nearing the close of my story, other than that I spent some time on the Western American coast, then began my journey toward Indianapolis, and en route, near Ogden, Utah, we met, following which came our very warm friendship, and our valuable investigation of the Catholic church and Catholicism."

Bishop Meldon had listened attentively to the rabbi's

story, and while he had intended to take careful notes, he was so absorbed in the rabbi's interesting narrative, that he wrote but a few lines. He had been deeply impressed throughout the disclosure. However, he dared to state, after expressing his great appreciation of the promised story: "Rabbi Ben Arden, I hardly know what to say at this time, for I know that you are again a disappointed man in your investigation of Catholicism, largely because I have been unable to answer your queries. But I shall search until I can find the answers, or, not finding them . . ."

Rabbi Ben Arden was touched. Putting his hand on the bishop's shoulders, Ben Arden said, sympathetically: "Dear Bishop, somehow, I feel censured deeply for disturbing your faith."

"Not at all, Rabbi; for I would not have missed this intellectual experience for any money, for now, I have absorbed deeply, the majestic mission you have given yourself, and your quest for the Priceless Pearl, which shall also become my quest. One thing I must ask you in all sincerity, Rabbi Ben Arden, and that is this: If or when you have found among any people the existence of that divine authority as it existed in the days of Christ and the apostles, will you promise that you will so advise me?"

"That, Bishop, has been asked me by several of the sages of oriental religions, and each time I have answered, as I now promise you, that you will not be forgotten."

"I am sure, Rabbi, I may depend on your promise."

"Indeed, you may, Bishop Meldon. And it will be, if it has not already occurred, when will come an opening of the heavens to men and the priesthood be restored by divinely appointed, perhaps by resurrected beings. Let me leave with you, Bishop, two very significant passages from the New Testament, first, when Peter was speaking to the crucifying Jews, as recorded in the third chapter of Acts; let me read it: 'Repent ye, therefore, and be converted, that your sins may be blotted out, when the times of refreshing shall come from the presence of the Lord; and when he shall send Jesus Christ, which before was preached unto you: Whom the heavens must receive until the times of restitution of all things, which God has spoken by his holy prophets since the world began.' Bishop Meldon, I feel that if that time of restitution is not now here, it is at our doors. Now, the next comes from John, in the book of Revelations, in the fourteenth chapter. John saw an angel. I shall read it: 'And I saw another angel fly in the midst of heaven, having the everlasting gospel to preach unto them that dwell on the earth, and to every nation, and kindred, and tongue, and people. Saying with a loud voice, Fear God and give glory to him for the hour of his judgment is come.' Now, Bishop, listen to this closing of John's words, 'and worship him that made heaven and earth, the sea, and the fountains of water.' In these last words, think, I pray you, of the God of Abraham, Isaac, and Jacob, in lieu of that man-made all-pervading essence."

The train pulled into Chicago, and the parting between these two was indeed touching.

CHAPTER XXI

HOMER BEN ARDEN had no more than stepped from the train in Indianapolis when his old friend John Mordon grasped him by the hand, for the two men had met as brothers.

"My dear Ben Arden," began Mordon, "welcome to our city. You can't know the joy I have in greeting you."

Immediately the rabbi returned warmly: "The joy is mine, John, I assure you, for I have longed for this day when we could meet again, and that in Indianapolis where I may realize the beauties of your metropolis you so often described to me in India."

"Give me your checks," said Mordon, as he extended his hands, "and I will have your baggage sent to my residence, then we will motor on through the main street of the city. I take it, however, that you must be much fatigued after your long voyage from Honolulu."

"Quite to the contrary, John, for last night I slept through the entire hours from dark to daylight."

"How jolly that, Homer," laughed the American in his genial manner. "We may have an interesting evening together talking of old times. What say you?"

"Nothing could please me more, John. By the way, you have a lovely automobile."

"Yes, one of the latest Packards. You know, Homer, I like to wear the new off, leaving the other fellow to wear out the old; American selfishness perhaps, but there is always a market for used cars. Besides you were coming to pay us the long expected visit, so I thought it opportune to buy this new car and become well used to its manipulation by the time you arrived."

"How kind that is of you, John, I really did not expect anything like this courtesy extended to me."

John allowed his car to slow up, as turning to the rabbi he said: "What, Homer? Have you so soon forgotten the debt of gratitude I owe you for having changed the entire course of my life? Moreover, you are as a brother to me, and I hope you feel such."

Homer's eyes moistened as he returned: "John, I did not expect this hospitality, for while it has been my lot to meet some very warm friends in my world-travels, yet few have sought me. So you may realize how I feel, at this moment, and especially to meet one who feels somewhat as I do."

"Homer, you must have had some great experiences, and when the proper time arrives my family and I long to hear you relate them. Of course, you will remain with us an indefinite period, for while I realize the urgency of your quest, a month's repose will be refreshing to you. You know, Homer, I have never lost sight of the marvelous quest you are making, and I want you to feel that your quest is my quest. It has certainly given me a different slant on life."

"You are very kind, John. By the way, you seem to handle your automobile with perfect ease. Do you not prefer a chauffeur?"

John Morden laughed heartily. "Not on your life, Homer. I don't want any chauffeur taking the joy out of my life, for I get too much kick out of handling the wheel myself. Then we have excellent paved streets, in fact, our entire nation is now cobwebbed with paved roads."

As the car stopped at the curb, Homer looked his amazement, while John spoke: "Well, Homer, here we are. How do you like my residence?"

"Marvelous, John. I see you have not been sparing in its cost, for it is palatial indeed."

John had taken great pride in his home. He returned: "I am happy to say it is all paid for, and besides it is home sweet home where love abounds. You know, Homer, business had been very good with me since my return from India, and much of my success I attribute to my new outlook on life. You little dream, Homer, what you put into my life."

"To the contrary, John, it is I who am indebted."

The rabbi found himself seated in a palatial parlor, and, left to himself passed several moments admiring the interior decorations, paintings, rare miniature statuary, drapes, and what not. He was brought suddenly from his seeming reverie, as John entered with his family; "Homer, this is Mrs. Mordon of whom we have so frequently talked. Mother, this is Homer. And Homer this is my son, John Junior, who has just been graduated with a degree, and lastly is our baby whom we have named Homer Mordon."

Mrs. Mordon was gracious: "We truly welcome you, Mister Ben Arden, and want you to feel thoroughly at home, just as though you were one of the family. We are plain people, waiving many of the usual conventions that characterize homes of this class." Turning to her husband, she urged: "John, show Mr. Ben Arden to his room, as dinner is ready."

"Well, Homer," laughed John Mordon as he passed a substantial serving of turkey, "this is somewhat different to some of those horrid fares we had at old Puri, is it not?"

The rabbi smiled as his mind went back to those

days: "Yes, John, it is. Yet I had some dishes in China that were almost as nauseating as those of the old fakirs we saw."

"Then, Homer, you carried out your plans to visit the Celestial Empire, did you?"

"Yes, indeed, John. From India I went to Peking where I had an intensely interesting experience and gained much information."

Mordon was quiet for a moment: "Is it not surprising what gems of truth and beauty one unearths from beneath the rubbish of oriental thought? You know, Homer, I learned to have great respect for the Brahmins and Buddhists."

"Yes, John, and in Mohammedanism, I found the beautiful, especially in the extravagance of their buildings. Then, with the Chinese I learned much that had never entered my mind. You know, some of those old oriental religions have foundations that are really worth weighty consideration."

During this table conversation, Mrs. Mordon had been an attentive listener: "Your experiences must have been of great value to you, Mr. Ben Arden. However, we have kept you talking to the extent that you have eaten very little." Homer smiled, for he had eaten heartily, John having forced a second generous serving of turkey with all that went with it. "To the contrary, Mrs. Mordon, I have eaten until I should feel ashamed of myself. You know, Mrs. Mordon, at least I wish to say that this is the first meal of home cooking I have had since my dear old mother died in Jerusalem years ago, so you may well know what a rare treat this is to me. Your cooking is just to my taste."

Mrs. Mordon was somewhat embarrassed, for she was very modest. "You are indeed kind, Mr. Ben Arden. I am not a city girl, for I was country raised."

John turned to his wife: "Let us hear no more 'Mr. Ben Arden.' Call him by his first name of Homer as I do."

"If our honored guest is agreed I, of course shall be happy."

"And nothing could make me more happy, Mrs. Mordon. Let me be simply Homer."

John was deeply interested in the rabbi's last experience with the Catholic bishop. He urged: "Homer, did you investigate Catholicism as thoroughly as you did the religions of the orient?"

The rabbi seemed a little reluctant momentarily as he responded: "Yes, John, and perhaps tenfold more intensive, for my quest was too much of an aggressive one. The bishop at the outset was so arrogant in his positiveness that he hurled a vicious challenge at me that I could not let go unaccepted. You know, John, I am not naturally an aggressive man. But with a store of truth I had gleaned in advance through my long studies, especially during the winter months I spent in Honolulu, I felt quite well informed."

"And the result, Homer?"

"Well, to make a long story short, the bishop little by little began to see the weakness of his church, for on every hand he met defeat. Beginning with their false conception of Deity; the Atonement of our Lord, its efficacy being denied in the act of their baptism to remove the stain of Eden that Christ atoned for; church organization; transubstantiation; supererogation; celibacy; indulgences; and the very unclean history of papal descent. I will say this for Bishop Meldon. He is an honest man and true, one whom I was proud to meet. He confessed at length, just before we parted that, if he could not find the answers to my questions, he would renounce his bishopric, and henceforth my quest would be his quest. In all my studies and invesigations I have come to the conclusion that if my Priceless Pearl is not on earth today, the time is not far distant when God will again speak from the heavens restoring his gospel in its fulness, with all gifts, powers, authority, and fruits that characterize its divinity. Somehow, in some way, I have a feeling that all my years of quest are not going to be in vain. While I have spent many thousands of dollars, yet were my last cent given and at the very last found my Priceless Pearl, I would be amply repaid for my effort."

The rabbi's extended review was intensely interesting to the Mordons, and finally, turning to his wife, John asked: "My dear, we have often talked of Homer's achievements, have we not, and what it has meant to me?"

"We have indeed," smiled Mrs. Mordon kindly, "and the explanations John made to me, certainly give me a new point of view on life. John is a different man altogether, and ever on the alert for the object of your quest. In fact, we both have made your quest our quest, believing that some day we, with you, may find it."

The conversation so much enjoyed lasted until after the midnight hour.

For several days, the rabbi was a guest of the Mordons, during which the city and its environs had been visited, for John, his wife, and the rabbi motored in all directions. Then a party of guests assembled at the Mordon's in honor of their distinguished guest.

CHAPTER XXII

DURING the several days the rabbi remained in Indianapolis, the old-time friendship between the two men had been much intensified, while the sweet spirit of Mrs. Mordon had given him a feminine touch that for long years he had missed, for hotel life, good and bad, had been his portion, until the comforts once more of a real home lent a satisfying feeling that must be lived to be appreciated.

The urgent invitation of Homer Ben Arden that Mr. Mordon accompany him to Boston was eagerly accepted, and on the following day the two devout friends were seated in their Pullman compartment. The conversation drifted to the quest; the rabbi at length saying: "John, the more I see of modern Christian denominations, the more apprehensive I become that I shall not find the Church of Christ therein. I have attended churches of every Christian sect available to me, covering, I think, nearly all modern Christian creeds, and really, I find nothing that vibrates on my heart. To me all seems a blank sham."

A potentate of a Christian church sitting near had overheard the rabbi's statement, then came forward saying kindly: "Gentlemen, will I be intruding if I enter your conversation?"

Sizing the gentleman up as one of "the cloth," the rabbi replied genially: "Not at all, your presence might be well in order at this moment. I observe, however, that you are a minister of the gospel."

The prelate passed his card which read, "Canon

Charles Greer of the Episcopal Church."

"Yes, yes," replied the rabbi, "I had quite a pro-longed discussion with one of your ministers in Australia, and a fine man he was too."

Following some brief preliminaries, the prelate began: "I overheard you say, Rabbi, that nothing in Christendom had a responsive ring to you. Of course, your being Jewish, naturally repudiates all thought of Jesus Christ, so your stand is after all quite what one may expect."

Homer Ben Arden turned to the canon, quickly retorting kindly: "I beg your pardon, Canon, but I am a follower of Jesus Christ and not of Judaism. Yet withal, I emphasize my conviction that all I have found in modern Christendom so-called, is a dead form, honey-combed with oriental thought and philosophy. In fact, as a world traveler and after the investigation of churches of the world, and especially Christian, I find nothing but man-made institutions that have usurped divine authority which, so far as I know, vanished with the Apostles."

"In which you are sadly mistaken, Rabbi," answered the canon, "for authority has come down in an un-broken chain from Peter of old."

"Of course, Mr. Greer, you refer to the arrogant claims of the Catholic Church, which, by the way, have nothing to stand upon. Moreover," smiled the rabbi as he looked into the canon's eyes, "I am rather amused to hear that, especially from the Church of England, for I should dislike bowing to a church that received its authority from the action of political government."

The rabbi's statement did not meet with the canon's approval. To the contrary he registered a resentful air as he replied: "Which of course I must resent, Rabbi. Isn't such a statement rather indiscreet on your part?"

John Mordon was at once interested, fully anticipating what the rabbi would reply: "I think not, canon,
for your church dates back to Henry the Eighth, who,
as a reward for his faithfulness to Rome had been given
the title of 'Defender of the Faith.' Am I not right?"

"Yes, Rabbi, your statement is quite right, especially from a standpoint of organization and of King
Henry."

"Now, my dear canon, Henry was a high magnate in
the Catholic Church, on this I am sure we are agreed.
But he became infatuated with one Ann Boleyn, and to
marry her he sought to divorce his wife Catherine. The
Pope refused, and that justly, to concede to Henry's request, and in defiance of papal decree, Henry, while yet
the husband of Catherine, married Ann Boleyn for which
act he was excommunicated from the Catholic Church.
This, Canon, you can not deny. Now, subsequent to
this, King Henry assembled the British Parliament in the
year fifteen-hundred-thiry-four, inducing that body to
pass the famed Act of Supremacy, thereby nationalizing
the Church of England, a church, mind you, of political
origin."

The canon reacted: "But, Rabbi, please remember
that nationalizing a religion is quite in order when there
is divine authority to officiate therein."

The rabbi looked at his friend Mordon who was
smiling at the implication: "But dear canon, Henry's excommunication from the Catholic Church automatically
cancelled any authority he might have held therein.

"As to King Henry's authority," returned the canon,
"I am fully convinced that there was no flaw."

Ben Arden look squarely into the canon's eyes.
"Why, Canon, even your own church admits the loss
as disclosed in one of your homilies on the perils of
idolatry." The rabbi drew a small book from his suit-

case always at his fingertips. "Let me read it to you: 'Laity and clergy, learned and unlearned, all ages, sects, and degrees of all Christendom, have at once been buried in abominable idolatry, most detestable to God and damnable to men, and that for eight hundred years and more.' This being the case, dear Canon, where was divine authority during that period. Moreover, you confess no new revelation or divine restoration of authority. So tell me what of your authority?"

With flashing eyes, the canon was about to withdraw, when the rabbi insisted that he remain. "Pray take no offense, Canon, for I am an earnest searcher for truth. For the Church of Jesus Christ with its powers unto salvation as in olden times; but to be frank with you I have failed to find it in modern Christendom."

"I take it, Rabbi, that you are expecting altogether too much of this modern age."

"Not at all, Canon Greer. In the first place your conception of God, as expressed in your first article of faith reads: 'There is but one true and living God, everlasting, without body, parts, and passions, of infinite power, wisdom, and goodness, the maker and preserver of all things both visible and invisible. And in the unity of this Godhead there are three persons, of one substance, power and eternity; the Father, the Son, and the Holy Ghost.' Mr. Greer, I consider this as being little more than the Christianized God of Buddha."

"A pretty radical statement," returned the canon with an air of resentment.

Rabbi Ben Arden looked squarely into the Canon's face again, as he continued: "Let us see, Canon. To you God is an all pervading, omnipotent essence, that Jesus Christ of all-pervading essence was made flesh, later, that he was resurrected and then came his glorious ascension. Do you agree, Canon Greer?"

"Yes, that is the truth as I understand it. The blessed Lord ascended into heaven."

The rabbi's mind was working rapidly: "Now, Reverend Greer, tell me dispassionately. If Jesus came from his all-pervading essence, then ascended into heaven, then what of him at this very minute? Has he his former physical qualities, or is he dissolved back into substance whence he came?"

Canon Greer lapsed in deep meditation. Finally he replied: "That is a pretty deep question, Rabbi. However, our church teaches that he is now of that substance to which you refer, and as taught by our first article of faith."

"Yes, yes, Canon. Your church teaches that. Now, Canon Greer, please answer me this. Subsequent to Christ's resurrection, according to both Matthew and Paul, the dead were raised in resurrection. The question is that if Christ was the prototype and examplar of resurrection, thence to dissolve into substance, what of the human beings who were resurrected. Are we to understand that they too are dissolved into some God-essence? Surely this is a timely question, Canon."

The canon was honest: "That is too mysterious for me to answer, Rabbi. However I am free to confess that such might be the case."

The rabbi was now intensely sincere as he asked: "Yes, yes, Canon, that I understand is the attitude your church takes. Now I ask in all sincerity that you indicate the line of demarkation between your dogma and that of the Nirvana of Buddhism that teaches the reversion of destiny in which all life is dissolved into essence. Or the Taoism of China that teaches that emptiness is the only reality of existence."

Several passengers had gathered during the course of the discussion, and registered disappointment when the canon arose, offering his hand, and withdrew.

With no reference to the retiring prelate, Ben Arden, turning to his friend, said firmly: "John, is there any wonder that the marvelous gift of the Holy Ghost can not be found in Christendom today? Listen to this from the *American Christian Quarterly,* for it is a sweeping confession: 'The whole church is in error. No one can throw the stone at the other. We could not have been in this plight with a multitude of divisions if we had not lost the path in which Christ walks. When we find our common guilt, we will repent and learn to do the will of Christ.'"

John Mordon nodded his head in approval: "A most sweeping statement, Homer, and nearly as pointed as the one I gave you in India delivered by a Reverend Martin, who said in substance, speaking of the loss of the Holy Ghost that the churches were like men trying to pump artificial blood through the arteries, or like men trying to run an engine without steam, that they were the churches of men and not of God. Homer, since leaving you in Calcutta, I have met ministers galore since you put me on the right track, and have always been able to maintain my ground. They all confess in the final analysis that the powers of the miraculous that characterize the true Church of Christ have been lost."

"John, there is one thing quite sure, and it is this: If God has not spoken from the heavens, again delegating divine authority to men to establish the dispensation of the fulness of times as taught by Paul as a latter-day event, then the church of God is not on earth. That we are living the hour of his judgment is axiomatic in world events, and it is in this day of judgment that the gospel is to be restored."

John Mordon sat motionless for several moments, at length asking: "Homer, do you anticipate being able to detect the true church when you find it?"

"Recognize it, John? That I shall, for in the glow of my extensive travels, and the research I have made of the true Church of Christ, I shall not fail."

"But from what source, Homer, do you expect it to come? You certainly must have formed some idea as to that."

"John, I have. I do not expect it to come from any embellished pulpit, nor under the voice of some hireling priest or prelate. But, conversely, from the most lowly source comparable to the fishers of Galilee. Of one thing I am sure, John. I shall find it in the hands of the meek and lowly."

CHAPTER XXIII

AS Homer Ben Arden and John Mordon stepped from the train in Boston, a young woman made her way through the crowd, grasped the rabbi by the hand, saying sincerely: "Mr. Ben Arden, you have no idea how glad I am to greet you in Boston."

"Why, Miss Banks," returned the rabbi with great satisfaction, "is it you? Really, this takes me immediately back to old Peking."

Taking John by the arm, the rabbi spoke: "Clara, this is my old friend John Mordon of whom I spoke—my companion in old India. You know, there we were inseparable friends. This is why I wired you that he was accompanying me to Boston."

Following the conventions of getting acquainted, Miss Banks began: "Really, friends, I think this a rare occasion for you two gentlemen to have a rendezvous in old Boston, and to me even more rare that I have the privilege of having been so closely connected with Rabbi Ben Arden in China, and having learned the value of his wonderful quest. Now, in the first place, you both are to be our guests during your stay in Boston. Father insists upon it, for I have so often told him of Mr. Ben Arden, and also what little I knew of the part Mr. Mordon played in the picture."

At the Banks home the rabbi and John Mordon were welcome guests, in whom Mr. Banks, a man of affairs, was intensely interested. For hours they talked of travel, countries, manners, ethics, and customs of peoples, for the host was himself one who had travelled much.

When the subject of the rabbi's quest came up, Mr. Banks urged to have the proposition given him first hand, even though his daughter Clara had so often spoken of it.

Profound silence maintained for hours as the rabbi recounted his life story, his experiences, and especially near the conclusion when he spoke of his eventual investigation of Christian creeds in which he stated that he had found little more therein that would lead to the realization of his quest than in oriental religions. His host nodded his head frequently in approval, for he and Clara had often talked at length of the condition when she had met the rabbi.

Just before retiring, Mr. Banks ventured: "Rabbi, I thought little of the status of the churches until Clara's return from the orient, when she seemed more than anything else deeply impressed with your teachings and quest. For some reason it sank deeply into my soul. All my life I have had little to do with what I considered man-made systems. With the added illumination I received from my daughter, I detected the lamentable loss of spirituality from the pulpits."

John Mordon had accepted an invitation, the following morning, to accompany Mr. Banks to visit some of the major financial houses of Boston, leaving the rabbi and Clara Banks at home alone. They spent several hours in the parks, and as they sat on a bench beneath the shade of a large spreading tree, where Clara began eagerly to disclose what she thought good news.

"Homer, you say that in all your research you have not discovered the slightest trace of your Priceless Pearl. Rather, Homer, permit me to say ours, for it is uppermost in my life now. In a word, your quest is my quest."

"I am indeed happy, Clara, to hear you speak thus. It makes me feel that I am not alone. How sweet it is to have someone think and feel as I do. That is something I fear you cannot fully appreciate. Now to answer your question. I am sorry to say that in all my travels and investigations my quest seems entirely fruitless. However, an intuitive something seems to assure me that I shall not have searched in vain."

Clara's eyes moistened as, looking into his large dark eyes, she explained: "Homer, I have some good news for you, that I feel sure will make you rejoice, for I have had some wonderful success of late in light being shed upon our quest."

The rabbi leaned forward seemingly to grasp what was coming.

"There are some young missionaries who have been holding street meetings near our home. To me they seem to have just what you are seeking for."

The rabbi's eyes flashed as he replied: "What! Is it possible that after these years of quest, I am to have a little encouragement?"

"Not only possible, Homer, but very probable, all of which I shall leave to your powers of discernment. These delightful young people hold their meetings each evening at five o'clock, and we have but an hour to arrive at their street corner. I propose that we return home for the automobile, besides I want father and Mr. Mordon to listen to them. They will be home by the time we return."

Fifteen minutes before the meeting hour the group were parked near the curb where the young people held their meeting. Already people had gathered, with more coming. Looking up the street, Miss Banks, pointing off, said. "Look. See that young man carrying a brief-case with the young man accompanying him? That is the missionary pair of whom I spoke."

The rabbi, Banks, and Mordon seemed amazed that

youths of these tender years would be holding religious meetings, and the crowd already being quite large, Mr. Banks asked that the missionaries speak from his open car, an invitation which was gladly accepted.

The young man, after a few brief preliminary remarks, said to his missionary companion, Neil Hamilton, would begin the meeting with a vocal selection.

Simply and sincerely, the young missionary sang,

"See, the mighty angel flying,
See, he speeds his way to earth,
To proclaim the blessed gospel,
And restore the ancient faith.
Hear, oh men, the proclamation
Cease from vanity and strife,
Hasten to receive the gospel,
And obey the words of life."

During the rendering of the four verses of the song, something seemed to burn within the rabbi's breast. He gazed openmouthed, eager to catch every word so well articulated in the rendition.

Then came a soulful prayer from the young man that, in itself, was comprehensive and touching, following which Mr. Hamilton sang:

"What was witnessed in the heavens?
Why an angel earthward, bound
Had he something with him bringing?
Yes, the gospel's joyful sound.
It was to be preached in power
On the earth, the angel said,
To all men, all tongues and nations
That upon the earth are spread."

The youthful preacher arose, and with profound earnestness that seemed to impress the people, spoke in clear, audible, well-articulated language:

"Kind friends, for a common country lad like me

to address the group of learned men and women I see before me, requires courage beyond my natural self, hence I am depending upon the Spirit of the Lord, and your sympathy to assist me in delivering my message to you good people.

"I am here to expound to you Jesus and him crucified. To call upon all men to believe in him, to repent of evil doings, by which I mean to reform life, that the misdeeds of today be not repeated tomorrow. Then to be baptized by immersion for the remission of sins by one having divine authority, that they may, by the laying on of authoritative hands receive the Holy Ghost, following which, if the convert be contrite and faithful, that gift is sure to come bearing testimony that the message I carry is true.

"Referring to the song, 'See, the mighty angel flying,' so beautifully rendered by my companion, I wish to emphasize the thought by reading of an event of which John the Revelator wrote that was to transpire in the hour of God's judgment that is today upon the earth, I feel sure you are agreed. The apostle saw our day when the gospel would not be found among men, and that the heavens would be opened for its restoration, that dispensation of the fulness of times of which Paul wrote. Here are the words of John: 'And I saw another angel fly in the midst of heaven, having the everlasting gospel to preach unto them that dwell on the earth, and to every nation, and kindred, and tongue, and people. Saying with a loud voice: Fear God and give glory to him; for the hour of his judgment has come: and worship him that made the heaven, and earth, and the sea, and the fountains of water.'

"This, my friends, implies that the call is to all humanity to cease worshiping the false immaterial god-substance without body, parts, or passions, and worship the true and living God in whose image men—male and female—were engendered. Furthermore, the text implies that were God's church on earth, the restoration of the gospel by the angel would be fruitless and unnecessary.

"I am here, friends, to declare that man is a literal descendant of God, hence he is the offspring of a divine family and to that heritage has a just claim. Nowhere in his teachings did Jesus differentiate between himself and his brethren, other than in degree of exaltation. Conversely, he taught men to pray, 'Our Father in heaven,' also 'I ascend to my Father and to your Father, to my God and to your God.'

"Christ was crucified, and later resurrected a tangible being, as were some of the righteous dead following his resurrection. Listen to Matthew's testimony: 'And the graves were opened, and many bodies of the saints which slept, arose and came out of their graves after his resurrection, and went into the Holy City and appeared unto many.'

"After forty days of resurrected life among his brethren, Jesus made his glorious ascension, and later he was seen to be in his place, on the right hand of his Father. Our Father, the very God I declare unto you in contradistinction to present-day pantheistic thought. The moment, friends, that you step aside from the truth that man is divine—of divine source—and is on the earth in mortal embryo, possessing within him the physical qualifications to eventually culminate into Godhood, that moment you place man in the realm of the beasts, which induces man to become an infidel, sensual, mean, unchaste, and murderous.

"But I declare unto you, with all the sincerity of my soul, that man is divine, and not a worm in creation. His mission is to fill the measure of his creation through mortality, resurrection, to eternal progression.

"In all humility I bear you my humble testimony that God lives, and that Jesus is the Christ; that they have appeared to men in our day; that the angel of which John spoke has actually come to earth, and that the gospel is again committed to men; that John the Baptist, also Peter, James, and John have, by the laying on of hands, restored divine authority to men. By that authority, friends, I was called from my father's farm to bring you this message without cost or price.

"Jesus said truly, 'If any man will do my will he shall know of the doctrine, whether it be of God, or whether I speak of myself.' This, my friends, is the criterion of measurement, and I promise you that if you will put the Lord to the test through humility, faith, repentance, baptism, with the conferring of the Holy Ghost by divinely delegated authority, you shall know for yourselves, for the Holy Ghost will bear this record to your souls.

"I testify that the gospel in its fulness has been restored to earth, with all its gifts, powers, and workings, even as in the days of the Master when by the mandates of holy men the very elements obeyed, the winds and waves were stilled. Today sick are healed, the lame have walked, the blind have received their sight, and the dead have been raised to life again.

"I solemnly bear this testimony to you in the name of Jesus Christ. Amen."

The street-corner service concluded by Elder Hamilton's singing in his mellow voice.

> "Know this, that every soul is free,
> To choose his life and what he'll be,
> For this eternal boon is given
> That God will force no man to heaven.
> He'll call, persuade, direct aright,

Bless with wisdom, love, and might,
In wondrous ways be good and kind
But never force the human mind."

The other young missionary offered a touching prayer.

As soon as the services were concluded, Homer Ben Arden siezed the lad by the hand, saying, "Young man, I have travelled the world over and have spent a fortune during years of time in an indefatigable quest for just what you seem to have. I am Rabbi Ben Arden from Jerusalem, and your name is—?"

"Paul Seymour," replied the lad, "and my companion is Neil Hamilton."

During the strange incident, the crowd had pressed close to the car, eager to catch every word. Mr. Banks said: "Will you young people kindly accompany us to my home? I am sure the rabbi as well as my family and friends are eager to hear more of your strange message."

The consent being joyfully given, the car pushed its way through the dispersing crowd.

CHAPTER XXIV

DINNER was over at the Banks home, and the young missionaries had gone for a drive with Claire Banks, leaving the three men to spend an hour with themselves during which an interesting discussion of the strange affair was the topic of conversation.

"Homer," asked John Mordon, "what do you think of it anyway?"

The rabbi, seated in deep meditation, seemed to arouse and replied: "John, I am amazed—dumbfounded, to think that after my years of quest I make this discovery."

Although not very demonstrative, Mr. Banks interrupted: "Gentlemen, I might be an undemonstrative business man, but if I ever heard dispassionate sincerity in my life that young man was a demonstration of it. Cool as a cucumber, unemotional, and yet he seemed to talk with the conviction of one who knows."

"Which to me," returned the rabbi, "is potent indeed. Moreover, his spirituality seems different from what I have heretofore experienced with men. Then Mr. Hamilton's voice is simply sublime."

During this conversation, Clara, followed by the missionaries, entered the parlor, and soon all were seated comfortably.

Ben Arden seemed to have his wits well sharpened for a severe investigation of the newly presented religion. Eagerly he forced the conversation asking: "Mister Seymour, what is the name of your Church?"

"May I first ask you," returned the missionary

kindly, "one important question before I answer you?"

"Why, indeed," answered the rabbi, "provided I can answer you."

"Then, Rabbi, what would you consider the name of Christ's church should be?"

Ben Arden pondered, then replied: "Well, I think at least it should bear Christ's name, should it not?"

"You are right there, Rabbi, and the name of his Church today, to distinguish it from his church in the days of the apostles, is, the Church of Jesus Christ of Latter-day Saints."

"What!" interrupted Mr. Banks with an indignant air. "Are you Mormons?"

"We have that honor, Mr. Banks," returned the missionary. "If you choose to call us Mormons, we reply cheerfully to the name given to us as a mark of disrespect, as was the name 'Christian' given to the early saints. Moreover, we do not mind in the least being called Mormons after so noble a prophet as Mormon, the ancient American prophet."

"But," continued Mr. Banks, "you of all people are the most hated and detested."

"Very true, Mr. Banks. My people have been much misrepresented and much misunderstood, in consequence of which, in this fair democratic land of America, the Prophet to whom the Lord appeared and spoke face to face, has been cruelly martyred and that at the instigation of Christian prelates, as well as have many of his followers. But, gentlemen, does that indicate that we are in error?"

Ben Arden did not give the host time to reply but ventured quickly with: "Not at all, young man. It is just what I anticipate in the Church of Christ." Turning toward Banks and Morton, the rabbi continued: "Friends, kindly remember the words of Christ when he said to his apostles: Blessed are ye when men shall hate you, and shall separate you from their company, and shall reproach and cast your name as evil for the Son's sake. Rejoice ye in that day for behold your reward is great in heaven, for in like manner did the fathers unto the prophets. Again: Blessed are ye when men shall revile you, and persecute you and shall say all manner of evil against you falsely for my sake. Gentlemen, one of the best witnesses to the Church of Jesus Christ has ever been persecution. You recall that when Paul came to Rome, they said to him: But we desire to know of thee what thou thinkest: for as concerning this sect, we know it is everywhere spoken against. Moreover, let us consider the hate that crucified our Lord, and martyred the apostles. So I suggest that we take all the hate and their persecution as evidence in their favor."

"May I intrude, Father?" interrupted Clara.

"Certainly, my dear," returned Mr. Banks, for we want a full and free investigation and discussion."

"Then, may I state, when the National Educational Association held its huge convention in Salt Lake City, you know, father, I was appointed by the press to cover it. It was a revelation to us all to observe the intelligence of the Latter-day Saints. Their educational system is a leading star in America. Their social order, especially represented in the organizations for the youth of their church, as regards the sane and constructive control of leisure time has no peer anywhere. Their great birthrate, and what is more their marvelous low death rate, their home building, the standard of their communities, prove them to be pioneers in modern irrigation. Then their purity and cleanliness of life and virtue place them, in my opinion, at the peak of American citizenship. With your indulgence, I wish to read to you what one of America's foremost educators, a delegate to that convention, wrote upon his return to Connecticut. I refer to the eminent Doctor Thomas A. Bicknell." Miss Banks stepped into her room, later returning with a pamphlet, from which she read: 'As a visitor in Salt Lake City, from New England, I am asked to state my impression as to the distinctive policy of the city and state founded by the pioneers of the Mormon faith and ideals. I do this most cordially, for I am not a stranger to what has been transpiring in the intermountain commonwealth, having studied this peculiar and remarkable development for a period of more than forty years. Four great purposes have been regent in Utah and its capitol—Salt Lake City—since its occupation by the pioneers July 24th, 1847. The first has been a positive abiding religious faith. The working creed of its people is the measure of its devotion to high ideals, and the creed is measured by its fruits as a tree. The pioneers of Utah were, most of them, of New England birth. Nearly all of them came out of the rural life of New England of a century ago. The six New England states with rural New York, nursed the childhood of the founders of the Mormon faith. Puritan and pilgrim, and the children of the Mayflower stock, made the first emigration across the plains to Salt Lake Valley. The ruling motive was religion, in creed and form not far removed from the Hebrew faith. Its bold declaration of the great principles of faith and practice drew to their embrace men and women of strong intellects and warm hearts. The new expression of old tenets won persecution and distress for the possession of the new faith, and only brave souls could stand the stress of the new cult. Utah and several of her sister states were founded by a people of Eastern birth, of brave purpose and undying resolve.

" 'What is the issue? A society of tens of thousands of

souls of the strongest moral fiber. It can be stated without fear of contradiction that the Wasatch range holds in its embrace a population whose standards of moral, ethical, and religious culture are unequalled on the American continent or any other continent.

" 'With religious convictions deep and controlling, the education of the people has been a radical element in Mormon faith. A schoolhouse was planted by the first house in Salt Lake City, and today education is fostered in supreme fashion, from the kindergarten through the university. Cities and towns vie with each other through education of the children, and of the state revenues, over eighty-seven per cent are devoted to education. In schoolhouse architecture and school equipment, Utah leads.

" 'The Mormon policy on the side of social order is recognized as the most thoroughly organized system in the world. Every intelligent man should study it for its recognition of the solution of economic and social problems. Its details of supervision are exact, thorough-going, and efficient.

" 'Beyond and above all in perfection of system and in realization of grand results, are the industry, frugality, and temperance of the people. The beehive properly symbolizes the spirit and practice of the Mormons. Go where you will, you will find no poverty, while wealth abounds in practical abundance. Homes are full of comfort and luxuries; art, music, and literature are the endowments of all. The wealth of the land has attracted the Mormons more than the wealth of the mines, and both are making wealth common and fairly distributed.

" 'Utah is a land of great possibilities. Its richest possession is its "Mormon population" of honest, pure minded, sweet hearted men, women, and children who have drawn on nature's forces for her greater service

and returns. They have, out of the lion's mouth, plucked
the honeycomb of sweet content and honest life, and
were the Master to walk the streets of Salt Lake City today, would he not say to all critics: 'Let him that is
without sin cast the first stone?' This has been lengthy,
friends," spoke Miss Banks with fervor, "But I feel sure
you have been interested in the account from so eminent
an authority as Doctor Bicknell."

"Good enough," replied the rabbi who had eagerly
absorbed every word as it fell from the lips of Miss
Banks. Then, turning to the missionary, he asked:
"Now, Mr. Seymour, do you mind my being somewhat
aggressively inquisitive in satisfying myself as to the
doctrines of your Church?"

"Not at all," returned the lad, "but please remember
that I do not profess to come within the intellectual
atmosphere of you learned gentlemen. Bear in mind that
I am but a farm boy from Utah, and uneducated for
the ministry."

The gentlemen looked amazed at the boy's remarks,
then the rabbi continued: "All the more to your credit,
Mr. Seymour. Now to continue. You have pretty well
satisfied me, in fact quite so, of your conception of the
true and living God, with his personality, and also of
Jesus Christ. But will you please inform me as to his
atonement?"

Young Seymour looked toward Neil Hamilton, his
companion missionary, then turning to the inquisitor he
replied: "Gentlemen, my companion, Elder Hamilton,
has made this one of his choice studies since he has been
in the missionary service, and I am sure he will be glad
to treat the subject, and I think to your entire satisfaction."

Elder Hamilton seemed to register some confusion,
with all eyes focused upon him. However, with a

prayer in his heart for divine guidance, he began: "Friends, I would explain it as follows: When in the *modus operandi* of God's procedure, a new world is to be created, the next step is to people it, for we teach that this is the real object of world creation. Man and woman must be placed upon it as progenitors of that world's inhabitants to be tabernacled in the flesh. I take it that none less than an immortal being would be worthy of such distinction. Of their own free will and choice a divine law, not of earth, must be transgressed in order that man become mortal to fill God's first injunction to multiply and replenish the earth and subdue it. Is that clear to you, Rabbi?"

"That seems plausible, Mr. Hamilton. I see no other way in which this might be brought about," returned the astonished rabbi.

"And in that fall," continued the young man, "he would naturally pass to full mortality, passing the same to his offspring, who, like Adam, the patriarch of this world with his God-given wife Eve, would also be fully mortal and unable again to operate the higher laws of heaven as before they had transgressed in Eden. Let us remember that our first parents, giving up their immortality, must have made a tremendous sacrifice that is beyond comprehension. He and his posterity could have risen to the full dignity of human achievement. But the time would come when they would have reached the fulness of their life circle. Then what?"

The listeners looked from one to the other, at length to the rabbi for the answer who faltered with: "A ponderous subject that, and I shall be obliged to ask that you answer your own question."

"Well, friends," continued the missionary, "our view is this, and I feel quite sure you will agree that it is rational. In the first place, eternal death faced them,

for when they died that would be their ending. Next,
in the divine fiat of God's great plan of peopling and
redeeming worlds, a redemption must be made for that
Fall. Hence someone greater than Adam and Eve must
atone for that transgression, or breaking of that divine
law that made them helplessly mortal. Now, in that
divine fiat, someone must die to satisfy the demands
of justice and judgment; so I ask you, friends, What
kind of being would be physically qualified for this
majestic mission? Remember that Adam nor his posterity could not raise above their mortal level, hence
they could not satisfy the exegeses of justice and judgment. Again I ask, what kind of individual could possibly bring about a redemption?"

"I am sorry," returned the Jew. "But you will, I
fear, have to answer your own pointed question."

"I shall do my best," returned Elder Hamilton. "As
I understand it, the being who could effect a redemption
must be sufficiently mortal to die, and sufficiently immortal to have power, of his own free will and choice, to
rise in defiance of the bands of death. So, friends, let us
consider the life of Jesus Christ, and allow me to read
the account of his coming as recorded by Luke. The
angel said to Mary: 'Behold thou shalt conceive and
shall bring forth a child, and shall call his name Jesus.
He shall be great and shall be called the Son of the Highest.' The Highest you will agree is none less than God
the Father. But to continue Luke's account, 'The Holy
Ghost shall come upon thee, and the Power of the Highest shall overshadow thee; therefore also that holy thing
which shall be born of thee shall be called the Son of
God.' Think of it, friends. The immortal God being
the Father, and the Galilean Mary being the mother,
which implies that all that was mortal in Jesus came
from Mary. His immortality coming from God his

Father by which death could not forbid his rising. Moreover, friends, please remember the words of Jesus speaking of that innate power: 'I have power to lay down
my life, and to take it up again.' Also, 'As the Father
hath life in himself, so he hath given the Son to have
life in himself.' In no instance did Jesus say his Father
would raise him up. No, but he did say 'I have the
power.' This friends, is the mission of a redeemer as I
understand it. Hence we teach with Paul, 'that as in
Adam all die, so also in Christ shall all be made alive.'
Jesus further emphasized the fact of this general salvation in the following, 'For the hour is coming in which
all that are in their graves shall hear his voice and come
forth. They that have done good unto the resurrection
of life, and they that have done evil unto the resurrection
of damnation.' "

"What," asked the startled Miss Banks, "a resurrection of the wicked? Could that be possible, Mr. Hamilton?"

"And why not, Miss Banks? The atonement of
Jesus Christ was infinite in that the entire human family, the just and unjust, come under this majestic atonement. Anything short of this would not be complete.
Please recall that John wrote that he saw the dead, small
and great, come forth, that even death and hell delivered
up their dead to be judged according to their deeds in
the flesh. Yes, that atonement must be universal and
infinite, for this was Christ's special mission."

"That is all quite clear to my understanding," spoke
the rabbi in his amazement. "Surely every soul must be
heir to salvation through the atonement of Jesus Christ."

"Friends," continued the missionary, "before I close
my review of the atonement, I wish to present for your
consideration a very beautiful piece of theological thinking from one of the successor presidents of the church

bearing on the subject at hand. This from President John Taylor: 'Is justice dishonored? No, it is satisfied, the debt is paid. Is righteousness departed from? No, it is a righteous act, all the requirements are met. Is justice violated? No, its demands are fulfilled. Is mercy triumphant? No, she simply claims her own. Justice, mercy, and truth harmonize as the attributes of Deity. Justice and truth have met together. Righteousness and peace have kissed each other. Justice and judgment triumph as well as mercy and peace. All the attributes of Deity harmonize in this great, grand, momentous, equitable, merciful and meritorious act.'

"Contemplate the majesty of it. Measure it by all laws of reason, scripture, and logic, for it is God's great majesty in redeeming the world."

There was a profound stillness while Mr. Hamilton gave his review, other than an occasional question, which he answered to the satisfaction of all, and while he read the words of the late President Taylor, the closest attention maintained.

Following a brief pause, the rabbi exclaimed: "Beautiful, sublime, and comprehensive. Really there seems nothing more could be said, and I am grateful to our missionary for his able and intelligent explanation of so sublime a doctrine."

All acquiesced in the rabbi's appreciation, while Elder Hamilton felt quite modest, even though his heart bounded within him.

CHAPTER XXV

FOLLOWING the brief recess in which refreshments had been served, the company was again in the parlor, in view of the further investigation of the Church of Jesus Christ.

Ben Arden was first to begin by asking, "Now, Mr. Seymour, rather I should address you as Elder Seymour, after absorbing the beauties of the Atonement so forcefully explained by our missionary friend, I ask if there remains anything further on the part of a soul struggling for salvation."

"A very important question," returned the missionary. "Of course, in the atonement, death lost its sting and the grave its victory, for in that sublime act death had been conquered in the vouchsafed resurrection of the human family. However, that is what to us is the complete removal of the original sin—the transgression of Eden, if you will. But there still remains individual sin that man commits independent of the atonement. We say in one of our Articles of Faith, 'We believe that man will be punished for their own sins, and not for Adam's transgressions. And again, 'We believe that through the atonement of Christ all mankind may be saved by obedience to the laws and ordinances of the gospel.' While in another article: 'We believe that the first principles and ordinances of the gospel are: first, Faith in the Lord Jesus Christ; second, Repentance; third, Baptism by immersion for the remission of sins; fourth, laying on of hands for the gift of the Holy Ghost."

"I presume," asked John Mordon, "that that is scriptural doctrine?"

The rabbi was foremost in forcing the answer: "It is, indeed, scriptural. You recall, of course, how Elder Seymour read us the words of Peter to the crucifying Jews, wherein this doctrine was fully discussed." The missionary continued.

"Passing by faith in God, Jesus Christ, and the atonement, the conscious investigator faces his life of sin that pricks his conscience. This is the first step in repentance, a godly sorrow. But to us, that repentance that has a salutary effect is actual reformation of life, in that the errors of yesterday be not repeated today. As Paul says, to walk in the newness of life. When a soul stands thus foursquare with his guilt before his Maker, he then is in a position where these sins may be effaced through baptism. Baptism for the remission of sins was the underlying thought in the days of Christ, as it is in his church today. It is a law of God to man, and so earnest was Jesus that he insisted upon his own baptism by John, not for the remission of his sinless self, but, as he said, to fulfil all righteousness, which applies also to us for the remission of our sins. You will recall, friends, that, according to Matthew, Jesus' last injunction was, 'Go ye therefore, and teach all nations, baptizing them in the name of the Father, and of the Son, and of the Holy Ghost.' While Mark, also speaking of these last words of Christ, wrote: 'Go ye into all the world, and preach the gospel to every creature. He that believeth and is baptized shall be saved; and he that believeth not shall be damned.' So, you see, friends, there is no escape from the truth and necessity of the ordinance if one desires salvation."

"And where does the baptized and sin-forgiven convert go from here?" asked Mr. Banks, earnestly.

"That," answered the missionary, "brings for consideration that wondrous gift of the Holy Ghost which Christ sought to impress upon his apostles when he told them he would send another Comforter that the world could not receive, the spirit of promise, that would lead them into all truth. This would show them things to come, even future events, and, last, but not least, to testify of Christ. It is little wonder he admonished his apostles that it was expedient that he went, for if he went not the Holy Ghost could not come, but after his departure he would send him—the Holy Ghost—admonishing them to wait for future ministry until endowed with power from on high. This, Mr. Banks, is the next step following baptism, the conferring of the Holy Ghost by the laying on of hands by one divinely authorized of God."

Clara Banks had listened with deep interest, when she asked at length: "Mr. Seymour, what of that Holy Ghost down through the ages?"

"Scan all ecclesiastical history down from when Christianity became paganized, and see how the churches have sought for the acquisition of this gift, but had sought in vain. Now, in conclusion, as to the gift of the Holy Ghost in our day, I wish to read to you of when the Prophet Joseph Smith had a prolonged interview with Martin Van Buren, President of the United States. Paul Seymour drew from his briefcase a small volume from which he read: 'In November, 1839, Joseph Smith went to confer with President Martin Van Buren regarding the persecution that had been suffered by the Saints in Missouri. While the two were in conference, Mr. Van Buren asked the prophet a pertinent question: "What is the difference between your people and other religious people?" Joseph Smith replied in one short sentence, "We have the Holy Ghost." This terse answer contains a volume. Joseph Smith concluded with, " 'I through my faith and prayer, have brought back to the world the unspeakable gift of the spiritual life. This is my most distinctive bequest to my generation.' ' "

Rabbi Ben Arden had listened with undivided interest, for each word seemed to bring him nearer to his conviction that he had at last discovered his Priceless Pearl. The narration of the restoration of the Holy Ghost struck deeply into his soul, yet, he ventured further for his satisfaction and information.

"My young friend, your narration is wonderful to me, more so than you can possibly imagine. You must pardon me if I seem insistent and aggressive. What I am now going to ask is this: To what extent have the workings of the Holy Ghost and the Holy Priesthood brought the fruits of the gospel, by which I mean comparable to those events in the days of ancient Israel, and especially in the days of Christ, when the very elements bowed to divine mandate in that the winds and waves obeyed, water was turned into wine, the sick were healed, the lame walked, the blind saw? Even after the ascension of our Lord, the same was marvelously realized under the hands of the apostles. Now, please tell me of these things in the restored gospel."

Neil Hamilton looked at Elder Seymour with a twinkle in his eyes, for he well knew this was one of his choice subjects. Elder Seymour began. "To me, Rabbi, this is one of the dearest and choicest experiences of my life, for I have witnessed the very things of which you speak. I may, perhaps, be considered bold in my testimony. In our day there has been as great or greater realization of the miraculous than was experienced in the days of Jesus. In our day, the sick have been healed, the blind have had vision restored, the lame have walked, men villainously shot by enemies have instantly been healed, demons have been driven from those possessed, even the dead have been raised to life again, and climate given to a parched and barren land."

The rabbi sat as one aghast, at length asking fervently: "Is such possible? I am amazed, yet why should I be when I feel so convinced that the Lord has spoken, and his Church could not be on earth without these very things. You speak of your own experiences with these powers. Will you please be explicit? This is very important to me."

"I shall be very happy to respond, Rabbi and friends. Listen to my story. My father died while I was a child, leaving my mother and two small children, I being the youngest. Unfortunately mother died, leaving us orphans. My old grandmother, a devoted convert to the gospel from England, sent for two aged elders to come and administer to her with oil and prayer. Arriving, they found mother had passed on, and only when the old venerable lady insisted, they exercised their priesthood, when suddenly mother opened her eyes, saying: 'Why did you bring me back?' Now, friends, psychologists and men of science might have some solution to offer of this strange event. But there is one thing they cannot answer, which is this: Father had come for mother's spirit, and as they passed to the spirit world, father hesitated, saying, 'Listen, the priesthood on earth has been so remarkably exercised, that the mandate of your death has been rescinded. You are privileged to return and rear our children.' Yes, friends, she did return and remained with us many years. I could relate similar experiences, several more of which have come under my own experience, though I am a young man."

During the elder's narration of his experience, so calmly and dispassionately told, without the least emotion, several eyes welled with tears. Even the rather

stern business man, Mr. Banks, had been deeply moved,
while Clara Banks wiped her eyes, for she, at length,
realized how near the rabbi, and she and John Mordon,
were to finding that Priceless Pearl.

When the rabbi gained control of his feelings, he
spoke calmly. "Wonderful, Elder Seymour, and I believe your story. I hope we may have several hours discussion in this sublime restoration of priesthood powers.
But now, may I ask you two more things that, to me,
must characterize Christ's church on earth?"

"I hope," returned the missionary calmly, "I may be
enabled to answer to your satisfaction."

"It is this, Elder Seymour: I had a splendid spirit-
ually minded father and also a loving mother who have
gone to the other side. Now, my question is this.
Should I come into the Church of Christ by baptism,
then what is to be the fate of my parents?"

This was a stunning question to some present. But
the missionary seemed eager to reply. "I shall refer to
baptism for the dead, that so strikingly maintained in the
days of the apostles. I mean, where the living performed
the work by proxy for their deceased ancestors. 'Else
what shall they do,' asked Paul to the doubting Corin-
thians, 'which are baptized for the dead, if the dead rise
not at all. Why then are they baptized for the dead?'"

"That is the very thing I wanted to bring out, Elder
Seymour, for I am fully in accord. It was manifest in
the early church. However, what is being done in this
regard in the church today?"

"That vicarious work, Rabbi, is paramount in the
Dispensation of the Fullness of Times. In fact, the dispensation hinges on that very thing. We have six magnificent temples built for that very purpose in which
ordinance work has been done for millions on millions
of those in the spirit world. This is one of the real

reasons for this dispensation, to save the world's dead throughout the ninety generations of men since Adam. However, this majestic service is twofold, to the living and also to the dead."

"By which you mean?" asked the rabbi.

"First, eternal marriage. For instance, were you to be married for a limit of ten years, the expiration of that time would cancel those marriage ties, would it not? Now, suppose you were married by the churches or civil authority 'until death do you part.' What then? Would not the contract be equally cancelled? When a husband, for instance, stands by the grave of his devoted wife, bids her farewell with this thought: 'You were my wife in mortality, but now our contract is ended—farewell.' What a tragic thing this must be. Remember, friends, God does nothing but that it is for eternity, and marriage is one of those eternal things. It must be solemnized in his holy sanctuary—a temple of the Lord, and sealed under divine authority. Later, I hope to refer to the restoration of the sealing powers as restored by the Prophet Elijah, but not at this point."

Mr. Banks and his daughter, Clara, exchanged glances, for he felt keenly sensitive in behalf of his deceased wife. "Is it possible," asked Mr. Banks, "that I may be assured of my deceased wife in eternity?"

"Indeed, it is," replied the missionary, "provided, of course, that you may, as a member of the church, prove yourself worthy to enter that holy sanctuary, for ordinance work in her behalf, thereby having special endowment work and sealing of husband and wife for eternity."

Rabbi Ben Arden was intensely interested in this narration. He urged hopefully: "Elder Seymour, in the case of my parents, of whom I have spoken, what of them? Is there some way of their being sealed as husband and wife for eternity?"

"Absolutely, Rabbi. In the first place, a proxy baptism for and in their behalf is made. Certainly, with the vast preaching of the gospel in the spirit world, they are anxiously waiting your work on their behalf, not only to effect their baptism, confirmation, and priesthood ordination for your father, but to seal for eternity that devout and loving couple. This, friends, is in progress in behalf of sealing millions of married couples in the spirit world for eternity, and children to parents. On and on this goes, in a majestic linking until all the families of the righteous people who have lived and died, have been sealed under the authority of Almighty God. We Latter-day Saints point to the near ushering in of the great millennium which shall be devoted almost entirely to the salvation of the sons and daughters of Adam from the beginning."

Deep silence maintained, at length being broken by John Mordon who, having absorbed the doctrine, asked, "What of my case, Elder Seymour? My wife and I are deeply devoted, yet married by civil authority—of course until death does separate us."

"I think I have made this quite plain, Mr. Mordon. You should go to a holy temple where God's sealing authority can seal for eternity. This is the sole solution."

John Mordon nodded his head understandingly, as did also Mr. Banks, while the rabbi sat as one transfixed. The rabbi looked at his watch, at length saying, "It nears the midnight hour. However, with your indulgence, Mr. Banks and friends, I wish to bring another problem that must characterize the Church of Jesus Christ in the last days, and that is the full and complete gathering and restoration of Israel. That problem not finding place in the great Christian churches of our time has been the means of driving thousands to infidelity on the ground that God had failed in his promises to restore scattered Israel, including the Lost Tribes. So you see, this, given in scripture, is to be one of the great events in the last days. Now, Elder Seymour, may I have your church's reaction in this regard?"

"Again, may I ask that Elder Hamilton treat that subject. Surely he will satisfy you in this regard," returned the missionary.

All eyes turned to the other missionary, who calmly began, "The gathering of Israel is one of the great movements of the revealed Church of God in our day. May I read from Isaiah in this regard?" He opened his Bible and read: 'And it shall come to pass in the last days, that the mountain of the Lord's house shall be established in the tops of the mountains, and shall be exalted above the hills; and all nations shall flow into it. And many people shall go and say, Come ye, and let us go up to the mountain of the Lord, to the house of the God of Jacob; and he will teach us of his ways, and we will walk in his paths: for out of Zion shall go forth the law, and the word of God from Jerusalem.' This, friends, has been majestically in progress for more than a hundred years, during which hundreds of thousands from all nations have been possessed with the spirit and urge to gather—yes—to the tops of the mountains which are exalted above the hills, even to the tops of the Rocky Mountains. Please remember that in Salt Lake City and Utah villages there are more than sixty languages spoken by people from far-off lands who have embraced the gospel and have been impelled to gather. Yes, friends, and this gathering shall go on and on for all the hosts of Israel—the children and posterity of Abraham to which the promise was made, which is one of the great themes of the Bible—shall have been gathered. All the tribes of Israel, shall be gathered. May I conclude by reading one more passage of scripture as to this majestic event now

under way. This is from Jeremiah: 'Therefore, behold
the day cometh, saith the Lord, that it shall no more be
said, the Lord liveth that brought the children of Israel
out of the land of Egypt; But the Lord liveth, that
brought up the children of Israel from the land of the
north, and from all lands whither he had driven them;
and I will send many fishers, saith the Lord, and they
shall fish them; and after I will send many hunters,
and they shall hunt them from every mountain, and
from every hill, and out of the holes of the rocks.' Please
note that this great event is to eclipse the vast hosts of
Israel that came out of Egypt. And friends, in all fervor, I state that this is the great mission of today in which
we are but two of many thousand of other missionaries
out among the nations to gather Israel—the blood of Israel from the nations. So, Rabbi Ben Arden, I hope you
see that in the Church of Jesus Christ this majestic
movement shall have its full and complete accomplish-
ment."

Rabbi Ben Arden sat motionless in his admiration
of this vast movement, while the others seemed enraptured with the revelation to them of it.

Rabbi Ben Arden made one more request: "It is too
late tonight, but the major thought before us is that if
God has spoken in our day, and that the gospel is restored in its completeness, we should have the story
of such restoration. What say you, Elder Seymour?"

"I shall be very happy to give full details of that
majestic restoration of the gospel of our Lord in our
day. But friends, it is quite a long story, yet a very
beautiful one which I feel sure will gratify you."

Mr. Banks was first to speak. "Though it requires a
whole evening, or a number of evenings, it is something
that should be given full consideration. If God has
spoken and the gospel restored, what is a little time to

learn fully of its details? But you splendid young missionaries, will you be willing to respond?"

Elder Seymour replied immediately, "Indeed. Remember we are missionaries, which implies that our time is freely given to the great mission to which we have been divinely appointed. When shall it be?"

"Why not tomorrow evening?" asked Miss Banks. "By the way, we have ample room, will you both remain with us tonight? Then on the morrow I am sure the rabbi will be happy to further pursue his quest for his Priceless Pearl."

"Were it not so late," returned Neil Hamilton, "we could telephone to the family with whom I am boarding. As it is I think we had best return. I cannot of course speak for Elder Seymour as he resides in another part of the city."

Mr. Banks insisted that, as the missionaries desired to return to their lodgings, that he take them in his car.

CHAPTER XXVI

RABBI BEN ARDEN and his friend John Mordon were comfortably seated in the Banks home, preparatory to Miss Banks arriving with the missionaries. The two men had talked with seriousness as to the discovery of what promised to be the very Priceless Pearl of the rabbi's quest, and each expressed amazement as to how a young man possessed such a store of knowledge covering point by point the gospel, and in it all they wondered whence came this information so minutely in keeping with the Church of the Master and the apostles. The rabbi suggested the probable solution of it all, saying: "John, there is but one answer as I understand it, and that is that the Holy Ghost, the source of all intelligence, must surely characterize the lives of these two young people."

When Clara arrived with the missionaries Mr. Banks came in, and soon all were seated comfortably. The subject of the evening, as by previous arrangement, was presented by Mr. Banks, asking that the rabbi be foremost in conducting the conversation of the evening.

The rabbi began, "Prophets and holy men through the ages have pointed to the last days, the dispensation of the Fulness of Times when God would speak from the heavens. If such an event has occurred, there could be nothing more seriously important to this world of men."

"But were this so, that God has spoken," asked John Mordon, "even were Christ to appear today, would he be generally received? Would he in this faithless, materialistic age, be received? Would he have a place to lay his head? Is it not probable that he might find a shorter road to Calvary, figuaratively speaking, than when he was in mortality?"

"That is quite possible," suggested Mr. Banks, "and for one I shall hold myself open-minded and, in fact, open to conversion to the fact that probably God has spoken."

Rabbi Ben Arden turned to Elder Seymour, "Now, my young friend, we hold ourselves in readiness for your story, and be assured that we shall be ardent listeners."

Elder Seymour and his companion had come fasting, and with a deep prayer in their hearts that words, well chosen and convincing, might be their lot. The elder suggested an opening prayer by Brother Hamilton. The fervency of his appeal touched all hearts as he supplicated heaven for the presence of the Holy Spirit.

Following the prayer, Elder Seymour suggested that Neil Hamilton sing an appropriate hymn. He responded with:

"O, how lovely was the morning,
Radiant beamed the sun above;
Bees were humming, sweet birds singing,
Music ringing through the grove,
When within the shady woodland,
Joseph sought the God of love."

He sang the entire song, while his auditors listened carefully.

"Were I to read the entire story as penned by the Prophet Joseph Smith," suggested Elder Seymour, "it would require perhaps too much time, even more perhaps than is necessary to be taken. However, I promise you that no essential detail shall be missed."

Mr. Banks, with a spirit of kindly resentment, suggested: "As I said last evening, we should hear the full story of how God is supposed to have appeared in our day, and how the gospel was divinely restored. Therefore, I suggest that no detail or word be eliminated from the promised story."

"Your point is well taken," returned the missionary. "However, the story is not so long but that there will be time for a few comments. I shall have something to say myself, I hope. So with your indulgence, I shall proceed with the story of the vision of God and resurrected beings in our day."

The eagerness of all, seemed to give Elder Seymour a deeper confidence in the task at hand. He, turning the pages of a small book, read Joseph Smith's own story:

" 'Owing to the many reports which have been put into circulation by evil-disposed persons, in relation to the progress of the Church of Jesus Christ of Latter-day Saints, all of which have been signed by the authors thereof to militate against its character as a Church and its progress in the world—I have been induced to write its history, to disabuse the public mind, and put all inquiries after truth in possession of the facts, as they have transpired, in relation to both myself and the Church, so far as I have such facts in my possession.

" 'In this history, I shall present the various events in relation to this Church, in truth and righteousness, as they have transpired, or as they at present exist, being now the tenth year since the organization of the said Church.

" 'I was born in the year of our Lord one thousand eight hundred and five, in the town of Sharon, Windsor County, Vermont. My father, Joseph Smith Sen., left the State of Vermont, and moved to Palmyra, Ontario, (now Wayne) County, in the State of New York, and when I was in my tenth year, or thereabouts. In about four years after my father's arrival in Palmyra, he moved with his family into Manchester, in the same county of Ontario. . . .

" 'His family consisting of eleven souls, namely my father Joseph Smith; my mother Lucy Smith (whose name, previous to her marriage, was Mack, daughter of Solomon Mack); my brothers, Alvin (who died November 19th, 1824, in the 27th year of his age), Hyrum, myself, Samuel Harrison, William, Don Carlos; and my sisters, Sophronia, Catherine, and Lucy.

" 'Some time in the second year after our arrival in Manchester, there was in the place where we lived an usual excitement on the subject of religion. It commenced with the Methodists, but soon became general among all the sects in that region of country. Indeed, the whole district of country seemed affected by it, and great multitudes united themselves to the different religious parties, which created no small stir and division amongst the people, some crying, "Lo, here!" and others, "Lo, there!" Some were contending for the Methodist faith, some for the Presbyterian, and some for the Baptist.

" 'For, notwithstanding the great love which the converts to these different faiths expressed at the time of their conversion, and the great zeal manifested by the respective clergy, who were active in getting up and promoting this extraordinary scene of religious feeling, in order to have everybody converted, as they were pleased to call it, let them join what sect they pleased; yet when the converts began to file off, some to one party and some to another, it was seen that the seemingly good feelings of both the priests and the converts were more pretended than real; for a scene of great confusion and bad feelings ensued—priest contending against priest, and convert against convert; so that all their good feelings for one another, if they ever had any, were entirely lost in the strife of words and a contest about opinions.

" 'I was at this time in my fifteenth year. My father's family was proselyted to the Presbyterian faith, and four of them joined the church, namely my mother, Lucy, my brothers Hyrum and Samuel Harrison; and my sister Sophronia.

" 'During this time of great excitement my mind was called up to serious reflection and great uneasiness; but though my feelings were deep and often poignant, still I kept myself aloof from all these parties, though I attended their several meetings as often as occasion would permit. In process of time my mind became somewhat partial to the Methodist sect, and I felt some desire to be united with them; but so great was the confusion and strife among the different denominations, that it was impossible for a person as young as I was, and so unacquainted with men and things, to come to any certain conclusion who was right and who was wrong.

" 'My mind at times was greatly excited, the cry and tumult were so great and incessant. The Presbyterians were most decided against the Baptists and Methodists, and used all powers of both reason and sophistry to prove their errors, or at least, to make the people think they were in error. On the other hand, the Baptists and Methodists in their turn were equally zealous in endeavoring to establish their own tenets and disprove all others.

" 'In the midst of this war of words and tumult of opinions, I often asked myself: What is to be done? Who of all these parties is right; or, are they all wrong together? If any one of them be right, which is it, and how shall I know it?

" 'While I was laboring under the extreme difficulties caused by the contests of these parties of religionists, I was one day reading the Epistle of James, first chapter and fifth verse, which reads: *"If any of you lack wisdom, let him ask of God, that giveth to all men liberally, and upbraideth not; and it shall be given him."*

" 'Never did a passage of scripture come with more power to the heart of man than this did at this time to mine. It seemed to enter with great force into every feeling of my heart. I reflected on it again and again, knowing that if any person needed wisdom from God, I did; for how to act I did not know; and unless I could get more wisdom than I had, I would never know; for the teachers of religion of the different sects understood the same passages of scripture so differently as to destroy all confidence in settling the question by appeal to the Bible.

" 'At length I came to the conclusion that I must either remain in darkness and confusion, or else I must do as James directs, that is, ask of God. I at length came to the determination to ask God, concluding that if he gave wisdom to them that lacked wisdom, and would give liberally, I might venture.

" 'So, in accordance with this, my determination to ask God, I retired to the woods to make the attempt. It was on the morning of a beautiful, clear day, early in the spring of eighteen hundred and twenty. It was the first time in my life I had made such an attempt, for amidst all my anxieties I had never as yet made the attempt to pray.

" 'After I had retired to the place where I had previously designated to go, having looked around me, and finding myself alone, I kneeled down and began to offer up the desires of my heart to God. I had scarcely done so, when immediately I was seized upon by some power which entirely overcame me, and had such an astonishing influence over me as to bind my tongue so that I could not speak. Thick darkness gathered around me, and it seemed for a time as if I were doomed to sudden destruction.

" 'But, exerting all my powers to call upon God to deliver me out of the power of the enemy which had seized upon me, and at the very moment when I was ready to sink into despair and abandon myself to destruction—not an imaginary ruin, but to the power of some actual being from the unseen world, who had such marvelous power as I had never before felt in my being—just at this moment of great alarm, I saw a pillar of light exactly over my head, above the brightness of the sun, which descended until it fell upon me.

" 'It no sooner appeared than I found myself delivered from the enemy which held me bound.

" 'When the light rested upon me I saw two Personages whose brightness and glory defy all description, standing above me in the air. One of them spake unto me, calling me by name, and said, pointing to the other —*This is my Beloved Son, Hear him!*

" 'My object in going to inquire of the Lord was to know which of all the sects was right, that I might know which to join. No sooner, therefore, did I get possession of myself, so as to be able to speak, than I asked the Personages who stood above me in the light, which of all the sects was right—and which I should join.

" 'I was answered that I must join none of them, for they were all wrong; and the Personage who addressed me said that all their creeds were an abomination in his sight; that the professors were all corrupt; that, they draw near to me with their lips, but their hearts are far from me; they teach for doctrine the commandments of men, having a form of godliness, but they deny the power thereof.

" 'He again forbade me to join with any of them; and many other things he said unto me, which I can not write at this time. When I came to myself again, I found myself lying on my back, looking up into heaven. When the light departed, I had no strength; but soon recovering in some degree, I went home."

Elder Seymour continued with the story of Joseph Smith, relating how the persecution of the young boy had begun as soon as he told people of his vision. How in spite of the vilification, the boy prophet had persisted in the truthfulness of his statements; and how a second vision had come, this time with the revelation of the hiding place of sacred records; how Joseph had gone to see the records and had been forbidden to take them until he had gone through a period of testing and preparation. Finally the elder quoted from Malachi, "Behold, I will reveal unto you the priesthood by the hand of Elijah, the prophet, before the coming of the great and dreadful day of the Lord. And he shall plant in the hearts of the children the promises made to the fathers and the hearts of the children shall turn to their fathers, if it were not so, the whole earth would be utterly wasted at his coming."

Although the reading took a long time, everyone of his auditors listened with the profoundest attention. When he finished, there was silence for some time, and finally Elder Seymour said, "Friends, this has been a very long story."

"Wonderful," answered the rabbi. "I am astounded; this story is so deep, yet simple and comprehensive."

Mr. Banks was foremost in replying. "To me, friends, it comes as a straightforward impressive message. You know, an impostor fears detail, and in that this man was so careful to give minute detail in all his story, forces me to believe that his story stands unimpeachable. It must surely be true."

"There is no doubt as to its veracity," said John

Mordon. "I would not have missed that story."

Miss Banks, who had taken every word of the story, while fatigued from the long strain, expressed her admiration of the visions.

Mr. Banks looked at his wrist watch. "If it is not too late for you young friends, I think this meeting should not close without the reaction of Mr. Seymour as to this marvelous occurrence.

"In the first place," began the missionary, "the Lord has spoken from the heavens. God the Father and his Son Jesus Christ appeared to the fourteen-year-old lad who had been brought forth to head the great Dispensation of the Fulness of Times. Second, the angel Moroni, he who John saw would fly through the midst of heaven, having the everlasting gospel to preach to men on earth, was the one who was charged with this restoration. Consider his teachings. Consider also that he it was who about the year three hundred eighty-five A. D. buried the sacred plates, where, in the latter-days, he showed them to the young prophet. Thirdly, consider the four times the message was repeated to the lad during that night and the following morning, that the same be indelibly engraved in the lad's heart. Fourth and of mighty importance, consider John the Baptist laying his resurrected hands on the heads of these two young men, and for the first time since the days of the apostles, the priesthood was again restored to earth. So we could go on and on. However with these high lights of gospel restoration, I think it best to conclude for this time. I leave the majestic story in your hands to ponder over until we meet again, provided you wish further discussion, as there is so very much that we have not yet considered.

"And when may we be so favored?" asked the rabbi.

"Elder Hamilton and I are at your service, so name the hour and you may depend upon our being present."

"As for me, friends," spoke Mr. Banks, "I would not miss any of this discussion, and in that I have an urgent business engagement that will take me from the city a few days, I suggest that it be postponed until next Monday evening. Are you agreed?"

It was fully understood, and Miss Banks returned the missionaries to their respective domiciles.

"Now," said the rabbi with deep earnestness, "for me, I feel like some child at the feet of some world professor. Elder Seymour, yes, and his companion, uneducated perhaps in the knowledge of the world, yet, under the Spirit of the Lord, have a power indeed. I take it that it would require many evenings to discuss the whole question. Yet on the other hand, perhaps the sooner one obtains the Holy Ghost which is the light of truth, the divine medium between the heavens and the earth, the better, for our good."

It was past the midnight hour when the three men retired after their discussion and experiences of the evening.

CHAPTER XXVII

DURING the intervening days, John Mordon had spent much time visiting the varied business houses of Boston, ofttimes taking business trips with Mr. Banks for both being men of affairs could naturally speak each other's language in the field of business.

Homer Ben Arden and Clara Banks had taken numerous motor trips through the interurban areas of Boston, and frequently they had halted for hours at a time reconsidering their outstanding experiences in China, and the rabbi told her of his varied experiences since their separation.

Evening came—the date of the rendezvous when the young missionaries were to make another visit to present other very important things pertaining to the revealed gospel of Jesus Christ. They had not long to wait, however, for Clara Banks was seen to drive up to the curb.

Greetings were cordially exchanged, when at once Mr. Banks, being a man of business affairs, began: "I feel fortunate in our having these two fine young Mormon missionaries again as our guests, and I feel that we yet have a treat in store, for certainly, in these short interviews, not one half of the great story, perhaps, has been told." Speaking to those who had assembled to listen, he said: "Now I feel sure that if we have any questions to ask our young friends, they will be as ready as heretofore, so I hope we shall feel free to ask questions."

At the request of Elder Seymour, the soiree began

with Neil Hamilton's singing beautifully:
> "The morning breaks, the shadows flee,
> Lo! Zion's standard is unfurled!
> The dawning of a brighter day,
> Majestic rises on the world."

During the rendition of the five verses of the song set to lovely music, profound thought seemed to impress the hearers as to the great importance of the splendid hymn.

"Friends" began Paul Seymour, "I trust that I may be inspired this evening, for I have had some thoughts that I feel will be enlightening to you good people on topics that we have not as yet considered. Now to begin. As you recall in the story of the Prophet Joseph Smith, the angel of the Lord promised that the higher or Melchizedek Priesthood was to yet be given. It was not long after the restoration of the Aaronic, or lesser priesthood by John the Baptist, that on the banks of the Susquehanna River in Pennsylvania, Peter, James, and John, the former Presidency of the Church, appeared, laying their resurrected hands upon the heads of Joseph Smith and Oliver Cowdery, ordaining them to this majestic priesthood, ordaining them elders and apostles in the new Dispensation of the Fulness of Times about to be ushered in. Thus the priesthood with all its keys and powers was again restored to the earth."

"And these two apostles, Elder Seymour," inquired the rabbi, "were they to be the beginning of the twelve apostles in our day?"

"Exactly so, Rabbi, and from this beginning other apostles were divinely chosen and ordained until the quorum was eventually complete. Not only that, but high priests, seventies, elders, priests, teachers, and deacons were ordained precisely as in the days of our Master. I hope I shall not be considered arrogant should

I take much of the speaking time this evening, for I feel that there are many things you might overlook in your queries. However, please feel free to interrupt as you wish."

Miss Banks, with a new supply of notebooks sat at her little table, was very careful that no word should be missed in the evening interview.

Elder Seymour continued: "Now, one of the great revelations of the Lord to the Prophet Joseph Smith—there being one hundred thirty-three in number—is one that is revealed as a transcript from the records of heaven, and in speaking of this vision, Joseph Smith bore the greatest testimony of Jesus Christ that has ever appeared in print. Here it is." The missionary turned to Section Seventy-six of the Doctrine and Covenants and read: "'And now, after the many testimonies which have been given of him, this is the testimony, last of all, which we give of him; that he lives! For we saw him; even on the right hand of God, and we heard a voice bearing record that he is the only begotten of the Father.'"

"Marvelous, wonderful," said Rabbi Ben Arden. "Could language more explicit be recorded? For me, I take that at its full value."

"Now to continue this testimony, and I hope you will please take careful note of what follows: 'That by him, and through him, and of him, the worlds are and were created, and inhabitants thereof are the begotten sons and daughters of God.' Friends, we teach that the word 'begotten' means all that it says."

There was a brief silence, when Miss Banks, looking up from her notes, asked, "How could such be, Elder Seymour? Could we have been begotten as in immortality?"

"Before answering you, Miss Banks, I suggest that

Elder Hamilton sing the third stanza of our cherished song, 'O, My Father'!"

In his well articulated voice Elder Hamilton began:
"In the heavens are parents single?
No, the thought makes reason stare,
Truth is reason, truth eternal,
Tells me I've a mother there."

Again there was silence; then Elder Seymour continued: "Yes, a mother there, and while we are praying to our Father in heaven, should we not also remember and adore our heavenly mother. Remember that no life can come but by the law of procreation, be it in heaven or earth. The only difference must be, that of our heavenly Parents we receive our spiritual bodies— spiritual bodies to contain our spirits, while in mortality bodies are provided to contain that spirit in its spiritual body. The Latin phrase, *Omne vivum ex ovo* or all living comes from an egg, is verily true. It is the experience of the race."

"Pretty deep doctrine," suggested Mr. Banks, "yet when we think of it, how could it be otherwise? I have never been in harmony with the doctrine that God said 'let there be flies and flies there were.' Even flies must have come about through the law of procreation, and God would be transcending his own laws were there an exception in creation."

"Passing this over for the moment," returned Paul Seymour, "let us go on to other things. However, ponder this great truth in your minds and should you be not in accord, I shall be glad to give further views."

John Mordon for the first time in the interview, gave his thought: "To me, folks, that is an answer to what has greatly perplexed me for years. Now the beauty of pre-existent life seems to me to have been succinctly and beautifully covered."

"Now to continue," spoke Elder Seymour, "you recall that the Angel Moroni said to the lad Joseph Smith, 'Behold I will reveal unto you the priesthood by the hands of Elijah the prophet.' This has been mentioned by Malachi that it was to come. Now the question arises. If John the Baptist and Peter, James, and John restored the Holy Priesthood with its keys, then what could Elijah restore?"

"A pointed question," returned the rabbi, "that for my part it will be up to Elder Seymour to answer."

Elder Seymour replied: "It was that Elijah held the sealing powers between heaven and earth as regards the sealing in holy temples for the living and the dead—sealing husbands and wives for eternity, as well as to seal living husbands or wives to their dead partners, or sealing those dead as husbands and wives, and children to parents, as Malachi says: 'Lest I come and smite the earth with a curse' and as Moroni said to Joseph, stating it differently, 'if it were not so the whole earth would be utterly wasted at his coming."

"And how, Elder Seymour?" inquired Mr. Banks.

"Without this sealing, Mr. Banks, the eternal linking of husbands and wives, of linking children to fathers back to Adam, would naturally disrupt God's great eternal plan for the ultimate redemption of the race. At this point, I wish to refer to another vision when this and other great events that were to precede the Lord's coming actually occurred. Here I shall refer to the one hundred tenth section of the Doctrine and Covenants, the book that contains the revelations of the Lord to Joseph Smith. In this manifestation the Lord once more appeared, telling Joseph Smith and Oliver Cowdery their sins were forgiven, telling them to rejoice, with other majestic instructions. Then suddenly appeared Moses who committed unto them the keys of the gath-

ering of Israel from the four parts of the earth. Next
came Elias who committed to them the dispensation of
Abraham saying that 'in us and our seed all generations
should be blessed.' Lastly came Elijah as before mentioned, conferring the sealing powers. 'Therefore' said
this prophet, 'the keys of the dispensation are committed into your hands; and by this ye may know that
the great and dreadful day of the Lord is near, even at
your doors.' Without these keys, my friends, Israel could
not be gathered; the mission of Elias with its power
could not take place; the mighty sealing powers by Elijah
as before mentioned could not be. Hence the great
importance of this heavenly conferring of authority.
This great event occurred in the temple at Kirtland,
Ohio, which had been erected for this very purpose."

A deeper silence maintained as the listeners absorbed
to the best of their ability the profound truth so very
new to them.

Rabbi Ben Arden was first to break the silence,
"Come to think of it, friends, all this must come to
fulfil God's written word in our Bible. To me this is
marvelous, majestic, and fills my very soul with awe and
amazement."

"Let us leave this manifestation for the present and
pass on to other things. However, perhaps there might
be something some of you would like to have us explain from the standpoint of the revealed gospel in our
day."

Ben Arden was foremost with a query. "Perhaps,
Elder Seymour, I may be considered impertinent, yet I
hope in no way arrogant in a question I wish to propound. One that I have asked of many preachers pro-
fessing to be divinely appointed Christian men of the
cloth, and that is this, very crisply given: What is salvation? None have been able to answer me."

Elder Seymour smiled and then began: "What an important subject that is! Yet one that the Lord has so fully and completely explained. In the first place, we have no place for the hell and damnation-eternal fire suffering expounded by the creeds; but to the contrary, we point to a full and complete salvation, for, with perhaps very, very few exceptions, the entire human family will enjoy some degree of God's salvation."

"That sounds more reasonable than what we have been taught in our churches," spoke John Mordon.

"Yes," said the rabbi, "if God is so narrow as to save those only who are communicants of some particular church, condemning all others to an endless hell, to me he would cease to be God."

"That is the very thing, more than all else," spoke Miss Banks, "that has made me alien to the churches that speak with such determination and precision that such is the lot of humanity. Think of Dante's *Inferno,* that tells the story. No wonder men are infidel."

"The Church of Jesus Christ is not interested in the faulty dogmas of men, but in what is truth. I have already referred to a revelation from heaven in which I read Joseph Smith's great testimony. This 'transcript from the records of heaven' gives minutely the status of the entire human family in eternity, in which you will see how great, merciful and kind is God in behalf of his children."

While Elder Seymour was turning to the revelation in his Doctrine and Covenants, there was a tense stillness, for what greater problem could possess the human mind!

"Here is what the Lord says, speaking of those who are heirs of the Celestial Glory: 'They are they who received the testimony of Jesus and believed on his name and were baptized after the manner of his burial, being buried in the water in his name, and this according to the commandments he has given—that by keeping the commandments they might be washed and cleansed from all their sins, and receive the Holy Spirit by the laying on of hands of him who is ordained and sealed unto this power. And who overcome by faith, are sealed by the Holy Spirit of promise, which the Father sheds forth upon all those who are just and true. They are they who are the church of the first-born. They are they into whose hands the Father has given all things. They are they who are priests and kings who have received of his fulness, and of his glory; and are priests of the Most High, after the order of Melchizedek, which was after the order of Enoch, which was after the order of the Only Begotten Son. Wherefore, as it is written, they are gods, even the sons of God. Wherefore, all things are theirs, whether in life or death, of things present, or things to come, all are theirs and they are Christ's and Christ is God's. And they shall overcome all things. Wherefore, let no man glory in man, but rather let him glory in God, who shall subdue all enemies under his feet. These shall dwell in the presence of God and his Christ forever. These are they whom he shall bring with him, when he shall come in the clouds of heaven to reign on the earth over his people. These are they who shall have part in the first resurrection. These are they who shall come forth in the resurrection of the just. These are they who shall come into Mount Zion, and the city of the living God, the heavenly place, the holiest of all. These are they who have come in an innumerable company of angels to the general assembly of the church of Enoch, and of the first-born. These are they whose names are written in heaven, where God and Christ are judge of all. These are they who are just men made perfect through Jesus the mediator for the new covenant, and

wrought out this perfect atonement through the shedding of his blood. These are they whose bodies are
celestial, which glory is that of the sun, even the glory
of God, the highest of all, whose glory the sun of the
firmament is written as typical.'"

"That," interrupted Mr. Banks, "refers only to the
elect of God, as I take it, yet that does not cover salvation to which our friend the rabbi refers."

"You are right there, Mr. Banks, and I hope in
giving this detailed revealed work I have not taken too
much time. I could have paraphrased it and perhaps
covered the ground to your satisfaction."

Rabbi Ben Arden spoke immediately. "Never. Let
us have the full account as the Lord has revealed it."

"Now comes the terrestrial world, whose glory as
written 'differs from the church of the first-born who
have received a fulness of the Father, even as that of
the moon differs from the sun in the firmament.' Please
follow closely, friends, for this is of utmost importance.
'Behold, these are they who died without the law. And
they also who are the spirits of men kept in prison,
whom the Son visited, and preached the gospel unto
them, that they might be judged according to men in
the flesh; who received not the testimony of Jesus in
the flesh, but afterwards received it. These are they
who are the honorable men of the earth, who were
blinded by the craftiness of men. These are they who
receive of his glory, but not of its fulness. These are
they who receive of the presence of the Son, but not a
fulness of the Father. Wherefore they are bodies terrestrial, and not bodies celestial, and differ in glory as
the moon differs from the sun. These are they who
are not valiant in the testimony of Jesus; wherefore, they
obtain not the crown over the kingdom of our God.
And now this is the end of the vision we saw of the

terrestrial, that the Lord commanded us to write while yet we were yet in the spirit.' Think, my friends, how very much of the human family this covers as heirs to that glory. But the end is not yet, for now I read further: 'And again, we saw the glory of the telestial, which glory is that of the lesser, even as the glory of the stars differs from that of the glory of the moon in the firmament. These are they who received not the gospel of Christ, neither the testimony of Jesus. These are they who deny not the Holy Spirit. These are they who are thrust down into hell. These are they who shall not be redeemed from the devil until the last resurrection, until the Lord, even Christ the Lamb, shall have finished his work. These are they who receive not of his fulness in the eternal world, but of the Holy Spirit through the ministrations of the terrestrial. These are they who are liars, and adulterers, and whoremongers, and whoever loves and makes a lie. These are they who suffer the wrath of God on earth. These are they who suffer the vengeance of eternal fire. These are they who are cast down to hell and suffer the wrath of Almighty God until the fulness of times when Christ shall have subdued all enemies under his feet, and shall have perfected his work. When he shall deliver up the kingdom, and present it unto the Father, spotless, saying, I have overcome and have trodden the wine-press of the fierceness of the wrath of Almighty God.'"

A greater and profounder silence than ever maintained, as thoughts flooded the minds and conceptions of the listeners. Elder Seymour and his companion seemed to enjoy the thought-provoking quietude. At length the silence was broken.

"How unlimited that is," suggested Mr. Banks. "Yet, is it possible that the very lowest of hell may come as heirs of a glory? It is beyond me, I assure you."

"That is stunning at best," injected John Mordon, while Miss Banks seemed to grasp the depth of meaning. All eyes turned to the missionary for a comment.

Paul Seymour began: "Now, I perceive your thoughts, friends. Yet, let us recall that the denizens of the depths of hell are, after all, sons and daughters of God and under the invincible dictum of divine justice and judgment. Now, let us consider that with even these mercy has a claim, and when the exigencies of justice and judgment have been satisfied, mercy will redeem them, and their lot will be in that lower glory to which they shall be assigned. So you see, friends, that salvation is almost infinite in nature, reaching for all except a very few who fall below any glory whatever. I refer to the few sons of perdition, that it were better had they never been born. And let us understand that there are very few who have had sufficient knowledge and intelligence to become sons of perdition."

Rabbi Ben Arden had been greatly moved in the narration, and frequently tears swelled his eyes, for it seemed that an inner something urged him to action. He startled all present by exclaiming from the depth of his soul: "It is enough. Elder Seymour, I present myself for baptism into the Church of Jesus Christ. In your opinion, am I a worthy supplicant?"

The startled missionary was deeply moved, as he answered, "Rabb Ben Arden, are you ready to have all the world turn against you? Are you ready to become a member of the Church of Christ in thought, deed, and action? Are you willing to pay a full tithing of one-tenth of your annual increase for the up-building and maintenance of the Church? Are you fully penitent, and with an understanding heart willing to go down into the waters of baptism for the remission of your sins, that you may have the gift of the Holy Ghost imparted by the laying on of authorized hands? Are you satisfied in your soul that I, a young elder in the church, one of thousands now dispersed through the nations, have that divine authority, to perform those sacred ordinances?"

Without further consideration, the rabbi replied: "All that, I assure you. I am willing and eager to give my all that I may have membership among God's people. Am I a worthy candidate? If I am, when may I be baptized?"

"Yes, you may be baptized, Rabbi, because I want you to know more fully the principles of the gospel and meet other missionaries, let us set the date ahead. We baptize about twenty miles from Boston. The arrangements I will give you later when I have discussed them with our mission president."

The rabbi wiped his eyes. The investigating, searching, determined, analyzing rabbi, had suddenly changed, and now was the personification of humility, peace and gratitude. He had at last made his great discovery of his Priceless Pearl that to be appreciated must, in the heart of such as he, be lived. Meekness and love pervaded his soul.

As the rabbi glanced at his friend, John Mordon, he saw conviction. As his eyes turned to Clara Banks, his heart bounded with joy as he saw her tear-dimmed eyes. Then he turned to Mr. Banks, in whom he saw conviction, yet a worldliness that was going to be hard to break down.

Elder Seymour arose, approached the rabbi, placing his hand on his shoulder, saying: "Homer Ben Arden, I thank God for the light of truth that has come to you. A majestic experience and mission await you, surely." The rabbi wept tears of joy.

Following this benign moment, Elder Seymour

looked at his watch. It was already late, yet he wished
to finish the evening according to his prearranged plans.
He spoke with great sincerity.

"While it is late, friends, I feel that I must infringe
on your time a little longer, as Elder Hamilton and I
leave for New York tomorrow where we are to attend
our mission conference. You know this mission with
more than a hundred men and women missionaries, is
but one in many large missions throughout the nations,
with thousands of missionaries, all for the love of our
fellow men, giving our message free—without cost or
price—to bring to them the knowledge of the gospel
as we have had the joy of doing here. However, that
is not what I wish to speak of."

Elder Seymour took from his briefcase four neatly
bound books which he held in his hands, saying:
"Friends, we have spoken of the Book of Mormon, and
it is with joy that Elder Hamilton and I present one
copy to each of you—Rabbi Ben Arden, John Mordon,
to you, Mr. Banks, and lastly one for Miss Banks. However, I wish in all candor and humility to say a few words
relative to this wonderful volume. Long ago, in ancient
America, lived a prophet—Mormon by name. When a
little boy, while the nation was under the throes of
devastating war, one Ammaron gave this Mormon, then
a lad of fifteen years, charge of the records of the ancient
American people. During nearly sixty years this Prophet
Mormon sought to abridge this history of the people
from six hundred years before Christ to near the fifth
century of our era. Knowing his time, as an old man,
was short among this still warring people, he conferred
the records to his son, Moroni, who at length, the last
of his people, deposited them in the hill Cumorah. It
was this same Prophet Moroni who, many hundred
years later delivered this abridgement, not one hundredth

part of the original historical record being abridged as written. It was this same Moroni, as told in Joseph Smith's story, who delivered the abridgment on plates of gold to Joseph Smith.

"Now, on the first page of the record, it says what the record contains, that it is to convince the Jew and Gentile that Jesus Christ is the eternal God. On the second page you will read the testimony of three witnesses, honorable men and trustworthy, who give testimony that an angel of the Lord came to them presenting the plates. Their testimony is convincing. On the same page you will observe the testimony of eight others.

"Kindly note further, that this abridgment of Mormon's writings, translated by Joseph Smith by the gift and power of God, is Mormon's Book, hence the name, The Book of Mormon.

"Now, to the record, it speaks of the rise and fall of peoples, their righteousness, their periods of unrighteousness. Mighty prophets moved among them with their sublime teachings of the gospel of our Lord, their hope and teaching of the coming Atonement of our Lord. Then, perhaps the most beautiful story of all time, is when Jesus Christ, following his resurrection in Jerusalem, appeared in person to this people and established the gospel in its fulness. Then follow the workings of that gospel among the people, until eventually unrighteousness followed. With a series of recurring and devastating wars, the people were largely destroyed, the American Indians today being the remnants of that race.

"Now, in conclusion, I present to you Moroni's words as he bade farewell to the world. It is a test by which one may know of the book's divine message and authenticity. Here is what Moroni wrote:

"'And when ye shall receive these things, I would

exhort you that ye would ask God, the Eternal Father, in the name of Christ, if these things are not true; and if ye shall ask with a sincere heart, with real intent, having faith in Christ, he will manifest the truth of it unto you, by the power of the Holy Ghost.'

"This, friends, is putting God to the test, and surely you will not be disappointed if you follow the words of Moroni. You will know of its truth. Elder Hamilton and I have carefully autographed each copy, and these we will present to each of you with our sincere compliments."

CHAPTER XXVIII

DURING the succeeding days, Rabbi Ben Arden found himself a busy man in his profound study of the Book of Mormon, in deep periods of meditation in the rapture of what to him was new life. His suggestion to the Banks family that he move to a hotel rather than remain in their home was met with stern resentment, for Mr. Banks and his daughter had learned to admire the sterling character of their guest, hence they insisted that he remain as one of the family.

John Mordon had returned to his business in Indianapolis, a happy and contented man in the thought that the rabbi had at last, as he was assured, found his Priceless Pearl in which quest, Mr. Mordon had, himself become a partner. Clara Banks was equally thrilled, for the rabbi's quest had become her own, and she was delighted that she had been the medium that had led him to his discovery.

The missionaries had returned from their conference in New York, and Elder Seymour had responded to a telephone call from Homer Ben Arden.

On his arrival, the rabbi gave the youth a very warm reception, at the same time expressing his gratitude for the privilege of reading the sacred volume of scripture so reassuring and convincing. The rabbi said with earnestness: "Elder Seymour, I have followed the advice of the angel Moroni, and a seeming something within me attests its divine origin. On the other hand, I am wondering why our Bible has not spoken of this wondrous scripture of old Amercia."

Elder Seymour's eyes seemed to snap at the query, as he replied: "Evidently, friend Ben Arden, you have overlooked what has been said, surely, for, as the Book of Mormon has proved to be the greatest witness for the divinity of our Bible, so, on the other hand, the Bible has testified of this new volume of scripture translated into our language. Now, as to what the Bible says." Elder Seymour took his Bible from his briefcase. "I read from the thirty-seventh of Ezekiel, where he speaks of sticks, as scripture in olden times were called —parchment rolled around wooden rollers, for, in that day, as you know, there were no bound books. Listen to what the prophet said: 'Moreover thou son of man take thee one stick, and write upon it for Judah, and for the children of Israel, his companions.' Rabbi, you will understand, I am sure, that this refers to your Jewish scripture. But to continue, 'then take another stick, and write upon it. For Joseph, the stick of Ephraim, and for the house of Israel, his companions; And join them one to another into one stick, and they shall become one in thine hand.'" Here, Elder Seymour placed the Bible and the Book of Morman together. "Yes, 'one in thine hand.' Let us read further. 'And when the children of thy people shall speak unto thee, saying, Wilt thou not show us what thou meanest by these things? Say unto them, Thus saith the Lord God; Behold, I will take the stick of Joseph, which is in the hand of Ephraim, and the tribes of Israel, his fellows, and will put them with him, even the stick of Judah, and make them one stick, and they shall be one in mine hand.'"

Ben Arden took the Bible from Elder Seymour, saying: "Please let me read that carefully. At length, he said in wonderment: "That is marvelous, indeed."

"Yes, Rabbi, it is," returned the elder, as he drew a

small book of ready references from his pocket which he passed to the rabbi. "At your leisure, friend Ben Arden, read the many passages in the Bible that refer to the coming forth of this, Mormon's abridgment. Especially, I draw your attention to the twenty-ninth chapter of Isaiah that previewed minutely what happened when Martin Harris presented the manuscript of a few pages to Professor Anthon of New York. This you will find striking, indeed." The missionary marked the passages in the reference booklet.

"I shall do that, Elder Seymour. Furthermore," spoke the rabbi, somewhat apologetically, "please do not think me over-inquisitive, or that I am in any manner a cynic or skeptic, nor that my faith has weakened in the least, for I am overjoyed in the thought that in a few days I may be baptized into the Church of Jesus Christ."

"I hope," returned the elder, "you understand that I am overjoyed to be of service, even to all who search the truth, for, as you know, there is no end to truth, nor will there be an end to the quest of truth even in the eternities."

The rabbi pondered deeply. "Yes, yes, it must be so, Seymour. So to begin. When one is baptized for the remission of his sins, how far succeeding that baptism does its efficacy extend?"

The elder had already anticipated a like question in this analytical mind. In fact, he had thought of speaking of that very thing. "Following faith, repentance made perfect in reformation, then baptism which remits past sins only, it is a purification of the suppliant that he may receive the Holy Ghost."

"That being so, Elder Seymour, where do we go from there?"

"That, Rabbi, brings us to the splendor of the

holy sacrament and the real intent and object of its institution."

"I have often pondered as to its efficacy. Please enlighten me."

"Rabbi, let us turn to any one of our more than a thousand organizations known as wards in which each Sabbath the holy sacrament is administered, and consider the broken bread and the cup passed to each member. First, it is the prerogative of the entire congregation to sing together some hymn directly upon the atonement of our Lord, some of the titles of these hymns being, for instance: 'He died, the great redeemer died,' 'In remembrance of thy suffering, Lord, these emblems we partake,' 'Oh, it is wonderful that he should care for me enough to die for me,' with a score of similar ones. Some of the wording of the verses is high lighted, as, 'Lord, forgive as we've forgiven.' Again, 'Pardon our weakness, forgive us of sin, and ere the sacrament passes each lip, seal us thy children without and within.'"

"Very beautiful," returned the rabbi. "From this, I take it that after baptism there is in this sacrament an element of forgiveness for subsequent transgressions. Am I right?"

"That very thing, Rabbi, provided, of course, that there is a contrite spirit and broken heart, for in this service we covenant with the Lord to continue a life of humility, faith, prayer, and thanksgiving. He who is authorized under authority of the Holy Priesthood to bless the sacramental symbols, after calling upon the Lord to bless and sanctify them to the souls of all who partake of it; that they may witness to Jesus Christ that they do remember him—his atonement—that they will take upon them his name; keep his commandments, that they may have his spirit to be with them. To such, Rabbi, comes, with this renewal of covenant a remission or forgiveness contingent to the penitence and fervor of the member. That, as I understand, Rabbi, is the full import of the holy sacrament that Christ was so eager to impress upon his apostles."

The rabbi pondered deeply, finally saying: "Elder Seymour, that is fully satisfying. The Lord has certainly provided for each minute contingency of his people! Now, my next query is this, will you please tell me something of the mode of living a life as a Latter-day Saint? I refer especially to the hygiene of your people, abstinence from things that are of a degrading nature physically?"

Elder Seymour smiled, happy that the subject had come up. He said with assurance: "Rabbi, more than a hundred years ago, the Lord revealed to the Prophet Joseph Smith what is known as the Word of Wisdom, which, in brief, is a code of health rules given without compulsion or restraint and adapted to the weak and weakest of all who are or can be called saints. In brief, it means abstinence from injurious foods; total abstinence from tea, coffee, hot drinks, liquors, and tobacco, which the Lord said 'is not good for man.' "

The rabbi had followed carefully, at length asking: "Now, Elder Seymour, what of its results with your people?"

"It is outstanding, Rabbi, for, as a result of its workings we enjoy perhaps the lowest infant mortality in the world, with a general death rate per thousand of less than seven. Rabbi, I was brought up under the Word of Wisdom, and I hope you will believe me when I affirm that I have never in my life tasted tea, coffee, liquor or tobacco, and that there are tens of thousands who can truthfully say the same."

"What is the actual efficiency of its observance, Elder Seymour?"

Paul Seymour answered quickly: "Rabbi, suppose we have a tender rosebush, and we sprayed it with ingredients that would cause its petals to fade and its leaves to fall. We would understand why, in our foolishness, we had done such a thing, would we not?"

"I learn," faltered the rabbi, with an air of dejection, "that I am up against a tremendous reformation."

Paul Seymour was keen to observe how the rabbi looked at his tobacco-stained fingers. Finally, the missionary said in all kindness: "Rabbi, the Spirit of the Lord will not dwell in unclean tabernacles."

Ben Arden started, hesitated, then turning to Elder Seymour, saying, "Brother Seymour, I give you my word."

After the missionary had left, Ben Arden sat alone in deep meditation for the errors of life seemed legion, and only the knowledge of the gospel had made them impressive upon his intelligence. While he was in this deep spell of thought, Clara Banks entered the room. "Why all this melancholy, Homer?" she asked. "You look as forlorn as the sphinx of Egypt."

Homer forced a smile. "Well, Clara, Elder Seymour has been here with his wondrous spirit and teaching."

"And?"

"His beautiful explanation of the why and wherefore of the holy sacrament was soul-inspiring, beautiful, and instructive. Yet, some of the things he taught me of what he is pleased to call The Word of Wisdom, pricked a guilty conscience. His words cut like a two-edged sword."

Clara seemed astounded. "Why, Homer, what is wrong?"

The rabbi looked at his tobacco-stained fingers. Then Homer explained the beautiful story and analogy of what the elder had taught of the hygienic qualities of the Word of Wisdom that had made the Latter-day Saints among the world's most hygienic people. Rabbi Ben Arden looked Clara in the eye fervently, asking: "Clara, will I, as a guest, be asking too much, or will it be an act of impropriety, if I ask that henceforth my drink be water or milk?"

"Why, most certainly, Homer, and you will not be alone in this at our table."

Rabbi Ben Arden arose, and without ceremony left the room, passing outside, and Clara Banks, curious as to his attitude, looked out at the window as he approached the incinerator.

At length, Homer Ben Arden returned, and with great satisfaction and fervor whispered, "Veni, vidi, vici," then he passed to his room.

Clara Banks was deeply meditative. She took from her purse her cigarette case, looked at it, then laid it aside with great determination.

CHAPTER XXIX

THIS was, perhaps, the happiest day in the life of Homer Ben Arden, for it was the day in which he would be privileged to enter the Church of Jesus Christ through baptism. He had arisen early and having gone to the Banks' library, had been in deep meditation as to his worthiness. "Have I repented sufficiently, a repentance through reformation and the humility of heart with a contrite spirit?" He looked at his stained fingers that he had tried to cleanse, nodding his head in satisfaction.

Breakfast was over and the rabbi and Clara Banks were seated awaiting the arrival of Elder Hamilton, who was to conduct the party to the place for baptism, for all arrangements had been made, and Elder Seymour having gone in advance to await them.

While they were waiting, they were surprised in the arrival of John and Mrs. Mordon from Indianapolis. Following the greeting, Miss Banks said kindly: "Why, Mr. Mordon, really, this is a surprise. We did not think of your coming."

"Do you think, Miss Banks, that the little disatnce between Boston and Indianapolis would prevent my being here for this occasion?"

Elder Hamilton arrived, and while the company was now awaiting the arrival of Mr. Banks from his office, the rabbi, desiring some information, took this occasion to inquire with deep sincerity: "My dear Elder Hamilton, will you kindly inform me as to the present status of the Church, as to its growth, its achievements,

its educational status, or anything you have in your heart
that we should know?"

Neil Hamilton smiled. "You are asking quite a
large order. However, our once localized Church in
the Rocky Mountains now has the satisfaction of being
a world religion, in that we cover nearly all civilization.
Besides our having over a hundred stakes, which, by the
way, is a well-bounded district in which there are many
wards, or Church groups. Each ward is as a church in
itself, as is each stake with its several wards. Then all
the stakes with their respective wards in one great composite is again the Church, and so on to the organization of the group or presiding priesthood, known as the
General Authorities."

The listeners were intensely interested, when Miss
Banks asked, "What is your Church membership in
all these stakes of which you mention?"

He replied, "That I cannot say exactly, but in the
stakes and missions of the Church we have just a little less than one million adherents, and the Church today is growing faster, according to membership, than
any other Christian Church. According to government
figures, the Church of Jesus Christ of Latter-day Saints
has grown in the last twenty years about two hundred
and ninety percent."

John Mordon, desiring specific information, asked:
"Mr. Hamilton, tell me something of your tithing system, and its use, please."

"To begin, Mr. Mordon, the Lord said through the
Prophet Malachi: 'Will man rob God? Yet ye have
robbed me. But ye say, Wherein have we robbed thee?
In tithes and offerings. Ye are cursed with a curse: for
ye have robbed me, even this whole nation. Bring ye
all the tithes into my storehouse, that there be meat
in my house, and prove me now herewith, saith the

Lord of hosts, if I will not open the windows of heaven, and pour out a blessing, that there shall not be room enough to receive it.' Our experience, friends, is that members who are faithful tithepayers of a full tenth of their increase annually, are the happiest of people. Now, to further answer Mr. Ben Arden, consider that from this tithing fund last year more than four million dollars were expended for the maintenance of temples, education, church buildings, hospitals, and charity. That vast fund is used, in a word, for the upbuilding of Zion in all essential phases. That fund circulated under the strictest auditorship, and precision."

The Banks and Mordon cars with their occupants, directed by Mr. Hamilton, arrived at the place of baptism thirty minutes before the appointed hour.

Elder Seymour had arranged for a traveling missionary male quartet to assist in the services.

Besides several of Mr. Banks' business friends whom he had interested in this strange affair, there were some members of the Church.

While Elder Seymour had escorted the rabbi to a near-by residence to change their clothes, the quartet sang some exquisite selections, among which were several classics.

Eventually, Paul Seymour and the rabbi appeared, dressed in immaculate white suits used for the occasion.

Following a few introductory remarks by a missionary, the quartet sang in good harmony and in full tones:

"Lo! on the water's brink we stand,
  To do the Father's will;
  To be baptized by His command,
  And thus the word fulfill."

Following the rendering of the several verses, another missionary offered a touching prayer of supplication and gratitude, and again the quartet sang:

"The morning breaks, the shadows flee,
Lo! Zion's standard is unfurled!
The dawning of a brighter day,
Majestic rises on the world."

Elder Seymour led the rabbi waist-deep into the water. Then came the choice words: "Homer Ben Arden, having been commissioned of Jesus Christ, I baptize you in the name of the Father, and of the Son, and of the Holy Ghost. Amen." Came then the complete baptism by immersion.

During this ceremony deep silence maintained, the solemnity of which had moistened many eyes. Especially were John Mordon, Clara Banks, and even Mr. Banks and Mrs. Mordon deeply touched.

While waiting the return of Elder Seymour and Homer Ben Arden, Neil Hamilton rendered the touching hymn, "O, My Father," following which the chorus rendered "The Pilgrim's Chorus" from Lombardi, "Invictus," and a few Latter-day Saints hymns appropriate to the occasion.

Then came the confirmation of the newly baptized, when a missionary laid his hands upon the rabbi's head, confirming him a member of the Church of Jesus Christ of Latter-day Saints, closing with the words, "Receive the Holy Ghost."

Following the confirmation, the rabbi advanced a few steps and, with bowed head, seemed to be offering a deep, sincere prayer of gratitude which brought everything as quiet as a shadow. Finally, dispassionately, he spoke: "Friends, I feel I must tell you that never in my life have I experienced the joy that I have experienced on this occasion. Perhaps you will understand it

better if I tell you something of the long search I have
made for the very priceless possession that is now, at
long last, my own. As some of you already know, I
am Homer Ben Arden, a Jew from Palestine, having
been on a world-wide quest of that divine power that
maintained with Moses in Egypt, with Elijah at Carmel,
and with many other of Israel's prophets. That power
having been entirely lost to men, until the advent of
Jesus Christ, when the winds and waves obeyed, water
was turned into wine, the sick were healed, the blind
saw, the lame walked, lepers were cleansed, demons
were cast out, and the dead were raised to life again,
climaxing in the majestic resurrection of our Lord, followed by his ascension into heaven.

"The more my college learning advanced, the more
I was convinced that these powers were unknown to
our age, which so impressed me that, despite my ordination as a rabbi with great promotions in the offing, I
apostatized from the Jewish faith, seeing therein but a
cold, clammy form, devoid of divine guidance, and, with
the proceeds of a fortune, launched my quest for what
I was pleased to name the Priceless Pearl.

"My quest began with the examination of the great
religions of India, one of which sways the minds and
hearts of one third of the earth's population. Some of
these mighty religions cannot be disposed of by casting
at them unsavory epithets.

"During the following year my quest took me into
China, the experience of which added vast stores of
knowledge. Yet, in all the great religions of the orient,
I found not the slightest clue that the power I was seeking had even been known to them.

"In India, I was fortunate in having a Mr. John
Mordon of Indianapolis as a safe, experienced, and congenial companion. While in China, I was also fortunate

in the kind, sympathetic guidance of Miss Clara Banks. I was gratified to learn that each of these estimable friends had absorbed deeply my mission to the extent that my quest became their quest. These true friends are now in this group.

"Through a happy combination of circumstances, I was brought into contact with Elders Paul Seymour and Neil Hamilton, missionaries of the Church of Jesus Christ of Latter-day Saints. These young people, now with us here, uneducated in the conventions of ministerial training, yet possess something so different from that found among other people—yes, some divine intelligence before which my college learning was forced to bow. My self-sufficiency and positiveness were unable to cope with the sweet sublimity and power of their teachings. My arguments and objections were nullified, and my queries adequately answered.

"The teachings of these missionaries were so scriptural, factual, and sublime as to cause me the deepest meditation, which led me to realize that I, at best, was but a prodigal, as it were, and had been feeding on corn husks—corn husks of materialism, as it were, that impelled me to say as did he of old, 'I will arise and go to my Father,' for I was profoundly impressed and convinced that God and his Son, Jesus Christ had, in our day, visited the earth, and that the Holy Priesthood had again been restored to men, by the operations of which the sick are healed, the lame walk, the blind see, demons cast out, and the dead raised. I was deeply touched in the story by Elder Seymour of his own mother having, by that authority, been raised from the dead back to life again. Friends, I was so moved to deep conviction that my long quest appeared to be nearing its end.

"When Elder Seymour told me that above all else in life, I needed divine guidance that can come only by

the gift of the Holy Ghost, a new resolution was born.
Who more than I had greater need of that benign
benediction?

"Following the teachings of my missionary friends,
came deeper faith in God, and Jesus Christ as the Messiah and Redeemer, and that, according to scriptural
forecast, the gospel of salvation with all its keys and
powers has been fully restored equal to that of past ages.

"Then came repentance, such as taught by my young
tutors. Not only a mere godly sorrow, but a reformation of life, mental and physical.

"I was profoundly impressed with their explanation
of the scriptural doctrine of baptism by immersion for
the remission of sins, and with the conviction that Elder
Seymour was endowed of ample authority to administer
the ordinance in my behalf, I presented myself as a candidate. This, friends, brought me to the baptism you
have just witnessed.

"I had no more than come from the water, when
the words of Christ to Nicodemus, that one must be
born again to see the kingdom of God, flashed before
me. It seemed to me that, with my spiritual eyes, at
least, the majestic view of the kingdom flashed pano-
rama-like before me. I have never before experienced
anything like it.

"Under the hands of several of the missionaries here
with us, you saw me confirmed a member of the Church
of Jesus Christ of Latter-day Saints, and heard the words
pronounced, 'Receive the Holy Ghost!' At once I experienced something very unusual, in that a sweet abiding something suddenly possessed me. It seemed that
the very windows of heaven were opened to me.

"Friends, I am not in the least of a temperamental
make-up, nor am I visionary or emotional. But this
thing causes me to feel floods of truth which I had never

anticipated. Fully, I recall the promise of the Holy Ghost to the ancient apostles.

"This is my benediction, hence, by virtue of my newly bestowed gift, and in the deepest dispassionate fervor of my soul, I testify to you that God lives; that Jesus is the Christ and Redeemer; that the Lord prepared the youthful Joseph Smith as the Prophet of this dispensation of the fulness of times, and, angel-taught, to establish his Church on earth; that the Holy Priesthood is once more operative in an unbroken connection between heaven and earth; that the mighty gathering of Israel, so dear to me, is established with salutary effects.

"Would that I had language to express the rapture, and the joy, gratitude, and thanksgiving that have come to me in this wondrous gift of the Holy Ghost.

"Humbly, I bear this testimony in the name of Jesus Christ, our Lord.

"Friends, my quest is over. I have found my Priceless Pearl."